SEVEN AGES

John Nicholson is lecturer in psychology at Bedford College, London University; he previously taught and researched at the universities of Oxford (where he was educated) and Reading. The results of his research have been published in scientific journals in Britain and Europe, and he writes regularly on psychological topics in several popular magazines. He is press officer for the British Psychological Society and acts as consultant to a number of organizations. Before becoming a psychologist, Dr Nicholson was a professional jazz and rock musician and composer, and music remains a major interest, along with reading and sport. He is also the author of *Habits: why you do what you do* (1978) and *A Question of Sex* (Fontana, 1979).

JOHN NICHOLSON

SEVEN AGES

FONTANA PAPERBACKS

First published by Fontana Paperbacks 1980
Copyright © John Nicholson 1980

Set in 'Monophoto' Baskerville

Made and printed in Great Britain by
William Collins Sons and Co. Ltd, Glasgow

For Clare

Contents

[Handwritten annotations:]
1. Say 0 — 12
2. c.13 — c.19
3. young adult c.20 — c.26
4. c.27 — c.38
5. c.39 — c.48
6. c.49 — c.65
7. c.64 — 0

Acknowledgements

I seem to have accumulated an embarrassingly long list of creditors both in writing *Seven Ages* and during the planning and execution of the research project on which much of the book is based. So far as the Colchester Survey on Aging is concerned, the research was paid for by London Weekend Television and carried out by Social and Community Planning Research. I am very grateful to Gavin Weightman, Mike Brennan and Jill Robinson of LWT, who made a TV series on the same theme as the book. I am also indebted to Roger Jowell, Barbara Mostyn, Alan Hedges and Jill Keegan of SCPR, but particularly to Jane Ritchie, who was responsible for the main survey and was enormously helpful to me at every stage of the operation.

Although SCPR carried out the research, I have other debts in the market research field. Arnold Cragg, Tim Dawson and Barry Ross, of Cragg, Ross and Associates played an important role in the early planning of the research, and I am very grateful to Wendy Gordon of the Schlackman Group and to Susie Fisher and Susan Holder of Youth Profile for giving me access to the results of two major surveys they had carried out on adolescence and motherhood, which I draw on in, respectively, Chapters 4 and 2 of the book.

Many friends and colleagues gave me material assistance and moral support while writing the book. They include: James Astor, Tessa Blackstone, Mark Boxer, Sheila Chown, Guy Claxton, Ernie Eban, Peter Evans, Brian Foss, Jacqui Graham, Paul Harris, Beverly Hayne, Virginia Ironside, Kate Loewenthal, Clare Mansfield, Anna Raeburn, Thelma Rumsey, Mary Sinclair, Tony Thomas and Clare Toynbee.

And I apologize to Kate Nicholson and Jane and Zeeb Kalim, who lived with me while the book was being written and gave me the benefit of their comments on the manuscript. Finally, it is a pleasure to acknowledge again the contribution made by Helen Fraser and Valerie White: no author could ask for a more sympathetic and understanding editor and typist.

INTRODUCTION

As Old as You Feel?

'Youth is a blunder; manhood a struggle; old age a regret.'

BENJAMIN DISRAELI

'If I did not keep telling myself my age over and over again, I am sure I should hardly be aware of it.'

ANDRÉ GIDE, at the age of seventy-three

This is a book about age. Not just old age or adolescence, though both of course come into it, but every period of life which separates the cradle from the grave. The main question I want to answer is this: does it matter how old you are? But there are a host of related questions we shall also have to investigate. How much does a person change as he or she gets older? And if we do change as we get older, is it the result of experiencing certain key life-events such as marriage, becoming a parent or reaching retirement, or is there some preordained human life-cycle which dictates that people of a certain age must share the same feelings and behave in a similar way, regardless of what has actually happened to them? Does it make any sense to talk about a 'typical' teenager or forty-year-old, and if it does, is it inevitable that the two will always be at loggerheads? Are some ages more difficult to live through than others; and how much truth is there in the currently fashionable view that our lives consist of a series of different stages, each of which begins with a period of crisis which we have to resolve – sometimes painfully – before we can settle comfortably into the next era of our existence?

Such questions may sound a bit far removed from everyday life. But the answers have enormous practical significance. Even if reaching a certain age brings new problems, if we can understand why these problems appear when they do, we can often minimize or postpone the unpleasant effects of growing older. One of my aims throughout the book will be to identify symptoms at one age which seem to predict problems later, and so provide an early warning system to help you to avoid them. And even where it seems impossible to avoid trouble altogether, there is usually a right and a wrong way to deal with it which may not always be obvious to the person who is experiencing it.

Another important objective is to try and capture the essential flavour of each of the different stages so that readers of one age can form some idea of what it feels like to be another. To do this, we shall have to examine each stage with a view to answering two questions about it. What are (say) adolescents like, and how does it feel to be an adolescent? These two questions may sound rather similar, but in fact we shall have to draw on two different kinds of evidence to answer them. The first is objective. There is a body of scientific evidence, gathered by psychologists, sociologists, doctors and others, which allows us to form some sort of picture of how the 'typical' child/ adolescent/thirty-year-old strikes the trained scientific observer. It is not difficult, for example, to plot the physical changes the average person experiences over his lifetime or to establish that our memories tend to improve over the early years, remain fairly constant over the middle of life, and then drop away in our declining years. We can also establish regular fluctuations in people's earning power or their sexual prowess over the years, and make certain deductions about how such changes might affect their leisure-time activities or what are likely to be their most pressing worries.

This sort of evidence makes an important contribution to the task of constructing profiles of Mr and Mrs Average at different points in their life-cycle, and it can also help us to understand people whose age is not the same as ours. For example, many of the misunderstandings which arise between adolescents and their parents might be avoided if the former made allowances for the effects of the physical changes which occur in the forties, and the latter made an effort to remember how awkward you can feel when your height has temporarily outstripped your strength. In the same way, communication between young and old is greatly improved when children realize that the process of becoming elderly is sometimes accompanied by certain changes in personality, and parents are aware that the thought processes of adults and children are not necessarily identical.

But I don't think that objective evidence of the kind I have been describing is much help in allowing us to get under the skin of someone of a different age. In fact, I very much doubt whether it would give us any confidence that we knew what it felt like to be another person of our own age.

Objective laboratory tests and tables of statistics are useful as a means of pin-pointing some of the changes which take place in our physical and intellectual capabilities over the years, but they do not answer the question of what it *feels* like to be six, sixteen or sixty. To do this, we have to stop observing people and instead start asking them questions. Which brings us to the second type of evidence I shall be drawing on in this book.

To establish the *subjective* importance of a person's age, we formally and informally interviewed some 600 men, women and children over the winter of 1979–80 in Colchester, the oldest recorded town in Britain, once a Roman settlement, later the home of Old King Cole, and now a town with a population of 80,000, the structure and social composition of which is typical of this country. Eighty people between the ages of nineteen and sixty took part in group discussions and in-depth individual interviews which formed the first phase of a survey carried out by the Social and Community Planning Research organization, and a further 461 participated in the main survey described in a technical appendix at the end of this book. Less formally, we canvassed opinion across an agespan ranging from five to eighty while making the TV series linked with *Seven Ages*. The answers we received to questions about how age affected all these people form the basis for much of the discussion throughout this book. But rather than anticipate the picture of the human life-cycle which emerges from this survey, let us first see what we might expect to find, on the basis of what others have had to say on the subject of age.

If the contents of newspapers and magazines are an accurate reflection of the subjects which concern their readers, we are all obsessed with age. Characters in news stories are identified by their age ('Mother, 34, runs amok in supermarket'), as if this somehow explained what they had done, while magazines are crammed with articles which offer age-related explanations for almost everything we think or do. Suppose, for example, you wake up in the morning feeling depressed for no obvious reason. There is no need to get alarmed It's your age that is causing it, however old you happen to be. Two? You are having problems resolving the trust-versus-mistrust psychosocial crisis. Twelve? Puberty is on the horizon. Twenty-two? Who would not be depressed when confronted by the intimacy-versus-isolation crisis which is alleged to over-shadow this period of our lives? Thirty-two? You are in the middle of the first major life review, facing the painful task of deciding whether you have chosen the right marriage partner or job. And so it goes on, if the magazines are to be believed, through the mid-life crisis, the menopause (male and female varieties), the pre-retirement era, the transition to life without work, and finally the decline through senescence and senility towards the merciful escape offered by the grave.

It would be unjust to blame contemporary writers for creating this gloomy picture of the human life-cycle. The idea that our lives move through distinct phases is as old as the written word. Egyptian, Greek, Roman and Medieval philosophers all subscribed to it, though they argued amongst themselves as to how many stages we pass through, and about the nature of the changes which occur at various points in life. What they have in common is a tendency to emphasize the difficulties which face people at different ages, and the assumption that generally speaking things get worse as the years go by. Thus in the Seven Ages of Man speech in *As You Like It*, Shakespeare's description of the puking baby and the whining schoolboy may not conjure up a very attractive vision of infancy or childhood, but both are surely preferable to old age, which he describes as 'mere oblivion, sans teeth, sans eyes, sans taste, sans everything'. Two thousand years earlier, in the earliest known medical papyrus on aging, there is a prescription for transforming old men into youths, which suggests that our generally negative view of growing old is not a modern fad.

But this is not to deny that our thinking about age is subject to historical change. There are fashions in the different stages of life, as can be seen from a brief survey of the last thirty years. In the 1950s it was teenagers who hogged the limelight. Books like *The Catcher in the Rye* chronicled the agonies of the adolescent years, while the James Dean movies represented The Generation Gap as an unbridgeable chasm. Journalists vied with social scientists to interview a terrifying new species of human beings who wore outlandish clothes and roamed the streets looking for old ladies to beat up. Teenagers continued to make good editorial copy in the 1960s – the Mods, Rockers and Hell's Angels saw to that. But increasingly they found themselves having to play second fiddle to their younger brothers and sisters.

The 1960s was the decade in which adults discovered the world of childhood. Of course children had always been of great importance to their own parents, but previously they had been thought of merely as embryonic adults, to be steered with a little help from Dr Spock through the tedious apprenticeship of childhood until they could behave like normal (i.e. adult) human beings. Much of the credit for changing this view of childhood belongs to the Swiss developmental psychologist, Jean Piaget, whose revolutionary ideas about the way children perceive and understand things eventually penetrated the consciousness of the English-speaking world, some forty years after he had begun to publish them in French.

Piaget suggested that children pass through a series of stages of intellectual development. Each of these is marked by a different style of thinking, all of which are recognizably different from adult thought. The idea that a child is not just less logical than an adult, but actually uses different varieties of logic fell on receptive ears. 'Progressive' primary school education was organized along Piagetian lines, and parents demanded guidelines from the experts which would enable them to identify the moments at which their children moved from one mysterious stage to the next. Meanwhile, child psychologists gave silent thanks to whatever god they worship for the largesse with which they were suddenly showered by research-funding agencies anxious to meet the public demand for information about child development. After years of academic neglect, childhood had become fashionable.

But the young have not had it all their own way. The results of the 1960 and 1970 censuses, both in America and the United Kingdom, confirmed a long suspected demographical trend: there are more adults than there used to be, and more of them are living longer than ever before.

In the United States, the percentage of the population over the age of sixty-five has more than doubled since the beginning of the century, while the absolute number of old people has increased more than sevenfold. Futurologists have consulted their crystal balls and come up with the prediction that about half the population of America will be middle-aged or older by the year 2100, and a similar state of affairs may be expected in other countries in which a low birth-rate is combined with advanced care for the elderly.

In the light of this, a boom in research into the nature of old age was to be expected, and it duly occurred in the 1960s and 1970s. The problems of the elderly may not have gripped the public imagination as powerfully as those of childhood or adolescence · we are too frightened of old age for that to happen – but there was an upsurge of magazines for the elderly, and the emergence of groups like the Gray Panthers in America has served notice that the old are now a force to be reckoned with.

Ironically, most of the millions of words describing the behaviour of human beings at the beginning and end of the life-cycle were written by researchers and journalists who themselves belonged to neither category. Until the mid-1970s, observers of the social scene could have been forgiven for assuming that the female menopause was the only problem we have to face in the adult years between twenty and sixty. But all this changed in 1976, with the publication of Gail Sheehy's immensely successful book, *Passages: the Predictable Crises of Adult Life*, and the subsequent appearance of books by the two American psychiatrists from whose work Ms Sheehy drew many of her ideas (Daniel Levinson's *The Seasons of a Man's Life* and Roger Gould's *Transformations: Growth and Change in Adult Life*). In the last few years, expressions like 'Mid-life Crisis' and 'Catch 30' have entered the layman's vocabulary, and there has been a growing tendency – especially in

America – to accept that the adult years should be seen as a series of stages separated by points of psychological crisis which have to be resolved before we can progress to the next period of stability. Linked to this is the idea that at each stage there are certain psychological tasks we have to work on, and common problems we all have to solve, before we can move on.

We have seen that the practice of dividing our lives into a succession of different phases is not a new one. Nor is the idea that each of these phases has characteristic problems. What is new in the spate of recent books on adult psychology is the suggestion that the difficulties we encounter at different times in life are the inevitable consequence of a universal developmental cycle which affects everybody, irrespective of the events which occur in a particular person's life. Take a man in his early forties, for example. Most men of this age have teenage children, and have also reached a point in their professional lives when they have a pretty good idea as to whether or not they are successful. But the theory states that if a man starts showing the symptoms of a mid-life crisis, this is not because he is anxious about his children, or because he realizes he has made a hash of his career. The cause of his condition is simply that he has reached the age of forty. In fact, in its strongest form the new theory of adult development states that a man of forty who has no children and has made a brilliant success of his professional life is just as likely to experience a spiritual crisis at this point of his life as a colleague whose children are drug addicts and who has just been made redundant.

The idea that everyone changes in roughly the same way at certain predictable ages, regardless of what they are doing with their lives, is a startling one, and not very appealing to those of us who fondly imagine that we have a fair amount of control over our destinies. Of course, the suggestion that *children* pass through a series of different stages of development is less disturbing, and few parents would deny that there are 'difficult' ages in childhood. But I think most of us would like to believe that by the time we have become adult, chosen an occupation and perhaps started a family, we have also arrived at a stable and distinctive personality. There may be aspects of yourself you want to change, and of course many adults make a conscious effort to improve themselves, sometimes quite successfully. But even if you think there's a devil in you, at least it is a devil you know and one whose behaviour you can predict, now and in the future.

The new theory of the adult life-cycle suggests that this is wishful thinking, because it implies that we never stop changing, and that we do so merely as a result of the passage of time – something we have no control over. But it is only a theory, put forward by psychiatrists on the basis of their study of a small number of adult Americans, many of whom were in psychoanalysis. What remains to be discovered is whether the common pattern of their lives is evidence for the existence of a universal human life-cycle which affects us all. It was to answer this question that the Colchester study of aging was undertaken.

At the beginning of the project I had an open mind on the subject. I was impressed by the fact that the seven ages of man had such a distinguished historical pedigree, and felt that Shakespeare's account of them still strikes a chord which the modern ear has no difficulty in recognizing. But it was the same speech in *As You Like It* which planted in my mind a doubt about the theory of the adult life-cycle, a doubt which grew larger the longer the project lasted. It occurred to me that the sequence Shakespeare described – infancy, schooldays, courtship, military service, magistracy, retirement and second childhood – could never have applied to more than a tiny fraction of the population, specifically upper-class males. I was also struck by the fact that Shakespeare was an actor by trade, which started me thinking that age might be vitally important to people in certain walks of life – for example, actors and actresses, models, soldiers and professional athletes, and any job where mental speed is at a premium – but much less important to the rest of us.

As the months went by and a picture gradually built up of what age means to ordinary people, it became increasingly clear that we are by no means slaves to our age, as the theory of the adult human life-cycle would have us believe. Most people, far from being obsessed by how old they happen to be, are quite surprised by the suggestion that their personality, behaviour or feelings have anything much to do with their age. They reject the idea that growing older changes their nature. One elderly woman reflected a widespread sentiment when she told us: 'I still feel the same inside, whatever my face looks like in the mirror.' Asked to describe ourselves, most of us seem to distinguish between the outside shell (what we look like), our functional performance (what we are capable of), and our actual selves. Few people think that 'the actual me') changes much over the years of adult life.

Nor did we find much support for the notion that things generally get worse, and life harder to bear, as the years go by. Inasmuch as they are aware of aging at all, most people see it as a means for coming to terms with themselves. As we get older, we get better at this, and become increasingly confident of being able to deal with problems and with other people. Young adulthood (the years between seventeen and twenty five, which will be described in Chapter 3) seems to be a period where we are particularly worried about aging, because we see it as the closing of options. But as we get older, we see it more as a process of emotional and social maturing, which is accompanied by physical and mental slowing down. People over the age of forty often say that they were at their peak physically and intellectually in their twenties and thirties, but they feel that this is more than compensated for by the fact that they are now more stable emotionally, more at ease socially, and more satisfied with themselves and with life in general. They tend to echo the wry sentiments of Henri Etienne, '*si jeunesse savoit, si vieillesse pouvoit*' ('if only the young understood, if only the old were able'), but seem to think that the advantages experience brings outweigh the disadvantage of being over the hill.

So this is an optimistic book, based on the finding of the research that we are not, after all, burdened by our age or necessarily made gloomy by the prospect of growing older. As we shall see, growing older does bring problems, but many of these can be solved by intelligent earlier planning, and they are at least balanced by the gains which increasing maturity seems to bring. And there is one other unappealing aspect of the cyclical theory of adult development which our research calls into question. When we *do* change in adulthood, it is not as a result simply of the passage of time, but rather because of major life-events, many (though not all) of which we wish upon ourselves. It could be leaving home to live on our own or taking on the responsibility of marriage, having a child or starting a new job, or it might be the death of parents, joining the army to do National Service, or having to respond to a crisis like divorce or a major illness.

Major events like these can change people, but this happens regardless of the age at which they occur. So a woman of thirty-three who has just had her first child may have as much in common with a woman of twenty in the same position as she has with a woman of her own age who has no children. For this reason, my account in *Seven Ages* of the different stages of life will give as much weight to the events which typically occur to people at certain ages as it will to describing the thoughts and feelings of the average forty- or fifty-year-old.

The book is in seven chapters which cover childhood (nought to eleven), adolescence (eleven to seventeen), young adulthood (seventeen to twenty-five), the era of parenthood (twenty-six to thirty-eight), early middle age (thirty-nine to forty-eight), later middle-age (forty-nine to retirement), and the retirement years (sixty/sixty-five onwards). These divisions are arbitrary, and I have attached ages to them only as a rough guide. Some of them I believe to be stages in a real sense, others may only be important by virtue of the fact that for most people they begin or end with a key life-event. The early sixties, for example, may have little significance for a self-employed writer whose literary output, lifestyle and health shows no change from the previous decade.

I have now outlined the currently fashionable theory of adult development popularized in books like *Passages,* and anticipated some of the findings of a major new research project which suggest that the theory is seriously at fault. Most of the present book is about adult life, but we do not enter the world as educated and socialized seventeen-year-olds. We must now turn the clock back and begin our journey through the seven ages of man and woman by entering the confused and confusing world of childhood.

CHAPTER I

The Discovery of Childhood

'Childhood shows the man, as morning shows the day.'
JOHN MILTON

Of all the ages of man, childhood is surely the most fascinating to those of us who are not ourselves experiencing it. But it is also the age least thought about by those who are going through it. Young children have very little concept even of the time of day, and although older children understand the more complicated notion of age, its significance to them is strictly practical. They are conscious of how old they are, may remember what they could or could not do when younger, and of course are always being reminded by adults that they are changing ('My, how you've grown!'). But even an eleven-year-old may be baffled by the paradox that he is different now, and yet the same person he has always been. Children look forward to birthdays and know that they will change schools when they reach 7 or 11. They may be very selective about friends, choosing only those of the same age. But they rarely think about age in the abstract – and would find it difficult to answer a question like 'What is it like being five?' This is rather frustrating for the researcher who wants to establish how it feels to be at this stage of the life-cycle, and it means that the first chapter of *Seven Ages* must inevitably be very different from those which follow.

We can learn a great deal about what each period of life is like from adolescence onwards, by simply asking people of that age about their feelings. This is what we set out to do in the Colchester study of aging, and as a result of that survey we have gained some insight into what it feels like to be in your thirties, forties or fifties. But the experience of childhood cannot be approached by this direct route. Infants cannot talk at all and toddlers don't have the vocabulary to describe psychological concepts even if they were interested in them. Children make enormous advances both in psychological awareness and in the sophistication of their language during the primary school years, but there are still significant differences between their thought processes and those of an adult. Adults tend to forget this, and as a result exaggerate their ability to understand the feelings of the prepubertal child. Freud's firm conviction that sexuality plays no part in the lives of children between the ages of seven and eleven should be a dreadful warning to any adult rash enough to imagine that he understands the mind of a ten-year-old.

For these reasons, most of the evidence that we shall be considering in this chapter comes from experiments and observation – an indirect rather than a direct route into the world of the child. The study of children has been one of the most fashionable areas of the behavioural sciences in the last twenty years; indeed, there has probably been more research into the first decade of life than into the rest of the human life-span put together. Nor has this enthusiasm for childhood been confined to scientists. The general public has shown an insatiable appetite for books about children, and the ideas of the two giants of developmental psychology – Freud and Piaget have acquired wide currency.

In this chapter, I shall steer clear of Freud's stages of psychosexual development and Piaget's of intellectual development. This is partly because they are so well known, but mainly because much of the evidence I shall be presenting suggests that both Freud and Piaget have given us a seriously distorted view of childhood.

A lot of this chapter will be what journalists call 'knocking-copy', intended to persuade you that some of your most firmly held convictions about children are wrong. Given all the millions of pounds which have been spent on research into child development, we are still astonishingly ignorant about what children are really like. But I think we now know enough to be certain that they are *not* the creatures described be either of the two major developmental theorists. And the fact that so many professionals and some parents have swallowed the ideas of Freud and Piaget without choking suggests that it is not just psychologists who misjudge children.

There are four beliefs I want to attack. Each concerns a very important aspect of children's behaviour, and I hope that in the process of seeing what children are *not* like, we shall be able to form some impression, however hazy, of the world of childhood, and perhaps get a more realistic idea of the extent to which what happens to a person as a child affects the sort of adult he or she becomes.

Why adults misunderstand children

Why are adults so often wrong about children, and why do they tend to underestimate what children are capable of? The real problem seems to be that most adults - including many psychologists who have studied child development – are unable to escape from their adult vision of how things are, and cannot make the necessary leap of imagination into the child's world. Young children are often said to be egocentric, which means that they can only see things from their own point of view. But a closer look at some of the experiments on which this accusation is based suggests that it is not children but the adults studying them who are blinded by egocentricity, and as a result misinterpret their behaviour. Let me give you just one example of this, which involves perhaps the most famous of all the experiments devised by Jean Piaget, the founding father of developmental psychology.

Although children are born with a highly developed perceptual apparatus which allows them to respond to the sights and sounds around them, they are less well equipped to make sense of what they see and hear. As we shall see later in the chapter, babies seem to have an innate understanding of some of the properties of the physical world. But others they grasp only with experience, as a result of observing that certain events always follow others. For example, a spoon dropped from a high-chair always drops to the floor with a bang, while a sharp object applied to the skin always produces pain. Piaget has suggested that the young child's relatively precocious ability to *see* things can actually prevent him from understanding how they really are. The child is overimpressed by what something looks like, and so cannot grasp that a change in an object's appearance may have no effect on its essential nature. Thus, according to Piaget, it is not until the age of about eleven that a child comes to realize that a ball of plasticine which is squeezed into a different shape remains the same lump of plasticine in the sense that its weight has not changed, and that it could be squeezed back into its original form without adding or subtracting anything to or from it.

The logical rule that things can remain essentially the same although they look different is called the principle of invariance, and the tasks which Piaget invented to discover whether a child possesses it are known as conservation tests. The principle is a vital one, because it applies to many of the most important abstract properties of objects we use to make sense of the physical world – not just weight, but also number and volume. If it is true that young children do not understand it, or other logical rules like it, then their thought processes clearly are very different from ours. This would have profound implications not only for the answer to the question, 'What are children like?', but also for how parents should treat their children and what they ought to be taught at school. But are children really as illogical as Piaget and his followers suggest?

Recent research suggests that they may not be. For example, in the traditional conservation test for number, a child is shown two rows containing an equal number of counters, and asked: 'Which row has more counters, or are they both the same?' Seeing them lined up next to each other, each counter in the left-hand row matching one in the right, even very young children have no difficulty in saying that the rows are the same. The experimenter then spreads out the buttons in one of the rows, so that it becomes longer than the other, and asks the same question again. This experiment has been carried out many times, and the usual finding is that children younger than six say that the longer row now contains more counters, even though they have seen that no counters have been added or subtracted.

But does this reply really mean that they are illogical? From an adult perspective, the child's reply *is* illogical but put youself in the child's shoes and the situation looks rather different. There are at least three reasons why he might give the 'wrong' answer, even though he understands perfectly well that the two rows still contain the same number of counters. The first concerns the wording of the question. How can the child be sure that this unfamiliar adult with his silly game and funny questions hasn't made a mistake? He may be asking which row has more counters, but surely what he really means is which has more *inches*. The child may see the adult's second question either as stupid or as a naive attempt to trap him. Rather than cause the stranger to lose face, the child may helpfully choose to reinterpret the second question, and to respond as though it concerned not number but length which he feels is probably what the adult intended, given what he has just done with his hand to the counters.

It may seem rather perverse to assume that young children have the logic necessary to get conservation tests right and then try to explain why they in fact get them wrong. But there are good reasons for believing that wrong answers are not the result of logical faults, and that when young children are asked what seem to them silly questions by adults, they go beyond the wording of the question and try to figure out what the adult is really after. This was shown in an ingenious experiment carried out by James McGarrigle and Margaret Donaldson, in which the second row of counters was spread out not by the experimenter but by a glove puppet, a 'naughty' Teddy who was represented as spoiling the game. When this happens, young children are much more likely to answer that the two rows still contain the same number of counters, presumably because they no longer feel worried about embarrassing the experimenter.

There is a third aspect of the traditional conservation task which suggests that it may have given us a very mistaken view of children's intellectual capacity. From the child's point of view, he is simply confronted by a strange adult who asks an identical question twice. Generally speaking, adults only ask a question once, provided that a child answers it correctly the first time. The only time they repeat it is when they are not satisfied with the answer they first get: 'What are seven fours, Stephen?' 'Twenty-four, miss.' '*What are seven fours, Stephen?*'

A child is likely to assume, when asked again about the number of counters, that his first answer was wrong and will try a different answer instead. So here we have another explanation of the child's 'wrong' answer. Again, the fault seems to lie with the adults who designed the test. If in fact we simply omit the first question, children are much more likely to judge that the two rows contain the same number of counters, even though they have seen the experimenter 'lengthen' the second row.

So we have Piaget to thank for the first myth about childhood. Children are actually capable of making a logical judgment based on two separate perceptual experiences much earlier than he suggests, and they are only misled by appearances in artificial experimental situations in which adults encourage them to respond illogically. This means that educationalists who argue that children under the age of seven cannot be expected to learn how to use a ruler, for example, have been misled into underestimating younger children's capabilities. Exactly the same can be said about the belief that young children are incapable of appreciating anyone else's viewpoint, and once again Piaget must bear the blame for encouraging – if not actually creating – a popular misconception. According to him, children are *egocentric* up to the age of eight, both literally and metaphorically. In its literal sense, this means that young children believe that another person's view of a scene is identical to their own, though the second person is looking at it from a completely different vantage point. In the classic Piagetian test, a child is seated at a table on which there is a three-dimensional *papier mâché* model of three mountains of different sizes and colours. He is asked to represent the scene, by arranging three pieces of cardboard shaped like mountains, both from his own position at the table (i.e. to recreate what he has been looking at) and from the viewpoint of a doll seated in a chair at one of the other sides of the table (i.e. to work out what the model would look like from someone else's point of view).

Confronted by this task, children younger than seven don't seem to realize there can be any view of the scene other than their own. When asked how the mountains look to the doll, they simply arrange the cardboard shapes to correspond with their own view of the model. But does this really mean that they cannot imagine any perspective other than their own? Certainly not. Recent research makes it clear that once again adult rather than child egocentricity is responsible for the child's mistake, because both the stimulus material and the way in which children are asked to reproduce it are inappropriate. As any parent knows, children are profoundly bored by landscapes and so probably pay little attention to the mountains. Even if they do, the mountainsides are largely featureless and lacking in adequate cues which the children could use to tell one from another. When they are confronted not by dreary mountains but by a model of miniature people in natural settings – a farmyard scene or a battle between Cowboys and Indians, for example – children as young as three or four have no difficulty in predicting what the scene must look like to a doll viewing it from a different angle, provided that the display is mounted on a revolving turntable, and their ability to establish how it looks to someone else is tested by asking them to turn the display round until they are looking at it in the same way as it appears to the doll. This is a very much easier test than Piaget's, but the fact that even three-year-olds unhesitatingly turn the scene round shows that they know full well other people have different viewpoints from their own, and are perfectly capable of working out what these are, given an appropriate opportunity.

The demonstration that some of the most important sections of the Piagetian edifice are built on the quicksand of inadequate experimentation has profound implications, not only for our understanding of children but also for educational practice. I suggested earlier that the insights provided by contemporary researchers into the nature of the conservation task indicate that we ought to think again about what five-year-olds are capable of learning. Equally, the discovery that young children are not, after all, egocentric may mean that the progressive education movement, which draws much of its inspiration from Piaget, has caused parents to be overprotective in the social demands they make on their children. In short, there may be more than a grain of truth in the charge made by traditionalists that in primary schools where the progressive gospel is practised as well as preached, five- to seven-year-olds are given more featherbedding than they really need.

This suspicion is reinforced by American psychologist William Damon's intriguing exploration of the social world of the child, which suggests that there is a third area of the Piagetian myth to be undermined, and one closely related to what we have just been discussing. Piaget claims that children younger than nine are egocentric not only literally but also metaphorically, in the sense that they cannot appreciate someone else's point of view in an argument, or understand that other people have legitimate interests which sometimes conflict with their own and cannot just be ignored. Piaget suggests that before this age children have no sense of justice as an abstract concept, and that they are prevented from behaving in a ruthlessly selfish fashion only by fear of punishment and by the subservience to authority that they have been taught. If we followed Piaget's teaching strictly we would have to believe that children need protection not only from teachers who try to teach them things for which they are not ready and from parents who expect them to show a degree of give and take of which they are incapable, but also from other children, whose amoral pursuit of their own interests must surely lead to confrontations which can only be solved by the application of the principle that might is right.

Piaget has proposed a series of stages in a child's moral development analogous to his stages of intellectual development, but in this aspect of his theory he has been less influential than his follower, Lawrence Kohlberg, who claims that it is not until the age of twelve that children begin to apply moral principles. The idea that children are naturally wicked and totally selfish is another of the myths I aim to expose later in this chapter, but we can begin its demolition now by noting that once again the theorists have got it wrong. It's the same old story of experimenters judging childen's behaviour by adult standards and jumping to the conclusion that because the child's world does not seem to be governed by adult principles of morality, it has no moral principles.

Kohlberg reached his conclusions about moral development by telling people of different ages stories involving moral dilemmas, and asking them to judge the conduct of the protagonists. They might, for example, be asked to pass judgement on the action of a man who steals from a chemist's shop some medicine which he cannot afford to buy for his seriously ill wife. Most children tend to say that he did wrong because he was breaking the law and might be punished for it; it is not until adolescence that some – though by no means all – of us start to acknowledge that his action might be justifiable according to some higher moral principle. But although stories like this may be quite an effective way of judging the moral development of adults living in Western societies, they are inappropriate for children – who have no experience of this sort of moral dilemma; nor are they a suitable means of assessing the ethical sophistication of adults in cultures with different values from our own. For example, people in India, where family land and cows are sacred and have a higher moral value than human life, might give some rather unexpected comments on Kohlberg's moral dilemmas. But this does not mean that they have no understanding of moral principles; it is simply that their social world is organized on different principles from ours.

Exactly the same can be said about the social world of childhood. If, instead of confronting a child with a moral dilemma dealing with adult concerns such as the value of human life or marriage, we seek his response to a familiar situation – for example, asking him how he thinks a packet of sweets ought to be shared out among a group of children including himself – we find that even a five-year-old understands the principle of fairness. It is true that most four-year-olds respond egocentrically in this situation, saying that they should get all the sweets, but by the time they are five most children seem to have developed a concept of justice which dictates that the sweets should be shared out equally. Interestingly, they seem to apply this moral principle more readily when asked about a hypothetical situation than when they are actually given a packet of sweets and told to distribute them among a group of children. You may not find this observation very surprising, but it directly contradicts another of Piaget's assertions, that young children only develop a theoretical understanding of moral principles after they have mastered their application in practice.

The second myth

If Piaget is largely responsible for our mistaken belief that children younger than seven are egocentric and illogical, then Freud must take much of the blame for the second popular misconception about childhood – that what happens to us in the first six or seven years of life has a greater influence on the kind of adults we become than our experiences at any other stage of development. Freud was not the first person to put forward this idea; its long and distinguished pedigree can be traced back to the writings of Plato. But it was the furore caused by Freud's description of infantile sexuality which really focussed people's attention on the first half of childhood, and his claim that all adult neuroses are acquired before the age of six which gave root to the idea that damage done in these years can never be undone.

Freud's single-minded concern with the sex instinct led him to divide childhood up into the stages of psychosexual development – oral, anal, phallic and genital – named after the areas of the body from which he believed children derived most erotic pleasure at different times. But the names of the stages carry a much wider implication than mere sexual gratification. They are also supposed to describe a child's most pressing concerns and interests at each stage of childhood. Thus the oral stage is dominated by the hunt for the nipple and the anal stage by a struggle to adapt one's bowel movements to meet parents' demands. The phallic stage is a disturbing period in which children are said to desire a sexual relationship with their opposite-sexed parent and to be frightened that their parent of their own sex will become jealous and mutilate them as a punishment. Children are said to resolve this conflict by coming to identify with the like-sexed parent, whose moral standards they adopt, developing a conscience in the process. According to Freud, once a child has resolved the problems of the phallic stage – at around seven – his sexual urges cease tormenting him and lie dormant through a period of latency. This ends with puberty and the beginning of the genital period, in which all the earlier aspects of sexuality eventually come together to form a coherent set of sexual attitudes and feelings.

Freud's account of childhood development should not be taken as gospel, though his description at least of the oral and anal phases fits quite neatly with the observations of later researchers. The links he drew between a child's experiences during the various stages of psychosexual development and his personality as an adult are more doubtful. During the oral phase, for example, an infant is entirely dependent on another person for satisfying his need for food, and Freud claims that the extent to which this need is reliably met will determine how trusting and optimistic he will be in later life. A child whose mother is slow or unpredictable in answering his demands for food will become a pessimist and always be suspicious in his relationships with other people, while one who learns that he has only to ask for food to get it will develop a rosier view of the world and its inhabitants.

Another key Freudian notion is *fixation*, which is said to occur whenever the most important needs of a particular period are either frustrated or over-indulged. Either experience can make the child reluctant to move on to the next stage, which in Freud's view is the major cause of subsequent personality flaws. For example, fixation in the oral stage may express itself in adult gluttony or alcoholism. Similarly, a child who is fixated at the anal phase, perhaps as a result of a prolonged battle over toilet-training, will develop what Freud described as the anal personality – a mixture of meanness, obstinacy and obsessiveness.

The hold which Freudian theory continues to exert on the general public's imagination and the extent to which his concepts have been assimilated into our everyday language make it impossible to ignore his ideas. But although he may have performed a service by drawing our attention to the fact that there is a sexual dimension to children's lives, his description of childhood is one-sided, and his views about what makes us become the people we become are seriously misleading.

His view that the years of early childhood are all-important is wrong for two reasons. The first is that, as we now know, what happens to a child at this point does not set his personality once and for all. As Ann and Alan Clarke put it in their excellent book *Early Experience: Myth and Evidence*, 'there is virtually no psychosocial adversity to which some children have not been subjected, yet later recovered, granted a radical change of circumstances.' Perhaps this is illustrated most dramatically by a pair of Czechoslovakian twins who were brought up in complete isolation, locked in a cupboard and deprived of adequate food, fresh air and sunshine between the ages of eighteen months and seven years. They were then rescued by the welfare authorities and entrusted to the care of a foster mother. At this point the twins could hardly walk, were terrified of people, communicated with each other only by gestures, and had a mental age of about three.

They must surely have been beyond redemption, if there were any truth in Freud's assertion that all adult neuroses are acquired before the age of six, let alone in J. B. Watson's even more restrictive claim that our emotional disposition is set for life by the time we are three. What actually happened in this case (and it is not unique) is that by the age of fourteen the children had normal IQ scores, were deeply attached to their foster mother, and had entirely normal dealings with other children and with adults. So much for the idea that the wounds of childhood never close.

Before birth

The second reason why it is a mistake to over-emphasize the years of early childhood is that this leads us to underestimate the importance of what has happened before a child is ever born. And to do so is to ignore at least three major influences on what makes us the people we are. The first of these is our genes. A person's physical appearance and capabilities contribute enormously to every aspect of his or her life, and while no one would deny that our physical development is greatly affected by the environment in which we find ourselves as children and as adults, the genes with which we are endowed at the moment of conception set a potential which, for some aspects of our physique, cannot be exceeded. If you don't like the colour of your hair or the shape of your nose, both of which are determined by your genes, you can alter them, thanks to cosmetics and the miracles of modern surgery. But it is simply not the case that anyone can become an Olympic champion sprinter, any more than any foal can be turned into a Derby winner.

It is not just physical characteristics which are determined by genes. Many aspects of personality – for example, sociability, emotionality, activity, soothability and attentiveness – also seem to be influenced by our genes, though of course a child born with a cheerful disposition may easily be turned into a miserable adult if his life is a series of misfortunes. Although a child's personality is partly shaped by the treatment he receives from those who look after him, he also, from the time he is born, has a distinct personality to which those on whom he depends respond. No mother needs to be told this. Here is what a young mother whom we interviewed had to say on the subject:

The oldest one is very placid, but the second one is entirely different. Right from a baby, the little one just wanted continual attention. Whereas the boy – I just sort of led him, changed him and put him to bed, and that was that.

In a very real sense, babies get the treatment they ask for, or at least the treatment which their caretakers think they are asking for, and their genes must be largely responsible for their early personality. So although someone's character can be affected by his early environment, the nature of this environment is partly determined by his own genes and by the embryonic personality they have given him. This is why most psychologists now insist that it is nonsense to talk about the influence of *either* heredity *or* the environment, as if one could operate independently of the other.

No one would dispute that the way parents treat their children has an influence on how they turn out. We know, for example, that inconsistent discipline in childhood is associated with later delinquency, whether the inconsistency arises from having one lax and one strict parent, or parents who fluctuate unpredictably between the two. Similarly, children whose mothers are restrictive, dominant, intrusive and possessive tend to become under-achievers. But perhaps the most important discovery to emerge from researchers' many detailed observations of the way in which parents and children interact with each other is that the power to influence is mutual. For example, a baby who is bounced a lot may become more active, but his own temperament may also lead his mother to bounce him more than his less active brother or sister.

Mention of a newborn's personality brings us to two other important influences on development about which Freud has little to say – the child's experience during pregnancy and the experience of birth itself. Development during pregnancy is under the control of the genetic code, and irreversible damage will result if this is tampered with by tetragenic agents such as thalidomide which causes the genes responsible for the development of arms and legs to stop producing protein. Other suspected tetragenic agents include: irradiation, which can result in the malformation of any organ, depending on its stage of development; German measles, which can damage the brain or sensory and cranial nerves, leading to mental retardation or vision and hearing disorders; cortisone, which may contribute to the formation of a cleft palate; and excessive doses of Vitamins A and D, which can lead to a cleft palate and eye damage (Vitamin A) or mental retardation (Vitamin D). Recent research also suggests that mothers who smoke and those who drink even moderately may harm any child they are carrying. American researchers have found that the babies of alcoholic mothers are 20 per cent shorter and tend to be less intelligent than the average baby. The babies of smokers may also be smaller than those of non-smokers, perhaps because a non-smoking mother gives the foetus its full quota of oxygen while the foetus whose mother is a smoker receives through the placenta a cocktail of oxygen mixed with tar and nicotine.

Once the first three months of pregnancy have been safely negotiated, life becomes less hazardous for the foetus. During the second three months, it grows rapidly, from three inches to fourteen and from an ounce to one-and-a-half pounds. It has periods of sleeping and wakefulness, cries, hiccups, sucks its thumb, and may even perform somersaults. It also has an outside chance of surviving if born at this juncture. During the final three months, the foetus grows in length by a further 50 per cent and gains about six pounds in weight. If born prematurely, it has a fair chance of survival since most of its organs are sufficiently developed to function independently should the need arise. The main problem is breathing. This depends on the brain stem having reached the appropriate stage of maturation, which explains why respiratory problems are usually the most serious to be faced in keeping a premature infant alive.

There is another aspect of the prenatal environment

which can make a significant contribution to the sort of baby a mother eventually produces – her own psychological state during pregnancy. We can dismiss the old wives' tale that the child of a woman who is frightened during pregnancy will have a birthmark shaped like the object which upset her. But the mood of a pregnant woman does seem to affect the child she is carrying, via the hormonal changes which accompany powerful emotions. These hormones are carried in the mother's bloodstream and can pass through the placenta to the foetus, even though there is no *direct* connection between the blood vessels of mother and child. Mothers who are subjected to severe or prolonged emotional stress during pregnancy are more likely to give birth to babies who are irritable and overactive or have feeding problems and stomach upsets. Highly anxious mothers also have a larger number of spontaneous abortions, a higher proportion of premature babies, and tend to spend longer in labour and have more complicated deliveries.

Such considerations place a question mark against the contemporary practice of insisting that virtually all births take place in hospitals. Most people are frightened of being in hospital because it suggests that they are in danger, and many patients are disturbed by the feeling that they are no longer in control even of the mundane arrangements of their everyday life. Whereas a hundred years ago most women gave birth in the reassuring familiarity of their own homes, with the assistance of a midwife and female friends or relatives, birth is now very much a medical event which takes place in alien if not actually frightening surroundings. No doubt the change is greatly to a baby's advantage if the birth is a complicated one, but the gain has to be balanced against the effect which hospitalization may have on a mother's frame of mind. The other drawback about hospital births is that some hospitals limit the amount of time a mother may spend with her child. Research suggests that this can make it more difficult for the two to form a close relationship, partly because the mother feels that her competence as a parent is being questioned. But restricted early contact with its mother can also be bad for a baby's health. The human skin is covered by a rich flora of bacteria and yeasts which a baby acquires soon after birth from contact with adults. Normally these come from his parents, but if he is handled mainly by doctors and nurses, he may acquire unhealthy bacteria from them instead – hospitals are notoriously unhealthy places – before his skin has had a chance to be colonized by the safer bacteria of his parents.

Two points emerge from this brief review of the life we lead before our official birthday. First, it is clearly nonsense to speak of the newborn infant as a blank slate on which anything can be written. For a child whose mother took thalidomide, the single most important determinant of the sort of life he will lead and the kind of person he will become is long behind him, and it is foolish to pretend otherwise. The same can be said of many children who have the misfortune to be born with a genetic abnormality or who suffer from any major chemical insult during the first three months of pregnancy. For a normal baby, the position is much less drastic, but, as every mother knows, no two babies are identical – physically or in personality. The second point is that the age and stage of the foetus is critically important. An infusion of certain chemical agents may be a harmless irritant one day, but it can permanently damage some important organ if it occurs a week later.

So far as being born is concerned, this may be an event of more importance to a child's parents than to the child himself, and we shall have more to say about its impact on couples in Chapter 4. For the child it represents a change of surroundings and of status. He has to abandon the familiar peace and comfort of the amniotic sac for the much brighter, noisier and totally novel outside world. What must be an uncomfortable journey through the narrow birth canal is followed by a quick succession of experiences none of which are calculated to please him. He is cleaned up, held upside down, poked, injected, measured and stared at. Apart from the change of environment, the most important consequence of birth for the baby is that he is now breathing for himself. This aside, he is no nearer to becoming a viable independent being than he was the day before, although he has survived one of the more dangerous events of his life (the risk of dying is greater at birth than at any other time until we reach the late fifties).

First come, first served

There is one other factor over which the newborn infant has no control but which may have a considerable effect on what sort of adult he turns out to be – his position in the family. Take a look at either the British or American *Who's Who* and you'll find that it's dominated by first-born children. In one of the largest psychological experiments ever conducted, the IQ scores of all nineteen-year-old Dutch males were measured when they began their (compulsory) military service. These scores were then plotted against each man's position in his family, and a very strong relationship was found between birth-order and IQ. First-borns were more intelligent than second-borns, who were more intelligent than third-borns, and so on, regardless of the total size of their families. It seems to be a universal finding that eldest boys in a family are more intelligent, more motivated to be successful, but also more anxious than younger children. The same applies for girls, but only if no boys are born later.

One way to explain the intellectual advantage of first-borns is to treat the family as a unit with an intellectual level to which all its members contribute. Two average parents might contribute say 100 points each to this, and a newborn first child perhaps 7 points. So the intellectual level of the family at this point is 207 divided by 3, i.e. 69. By the time a second child arrives on the scene, the contribution made by the first-born might have risen to say 29 points. This plus the 200 points of the parents and the 7 of the second child makes a total of 236. But this now has to be divided by 4, so the overall intellectual level of the family drops to 59, which means that the second child is spending his early months in a less stimulating intellectual climate than that enjoyed by his elder brother at the same stage. It also means that from the second-born's point of view, the longer the gap which separates his birth from that of his elder brother the better. Suppose in the present example the parents had waited another year before having the second child. By this time the elder child might have contributed 45 instead of 29 intellectual points so that the younger one would arrive in a climate of 63 instead of 59. This suggests that the common belief among parents that it is a good thing to have children as closely spaced as is convenient may work to the advantage of first-borns, but be less helpful for their younger brothers and sisters.

There is another way of looking at the advantage of the first-born child and the effects of spacing between children. Very recently, a group of American researchers took blood samples from more than 250 babies immediately after they were born, and found that first-born boys had significantly higher levels of the male sex hormone testosterone circulating in their bloodstream than later-borns. This testosterone measure has nothing to do with the length of labour, birthweight or the age of the mother, but it is closely related to the spacing between births. The shorter the interval between the birth of two brothers, the less testosterone the second has in his bloodstream. We also know that if girls are exposed to unusually high levels of male sex hormones before they are born (as a side-effect of certain drugs their mothers are prescribed), they tend later to be more successful academically than average. However, it would be quite wrong to jump to the conclusion that the more testosterone you have the cleverer you are likely to be, because although testosterone is a male sex hormone, there is absolutely no evidence that boys are more intelligent than girls, or that men are cleverer than women.

At present we do not know whether the advantage of first-borns really has any biological bias. Even if it has, this must be augmented by other factors such as starting life with an exclusive claim to parents' attention, and an opportunity to practise leadership skills on a follower who will accept orders without question. Nor is it only eldest children who gain an advantage in later life from their position in the family. Youngest children are often especially close to their mothers, which builds up their self-esteem and so prepares them for later success. So far as second-borns are concerned, it seems to be an advantage to be the opposite sex to your elder brother or sister, perhaps because this increases your novelty value. But same-sex second children need not despair. The trends I have been describing are all based on averages, and we all know plenty of exceptions.

Second-borns very close in age to their elder siblings can also gain some consolation from the results of a recent survey carried out amongst middle-class teenagers in Boston, USA. Here the researchers found that when the gap between siblings was less than eighteen months, the elder children had a greater intellectual advantage over the younger than when the gap was more than thirty months. However, they also found that close spacing could work to the advantage of younger children. Specifically, closer spacing seemed to make younger children better at team games and more ambitious professionally than those less close in age to their elder siblings. The more closely spaced younger children were also more self-sufficient, more sober and serious, but less concerned about social protocol than the less closely spaced. I am not quite sure where this leaves parents who are trying to plan their families to the best advantage of all their children, but one thing is certain: we cannot ignore birth order when trying to understand how and why we become the people we are.

All this is to set childhood in perspective. I don't want to belittle the importance of the years between birth and puberty, but since we are concerned with the entire life-span we obviously cannot ignore prenatal factors which make a significant contribution both to what happens to us as children and to what sort of adults we become. It is equally important not to approach childhood blinkered by the Freudian myth that the events of a child's life set his personality in a way which cannot subsequently be altered. The astonishing resilience and powers of recovery shown by the Czech twins mentioned earlier leave no doubt that children are more flexible than Freud would have us believe. This case, and others like it, also suggest that it is wrong to assume either that all adult neuroses have their roots in childhood, or that there is no point in trying to remedy the effects of a scarred childhood.

A myth is as good as a milestone

There are two ways of approaching the childhood years. The first is to split it up into a series of chronological stages and identify the development landmarks of each. For example, we might say that infancy (nought to two years) is the period in which children become attached to people ('Can I trust them?'), in which they learn to walk and use their hands, and in which the child comes to realize that objects do not cease to exist when he is not looking at them. Similarly, we could describe toddlerhood (two to four) as the period when a child learns to talk and to acquire a degree of self-control ('Will they let me?'), early school (five to seven) as the period when he becomes aware of sex-roles and capable of combining two separate pieces of information to draw a logical conclusion, and middle school (eight to eleven) as a period in which the emphasis switches to the development of social skills and the acquisition of sound learning habits ('Can I do it?').

The drawback to this approach is that it implies far more uniformity and consistency of development than children actually show. The third myth about childhood is that children move through a regular sequence of easily identifiable stages, changing their behaviour as they move from one stage to the next but acting consistently across a wide range of situations at any point of time in accordance with the 'characteristic' behaviour of the particular stage they are in. Linked to this is the notion, dear to the hearts of IQ-testers, that children are also consistent over time, so that a lively and bright infant will tend to turn into an active and intelligent nine-year-old, while an infant who shows unusual distress when his mother leaves the room will later become an emotional adolescent. The reality is rather different. In fact there is enormous variability both between different children and among the various aspects of development in a single child. We all know about early and late maturers, and most parents will have noticed that girls develop faster than boys in almost all respects. But it is also quite common to find children who are precocious in one way but backward in others, which makes it difficult to say what stage they have reached. To take just one example, Piaget – the arch stage-theorist – claims that a child's thought processes change as he grows older, in an orderly and fixed sequence, because his ability to think stems from underlying intellectual structures so broad that they affect every aspect of his intellectual competence. This means that a child who is able to perform a task characteristic of one stage – for example, using a ruler to build a tower of blocks in one corner of a room the same height as a tower in the other corner – should also be able to perform all the other tasks characteristic of the same period – for example, realizing that if Jane is older than John, and John older than Kate then Jane must also be older than Kate.

Mastery of one task ought to mean that a child has acquired the intellectual structure which would allow him to perform all others like it, if Piaget is to be believed.

It now seems clear that here, too, Piaget is wrong. Researchers have found that when a child is taught a particular logical skill there may be little or no transfer of knowledge to other supposedly equivalent skills. And if we measure the logical skills of a group of children, there is often no fixed pecking-order for intellectual skills. Mary may be better than Clare at one task but less accomplished at another, even though the two tasks are supposed to involve the same underlying intellectual structure in Piaget's scheme of things. Instead of talking about a single all-embracing structure, psychologists now tend to view a child's intellectual development as a series of 'valleys' in each of which progress is made at different rates. And if it is wrong to think of intellectual development in simple stages, how much less likely is it that we can fit every single aspect of a child's development into easily recognizable stages?

The fact is that children are growing up all the time, physically, emotionally and intellectually, and there are no naturally occurring sharp divisions between one phase and the next, sad though this may seem to scientists who like things to be more neatly arranged. When children do start behaving differently, it's usually because of some change in their lives, like starting school or moving to a new one. But these changes are imposed on them by adults who assume that they are now about the right age to move on. So a child's sense of growing up, and feelings about what he or she ought to be able to do at a given age, are both greatly affected by the assumptions parents and teachers make about the 'natural' course of development, and the psychological theories on which these assumptions are based may well be wrong.

And it is not just that the same child can behave inconsistently in different situations, being precocious in some respects but relatively immature in others. There is also surprisingly little consistency in behaviour across the whole span of childhood. Certainly children have distinctive personalities from the moment they are born, as a result of their genes, their experiences in the womb and during birth (the drugs a mother is given during labour can still be affecting the disposition of a child several weeks after it is born), and the conditions into which they are born. The differences between them become more marked as they get older. But is there any connection between what we are like as babies and what sort of child, adolescent or even adult we turn into? Researchers have explored this question with regard to intelligence, personality and academic attainment, and their findings have a bearing both on our discussion in this chapter, and on our understanding of the factors that make people differ from each other later on.

Perhaps the most important finding is that measures of what children are like before they start school seem to offer very little clue as to the kind of people they are going to become. It is not easy to measure the intelligence of the pre-school child, but we can get a general idea of how advanced he is compared to other children of the same age by seeing whether he can tie his shoe-laces, dress himself or perform other essential skills. We can also take measures of how attentive, irritable or active he is. But none of these measures predict what a child will be like at the end of childhood, let alone what sort of adult he is going to become. Once we get to adolescence, personality tests become quite effective predictors of adult characteristics, but the fact that a child's nature before he reaches school tells us so little about his subsequent development is surely the final nail in the coffin for the view that the first six years of life are all-important in determining a person's character.

Measurements taken towards the end of childhood are a very different matter. The IQ score of a ten-year-old is an excellent predictor of his IQ at maturity though other measures, such as motivation and examination results, vary considerably during the years of adolescence. However, all these findings are reached by looking at large groups of children. When we examine more closely what is happening to individual children, it becomes clear that the pattern of apparent moderate consistency over the school years actually conceals three very different patterns of development. Some children show a rock-like consistency, maintaining the same IQ, degree of motivation and position in their classes. Other children show enormous fluctuations, while most lie between the two extremes. Why this should be so we simply don't know. It is possible that some people have greater variability built into their genetic code, and of course we would expect children whose environment changes dramatically, like the Czech twins mentioned earlier, to be affected by such a change. But most children grow up in fairly constant surroundings, so the finding that there is very little connection between the child of three and the adult of twenty means that we can no longer accept the old axiom that the child is father to the man. The quotation from John Milton with which I began the chapter is surely much closer to the mark. No Englishman needs to be told that a sunny morning does not guarantee that it will not rain before nightfall.

The myth of the antisocial savage

The fourth myth about childhood takes us back into infancy, and it brings us close to the doctrine of original sin. We saw earlier that four- and five-year-olds are much less self-centred than is often thought. Now we must consider whether even a newborn baby is the unscrupulous, totally self-centred autocrat he is sometimes made out to be, aware only of other people's existence insomuch as they supply his needs, and requiring a lengthy programme of socialization to turn him into a recognizable human being.

To see that this is not the case, we must abandon discussion of the development of personality and intelligence, and turn instead to the area of social behaviour – behaviour with other people. This is an area of critical importance, not only because our sophisticated social skills constitute one of the most important distinguishing characteristics of the human species, but also because the single most important task which confronts the newborn infant is ensuring that he receives a regular and adequate supply of food. For this he is obliged to rely on the good offices of another person or other people, a state of dependence which lasts longer in Man than in any other species. Fortunately, he has two allies working on his behalf – his own and his mother's nature. So far as the second is concerned, however, he may be on shaky ground. For although the hormonal changes which occur in pregnancy biologically 'prime' a woman for giving birth and prepare her for breastfeeding, there is actually no very convincing evidence for the existence of a maternal drive, as I have explained in my book *A Question of Sex*. Moreover, in the past many women died in childbirth, and many now choose not to breastfeed their children, so it is clearly vital that babies should be able to endear themselves to adults other than their mothers, in case the occasion demands it.

Until quite recently, this would have seemed unlikely. It used to be thought that newborn babies were interested only in themselves and their own needs, and that they had to be taught to be responsive to other people. Old-fashioned prescriptions for bringing up children placed a heavy emphasis on *socialization*, the process whereby the initially wilful and totally self-centred infant is made to recognize that other people have interests which sometimes conflict with his own, and is gradually forced to become social and sociable by the appropriate use of punishments and rewards.

This view of a child's nature now looks to be very wide of the mark. The contemporary view is that we are genetically programmed to become social beings, and come into the world already equipped with enough social skills to ensure that feeding and caring for us is actually quite a rewarding experience, even for someone who is not related to us by blood-ties. Precisely what a newborn baby is capable of before he has had a chance to learn any skills is one of the most controversial subjects in the whole of psychology. We know that he doesn't have to learn how to breathe or to suck a nipple, but experts still argue among themselves about what else comes naturally to him. Generally speaking, the closer scientists have studied babies, the more impressed they have become with babies' natural abilities. Many of these are too subtle to be picked up by the untrained eye, even when that eye belongs to so devoted an observer as the baby's mother. But careful experimentation and repeated viewing of videotapes showing babies' behaviour leaves little doubt that newly born humans have far more resources than we imagined even as recently as a decade ago.

For example, a newborn can tell where a sound is coming from and will turn his head towards it, showing that he knows it usually means there is something to look at. He also seems to know from the beginning that an object or person coming towards him is probably going to be tangible, and he will reach out to touch it. If held up, he will take steps along a table, but this primitive 'walking' soon disappears, perhaps because he is given no opportunity to practise it, since he spends most of his time flat on his back. Newborns can also reach out and grasp things (though their reaching is not very accurate and they seem unsure what to do with an object once they have it in their grasp). This is another skill which is present at birth but then seems to be lost for a while. Again, the problem may be that a baby gets little chance to use or practise his grasping behaviour, because potentially graspable objects tend not to remain within his reach long enough for him to grasp them. A good way of assessing an infant's understanding of the world is to disrupt the normal pattern of things and observe which distortions of reality startle him, and which leave him unmoved. For example, by placing a sound-proof glass screen between a baby and his mother and projecting her voice through a stereo system, we can make her voice appear to be coming not from her mouth but from some other part of the room. The newborn child does not react to this, but three weeks later he is clearly surprised, which means that the child learns in the early weeks of his life the fact that voices tend to come from mouths.

Nevertheless, a baby arrives in the world with impressively advanced abilities, both in perception and in movement. More surprising is some of his earliest behaviour which clearly shows that, far from being totally self-centred and oblivious to other people's existence, he is actually well aware of, and anxious to please them. How else can we explain the pheno-menon known as interactional synchrony? This grandiose term refers to the fact that when two people are having a conversation the person who is speaking makes certain body movements which the listener unconsciously imitates. The movements involved are tiny adjustments of posture or a tilt of the head, and close examination of films of people talking shows that we habitually engage in such dances. Given the complexity of the behaviour and the fact that even as adults we are totally unaware of doing it, the finding that newborn infants show perfect interactional synchrony is astonishing. Although it will be months before they start talking, from the day they are born babies actually move their bodies in time with the speech rhythms of an adult who is speaking to them. Moreover, it is only human speech which produces this response. Tapes of isolated vowel sounds or regular tapping leave them unmoved, which suggests that we have here an innate skill designed to establish communication with other people. A baby's mother may never have heard of inter-actional synchrony but she knows – and loves – the feeling that she is communicating with her baby, and this exciting new research confirms that she is not just indulging in wishful thinking. Not all babies are good at interactional synchrony, however, and those who are not run the risk of being called uncuddly or unresponsive. But most babies do it spontaneously, providing very powerful evidence that we are naturally social creatures, and do not have to learn to be responsive to other people.

Another sign of this is that babies start imitating other people in the first week of life. If his mother sticks her tongue out at him, a baby soon begins to stick his tongue out at her, and if she varies the routine by fluttering her eyelashes, he will do the same. This is remarkable because it is very unlikely that the baby will ever have seen himself in a mirror. So how does he make the connection between his own tongue and the pink object he sees protruding from his mother's lips? How does he know he has a tongue? It suggests a formidable amount of built-in intellectual organization, and babies' obvious enjoyment of imitating not just their mothers but anyone else who is prepared to join in the game further supports the belief that we are naturally social. Readers with children are unlikely to be surprised by this suggestion, but it strikes at the very heart of the traditional psychologist's view of the human infant as a completely self-absorbed creature who must be taught to be social.

Of course it is not just babies who enjoy imitating others – many adults fancy themselves as mimics; but children spend progressively less of their time imitating others between the ages of four and eleven. You can recognize the leaders in a group of children because they are the ones most imitated by other children. But the leaders also tend to be imitators too, and may even acquire their power in the group partly as a result of their prowess at mimicry.

No doubt child psychologists have much to learn from parents when it comes to assessing the capabilities of young children, but their experiments show that parents are not always infallible judges of their own children's behaviour. We have already seen that some aspects of a baby's behaviour are too subtle to be detected by the untrained observer, which means that his social skills are not fully appreciated by his parents. However, most parents tend to overestimate their babies' social accomplishments in one rather crucial respect – smiling. Babies produce their first smiles a few days after birth. But these are not full smiles (they involve the mouth and cheeks, but not the eyes), and they occur spontaneously, regardless of whether the infant is awake or sleeping, probably as a result of spontaneous discharge from the central nervous system. The full smile does not appear until the third week, when it is elicited by sounds from the outside world, especially the female human voice. At this stage, babies smile in response to what they hear but not to what they see – they are as likely to smile at the sound of a voice whether or not they can see the face from which it comes. Three weeks later the position is very different. For a six-week-old baby the sight of a human face is a most effective stimulus for eliciting a smile.

At this point, virtually every mother is convinced that when her baby smiles he is smiling *at her*, and she is delighted by this, thinking it means that her child not only recognizes her, but is pleased to see her. Kill-joy psychologists take a rather more cynical view, pointing out that although babies of six weeks certainly smile when they see a human face, they are just as likely to do so when presented with a crude mask or even a plate with two blobs on it! It is inconceivable that the child has simply mistaken the plate for a face, failing to notice that it is missing a nose, ears and mouth, since we know from his powers of imitation that he has been alert to these features for more than a month. In fact, experiments show that babies of this age are more likely to smile at a white card with three pairs of black dots on it than they are at the sight of the human face. So parents probably misinterpret the smile of a six-week-old. He smiles when they approach not because he is glad to see them or wants to be friendly, but simply because their faces happen to contain two dark areas the irises of their eyes surrounded by white areas.

A mother may be beguiled by her baby's early smiles into

thinking that he is responding to her when he is not, and therefore overestimate his sociability. But many mothers make just the opposite mistake about crying. The traditional view is that crying is just an irritating and undesirable item of a baby's behavioural repertoire which must be stamped out as part of the process of socializing him. If this were true, the best plan would be to ignore a baby when he cried since paying attention to him would only encourage him to cry more in future and so produce a spoilt, whining child. However, it turns out that this treatment has just the opposite result. The babies who cry least at the age of one are those whose mothers have responded promptly and reliably to their cries during the preceding twelve months; those who have been ignored, far from being discouraged from crying, actually cry more. The most likely explanation of this is that after the first three weeks, when crying is usually a sign of discomfort, a crying baby is trying to communicate. If his cries are responded to, the message he receives is not just that crying works but that communication with other people is possible. This encourages him to develop alternative methods of communication, and indeed researchers find that babies whose mothers are most responsive to their cries not only cry less by the end of the first year but also tend to have developed the most efficient alternative ways of communicating, for example by means of the expressions on their faces. So crying, too, is a sign of sociability, at least during the first year. Later, however, it means something very different. Older children cry when they are frustrated or when they fail to make their point using the more sophisticated methods of communication they have developed. So whereas parents would be well advised to respond promptly to the crying of a baby of less than one, a change of strategy is called for in dealing with older children. With them, being over-solicitous may indeed produce a fussy child, as the traditionalists maintain.

One final piece of evidence ought to remove any doubts

that we arrive in the world strongly predisposed to be sociable. This concerns the notion of obedience. According to the traditional view, babies are totally selfish creatures, interested only in seeing that their own needs are met and indifferent, if not positively hostile, to other people's wishes. Unfortunately for them, the people they have to depend on *do* have wishes, which need to be humoured to keep their good will. Obedience then is another unpalatable lesson the child has to learn as part of his socialization programme, or so socialization theorists would have us believe. Once again, careful observation of how infants actually behave during the first year of life shows how wrong the experts can be. Researchers who have watched mothers with their babies at regular intervals during the first year of life report that by the end of the first year nearly 70 per cent of a mother's commands are obeyed. Moreover, mothers who are sensitive to their babies' crying receive much more obedience than those who are less responsive. An additional bonus for responsive mothers is that babies who are treated in this way are more prepared to explore their surroundings on their own and make less fuss when she leaves the room. The reason for this is that such a baby is more secure. This security is based on trust, which simply means he is confident that he can predict his mother's actions, including her absences and returns and her response to his efforts to communicate with her. So crying in a young baby, far from being something we should try to stamp out, is actually an important part of his repertoire of social skills.

Many parents express the view that their children are not at all like they were at the same age. They say, half-enviously, half-approvingly, that kids have never had it so good as they do today. But are they right?

So far as the trappings of his life are concerned, no doubt the contemporary child's surroundings are very different from those his parents experienced, and light years removed from

the conditions in which his grandparents were raised. He
has TV and the pocket calculator, as well as the benefit of two
of the major economic and social trends of the post-war era –
the general increase in economic prosperity and the liberal-
ization of adult attitudes towards children. Not only does he
have more spending power than his parents had at the same
age, but probably more freedom to decide what to buy.
But there is no real evidence that the essential psychological
experience of childhood has changed as a result of these
changes in the veneer of everyday living. The tasks a child
faces remain the same: survival, getting on with people and
learning how to integrate their wishes and feelings with his
own, developing an individual personality, and mastering
the physical and intellectual skills he will need to function
as an adult. Nor have the constraints imposed on a child by
dependence on others and by his physical and mental im-
maturity changed.

However, the sight of the Colchester children we studied
playing centuries-old games has to be set against the fact that
today's children start junior school at an age when their
predecessors might already have joined the work-force. It
would also be foolish to ignore the enormous cross-cultural
differences which exist in what is expected of, say, a seven-
year-old. A colleague recently told me of a little girl he had
met in Guyana who had been orphaned at five and had
become a successful business-woman in the street-market by
the time she was seven. She was then adopted by an American
couple who set about transforming her into a 'normal' child.
Within months she lost her worldlywise sharpness and self-
sufficiency, and had come to depend on them for help with
tasks she had previously been perfectly capable of performing
herself. This story highlights the plasticity and adaptability
of children, but it also emphasizes the enormous influence of
chance environmental factors on how a child develops, and
provides further evidence of how unwise it is to describe
childhood in terms of biologically fixed stages. Of course, we

don't know how the Guyanese girl's feelings about herself or the world were affected by so abrupt a change in her circumstances, any more than we can compare the feelings of a seven-year-old today with those of a child fifty or a hundred years ago. But I strongly suspect that adults who say they are astonished by their children have a rather distorted memory of their own childhood, and that if some miraculous time machine allowed the modern child to meet his parents when they were his present age, the two generations would not really be so different.

This has been a rather unusual chapter, both in comparison to the rest of this book and because I have not followed the conventional practice of describing childhood as a series of stages. I have tried to explain why I think the stage approach is misleading, and have identified four key beliefs arising from the stage theorists' work which have shaped the way we think about childhood, all of which I believe to be mistaken. So far as its influence on the rest of the human life-cycle is concerned, I think that the importance of the first half of childhood has been greatly exaggerated, while the significance of the second half is best assessed in conjunction with a child's experience during adolescence, which we shall consider in the next chapter.

CHAPTER 2

Finding Yourself

'In case you're worried about what's going to become of the younger generation, it's going to grow up and start worrying about the younger generation.'

ROGER ALLEN

Some social historians believe that childhood is a modern invention, that until recently children were regarded simply as small adults. People also claim, with slightly more justification, that adolescence is a new invention. The arguments are similar, but the issue is more piquant because whereas childhood is something we would be proud to have invented, adolescence is thought to be a problem period, for those who are going through it as well as for those who have to deal with them. So if we have invented it, we might well curse our stupidity for saddling ourselves with the burden of The Teenager.

It is important to distinguish between adolescents and teenagers, because although the two terms refer to the same period of life, different claims have been made about their historical status. The claim about adolescence is that it only came into existence in the nineteenth century, while teenagers, according to one pundit, 'were born in 1942, marketed in American in 1947, discovered in small flocks in Britain in 1956, cosseted and comforted during the 1960s, began to weaken as youth unemployment climbed in the 1970s, and can now be pronounced extinct'. The word 'teenager' was only coined during the Second World War by market researchers who wanted to describe young people with money to spend. Sociologists are now suggesting that we should drop it, on the grounds that teenagers were a phenomenon unique to a period of affluence which has ended. I doubt whether teenagers are really worse off now than in the 1960s, but perhaps the language would be none the poorer if the term were allowed to die.

Adolescence however is a different matter. The word means growing up, and it has impeccable Latin origins, though the period of life it is used to describe has changed over the centuries. For the Romans, it covered the period beginning at seventeen and ending at about twenty-eight, although they occasionally used it to describe men as old as forty, perhaps in recognition of the fact that some of us are late developers. In the Middle Ages, the period of youth lasted from the end of dependence at seven or eight to the achievement of independence and marriage in the mid- to late-twenties, and little distinction was drawn between older and younger youths. After the Industrial Revolution, the traditions according to which youth lived were redrawn along class lines. The lower classes developed a youth culture organized around street gangs whose members ranged in age between the early teens and mid-twenties. For the sons and daughters of the *nouveau riche*, youth was a rather different experience. Girls were kept at home until they married, while boys left home in their mid-teens for university or an apprenticeship. The early public schools catered for boys between eight and nineteen, and it was not until boarding-school education became fashionable among the middle classes after the 1830s that the age of thirteen assumed any significance. Once the distinction between primary and secondary education had been introduced, a lower limit was fixed for adolescence, which has led to the claim that the reform of the English public school system initiated by Dr Arnold at Rugby was responsible for the invention of adolescence.

Of course it all depends what you mean by adolescence. The dictionary follows the Latin and defines it as youth or the process of growing up. So far as psychological development is concerned, the latter could refer to the whole of life. However, the term has recently become associated with physiological development, and it is often used to describe the period between the onset of puberty and physical maturity, which is reached at about twenty-one in females and slightly later in males. But there are at least two other ways of defining adolescence. We could adopt a more psychological approach and confine it to the period when someone is obviously suffering from the storms and stress which are supposed to be the hallmark of the 'typical' adolescent. The problem with this approach is that there is no universal experience of adolescence. Many children pass through the teenage years without any outward signs of disturbance, and so, by this definition, miss out on adolescence altogether. It is also worth noting that even when they do appear, the psychological 'symptoms' of adolescence usually start some while after the physical changes which mark puberty.

The other alternative is to treat the years between puberty and the mid-twenties as two periods, one ending with the completion of full-time education and the next with marriage. This is the practice I shall be following in *Seven Ages*. In the present chapter we shall largely be concerned with people between the ages of about eleven and seventeen, while the next chapter will take us up to the age of approximately twenty-five. Of course not everyone leaves school before seventeen or gets married by the time they are twenty-five. Some get married at sixteen. and a few are still studying when they are twenty-five.

If we follow the popular view that adolescence is a time when the young make life hell for their elders, then it obviously isn't a modern invention. The shepherd in Shakespeare's *The Winter's Tale* laments: 'I would there were no age between sixteen and three-and-twenty, or that youth would sleep out the rest; for there is nothing in the between but getting wenches with child, wronging the ancientry, stealing, fighting.' Contemporary surveys of adolescent behaviour confirm that all these forms of delinquency are still going strong. Equally, the descriptions we have of what young gangs of rival supporters did to each other at the chariot races in Ancient Byzantium, compared with which the Rangers-Celtic match is a vicarage tea-party, leave no doubt that adolescent trouble-making was recognized long before the Middle Ages.

However, there are several reasons why adolescence might have become a more distinctive period of life in the recent past. After all, it is only since the middle of the last century that adolescents have been shut up together in institutions, and thus been given an incentive to form a distinctive ethos and perhaps become intolerant of people who are older – or younger. Moreover, the age at which children reach puberty has fallen sharply over the last hundred years – a change known as the secular trend. The psychological changes of adolescence may not be dependent on the physical changes, but the secular trend is alleged to have extended the period between reaching sexual maturity and being emotionally and economically ready to support children, and hence to have increased the need for an agreed 'quarantine' period between being a dependent child and an independent adult. Certainly adults have paid more attention to adolescence as a stage of life over the last century than before. The turn of this century saw a flood of legislation to protect adolescents' interests as well as the formation of such youth movements as the Boy Scouts which were designed to turn them into healthy and wholesome adults.

But none of these arguments prove that adolescence is a modern invention. In the Middle Ages it was common for children to leave home and become apprentices or domestic servants around the age of thirteen or fourteen, which meant that there were large numbers of teenagers living away from home, with their masters or in lodgings.

The hours they worked left them little time of their own, but the apprentice riots which were commonplace on holidays in the sixteenth century are ample evidence that boys would be boys even then (the involvement of girls in gang warfare is a comparatively recent development). And while the age at which sexual maturity is reached may have fallen by several years over the last century (we do not know what changes occurred earlier), so has the average age of getting married.

So even if the psychological aspects of adolescence are closely linked with reaching sexual maturity, and if adolescence is only significant inasmuch as it reflects the frustrations of having sexual potential without the means to express it legitimately, the secular trend may have brought adolescence forward but it has not made it longer. What *has* changed over the last century is that adolescence has been democratized. The abolition of child labour, the introduction of education for all and the progressive raising of the school-leaving age, and the setting up of institutions like juvenile courts have all ensured that everyone is now guaranteed an official period of youth.

From a sociological point of view, things have undoubtedly changed. Whether there has been an equivalent psychological revolution is less certain, because we do not know what effect working had on lower-class children, and certainly cannot assume that it prevented them experiencing the increased psychological awareness and feelings of uncertainty that we associate with the 'typical' adolescent.

But what exactly is The Problem of adolescence? Are all adolescents surly, depressed and delinquent, and is there really a generation gap which makes it impossible for them to get on with their parents and teachers? If disagreements are inevitable, what is it that the two generations disagree about? Most of this chapter will be devoted to the psychology of adolescence, but first we must consider the physical changes which form the backdrop in front of which the cheerful and willing ten-year-old is transformed into a rather less predictable and agreeable animal. Contrary to popular belief, children do not grow in fits and starts but – until puberty – grow steadily and continually. And even though five- and six-year-olds are very interested in sex roles and anxious to behave like a little boy or a little girl, at this age the two sexes are actually very similar in shape and physical capacity, and their internal hormone balance is much the same.

Growing apart

All this changes with the adolescent growth spurt which marks the end of childhood. It is set in motion by a sudden upsurge in production of either male or female sex hormones (androgens and oestrogens), which causes the internal environments of the two sexes to diverge sharply and leads eventually to the distinctive masculine and feminine shapes, as well as to reproductive maturity. The process starts first in girls, who on average go through all the physical changes two years earlier than boys. But the age at which the growth spurt (and puberty generally) begins varies enormously amongst perfectly normal children of both sexes. In boys, for example, it may begin as early as ten and a half or as late as sixteen, so that one boy may have almost completed his physical development before another has even begun the growth spurt. Neither child is at all abnormal, though being an early or a late developer has certain psychological consequences which we shall consider later.

For the average girl, the growth spurt begins shortly after her eleventh birthday and ceases when she is about fifteen-and-a-half. For boys the whole process occurs about two years later, though neither sex stops growing altogether at the end of the growth spurt. Our height continues to increase, on average by about five centimetres, until we reach the age of thirty, after which it remains constant until about forty-five, when it may begin to decline as a result of changes in our bone structure. Changes in height and weight are accompanied by changes in body proportions and shape. The head, hands and feet reach adult size first, while arms and legs grow faster than the trunk, which explains why adolescent boys stop growing out of their trousers a year before they stop growing out of their jackets. There are two other points to notice about the growth spurt. Because girls reach it first, there is a period when they tend to be bigger and sometimes stronger than their male counterparts. And because different parts of the body grow at different rates, many adolescents go through a period of feeling that their hands are too big, or that they are all feet. Adolescent gawkiness is not just imagination, any more than adolescents who are clumsy are being deliberately annoying. Parents who fail to allow for this have only themselves to blame if their children round on them, while adolescents can console themselves with the thought that a brief period of physical ungainliness is the price everyone has to pay for reaching maturity.

Among the most significant changes which take place during the growth spurt are those which indicate the approach of sexual maturity. The appearance of the first pubic hair is usually the earliest sign a child receives of impending puberty, though it may be the appearance of a breast bud in girls or a marked acceleration in the speed with which his penis is growing for boys. This occurs at about twelve-and-a-half in the average British boy, though it may come as early as ten-and-a-half or as late as fourteen-and-a-half. The average British girl will first notice that her breasts are beginning to swell at eleven, though it can happen as early as nine or not until she is thirteen. Puberty finishes for the average boy at fourteen-and-a-half, within the range of twelve-and-a-half to sixteen-and-a-half, while girls have their first period relatively late in puberty.

The average age of reaching menarche currently varies between 12.8 and 13.2 in Europe and North America, and it can be quite a traumatic event. Here is a working-class Colchester woman's description of the occasion:

> I was only eleven when I had my first period. That was really hell . . . I can remember this hot burning sensation going through me. It was horrible. And I got home and I yelled at Brenda when I got to the loo – 'Oh dear', I said, 'I'm bleeding. My bottom's bleeding.' I was terrified . . . I had been told nothing, you see.

In one sense, a girl's first period is a false alarm because it is often the beginning of a phase known as adolescent sterility or partial sterility. This lasts between twelve and eighteen months, and during it periods occur without an egg being shed from the ovary. The biological explanation of this phase is still a mystery, but it is certainly not safe for a newly pubescent girl to rely on it as a means of contraception, since not all girls are affected by it and its duration is unpredictable. Despite the fact that girls are two years ahead of them in most respects, boys tend to become fertile earlier, because for them fertility occurs near the beginning of puberty while it is one of the last of the chain of events leading up to sexual maturity in girls.

We noted earlier that children in industrialized societies have been growing and maturing earlier over the course of the last century. Over the last eighty years, the height of the typical six-year-old brought up in average economic circumstances has risen by one or two centimetres every ten years, which means that today's average six-year-old is about twelve centimetres taller than a child of the same age at the turn of the century. Similarly, there has been a spectacular decline in the age at which the average girl reaches menarche, girls now tending to have their first period some two-and-a-half years earlier than they did in 1880.

It is hard to provide a comparable figure for boys since spermatogenesis, which marks the beginning of their potential fertility, is less easy to assess, and a boy does not have the equivalent of a first period, though we should remember that the discovery of adolescent sterility in girls means that menarche is not the definitive sign of fertility it was once thought to be. However, the pattern over the centuries of the age at which boys' voices break suggests that they, too, have been affected by a secular trend. Surviving records from J. S. Bach's time as choir-master in Leipzig (1723–50) reveal that hardly any of his choristers' voices had begun to break before they were sixteen. For most of them, the transformation from upper to lower register was well under way by the age of eighteen, but there were still some trebles and altos at nineteen and even twenty. Figures collected in London in 1959 give 13·3 as the age when the average boy's voice is half-way through the process of breaking. Voice-breaking is one of the later events of puberty for boys, and the full process can take up to a year. It is not a very reliable criterion of puberty, though it was often used as such in the days when people thought it improper to examine a boy's genitals.

The experts disagree about why we now reach maturity so much earlier. Economic factors may play a part, but this cannot be the whole story since all social classes have been affected by the trend. It is however true that in Britain the effect has been less dramatic among the well off than amongst the poor, which supports the view that adolescence has been democratized in the twentieth century. Another more fanciful suggestion is that the increased sexual stimulation offered by modern society lies behind the secular trend. But although we know that hormonal changes can be set in motion by events in the outside world, girls in co-educational schools do not begin to menstruate any earlier than those in single-sex schools, even though they are surrounded by the creatures most likely to cause their thoughts to take a sexual turn. Another possible factor is the climate. The average world temperature has been rising steadily over the past century, but since Eskimo and African girls reach menarche at approximately the same age, this too is an unconvincing explanation of the secular trend towards earlier maturity.

Changes in family size offer another explanation. It is well established that girls in small families tend to have their first periods earlier than those in large ones, and families have become smaller over the past century. There is no obvious reason why family size *per se* should have any effect on the onset of puberty, but one of the consequences of smaller families is that the children in them tend to be better fed, and an improvement in diet – especially in infancy – is the most plausible explanation currently available of why we reach maturity earlier now than we did a hundred years ago. Whatever the reason, it seems that the secular trend has come to an end, at least in industrialized countries. The young Londoner today can expect her first period a year earlier than her mother, but at approximately the same age as her elder sisters. But the secular trend cannot be dismissed as merely an historical curiosity since it has produced a situation where about one girl in four now begins menstruating while she is still at primary school.

Early and late developers

We have seen that there is enormous variation between children in the age at which they reach puberty. There is nothing abnormal about being an early or a late developer, but the age at which an individual reaches physical and sexual maturity can have an effect on his or her life not only at the time but later. Boys and girls who are early physical maturers tend to have slightly higher than average IQ scores both as adolescents and as adults. But it is not the case that early maturity causes greater intelligence, since the small but reliable advantage enjoyed by early maturers is present long before puberty begins. The tendency is for cleverer children to reach maturity earlier, rather than for early maturers to become cleverer.

The position is further complicated by the fact that early maturers also tend to come from smaller families, so it would be a mistake to exaggerate the effect which the age of reaching maturity has on someone's intelligence at the expense of all the other factors which may be at work. Remember too that the difference in IQ scores between early and late maturers is small, and applies only to the average score obtained by large numbers of children reaching puberty relatively early or late. The variation within the two groups is incomparably greater than the difference between them, so many late-maturing children will be much brighter than those whose physical development is ahead of theirs. However, research confirms that there is a link between physical and mental development. For example, girls who have reached the menarche perform better on IQ tests than those of the same age who have not, and one researcher has gone so far as to claim that during the period of the growth spurt each extra inch of height gives the early developer an advantage of one-and-a-half IQ points over a late developer. There is no difference in height between early and late developers when both have finished growing, but even among adults there is a small but significant correlation between height and IQ score.

The fact that taller people tend to be slightly more intelligent may simply reflect the fact that they also tend to come from the higher social classes, but it could also be a hang-over from adolescent experience. Children who reach maturity earlier gain kudos with their peers, and are more likely to be accepted as leaders. Both girls and boys are keenly aware of their own and their friends' physical development. Here is a sixteen-year-old boy reminiscing:

About fourteen I started to notice body-changes – side-burns and that. Lifting your hair up every morning to see if they'd grown or just to see if they'd got any fluffier. A friend at school had a hairy chest and really bushy side-burns and a moustache at thirteen.

Early maturers gain confidence and the opportunity to expand their social skills, which may explain why early developers tend to be less neurotic and more sociable than late developers when they become adults. Teachers, too, may unconsciously favour the early developer. Ideas put forward in a mature baritone are more likely to be taken seriously than those presented in a shrill treble, while female teachers admit they feel a closer bond with girls with whom they know they share the most noticeable mark of womanhood.

We cannot say that early maturity *causes* children to be cleverer, any more than we can be sure that the physiological changes which herald the arrival of adolescence directly trigger off the psychological, emotional and intellectual developments which occur. But early maturers gain certain advantages which they may never lose, especially if they are boys. Early maturing girls also tend to be better adjusted than late maturers, but the effect is less marked than in boys, perhaps because there is more ambiguity about the role which girls and women are expected to play in our society. However, the results of a recent study offer some consolation to late developers. Early maturers may do slightly better on IQ tests, but there is at least one important aspect of intellectual ability where it seems to be an advantage to be a late developer. The ability to visualize and manipulate objects in space without the use of language is thought to be important for handling mathematical and scientific concepts, and is also considered useful for artists, architects and chess-players. On tests of visual-spatial ability, it is late maturers of both sexes who come out best.

It is not certain why late maturity should be associated

with superior visual-spatial ability, though some psychologists tell us that the later our brains reach maturity, the less likely it is that those areas of the brain which handle visual-spatial tasks will be made less efficient by having to cope with other tasks as well. If this is so, then it seems that Nature has given boys – who of course mature later on average than girls – a considerable intellectual bonus, especially in the world of high technology where such a high premium is attached to scientific ability and numeracy. Educationalists have been greatly reassured by the suggestion that there is a biological basis for male visual-spatial superiority, because it lets them off the hook of having to explain why it is that only a quarter as many girls as boys take physics and maths at A-level, and thus exclude themselves from many prestigious jobs. But recent research from America suggests that we can't after all blame biology for adolescent girls' tendency to fall behind boys at maths and science while continuing to outshine them in most other subjects. We now know that adolescent American girls do just as well as boys at tests of mathematical ability, provided they have taken the same number of maths courses at school. The real difference between the sexes is that far more girls than boys are allowed to drop maths early in their secondary school education, so it is hardly surprising to find that boys pull progressively further ahead.

The question of why more girls than boys want to give up maths at a time when the two sexes are doing equally well at the subject is a complicated one. But it is well worth pursuing, because the answer not only gives a fascinating insight into the pressures exerted on older children and young adolescents but also goes some way towards explaining how it comes about that boys and girls enter adolescence with very similar abilities and potential, albeit at different ages, but often leave it with very different qualifications and aspirations. I suggested in the last chapter that we may get a better understanding of the years of late childhood by considering them as the forerunner of adolescence rather than as an extension of what has gone before. The force of this suggestion will become clearer when we come to look at the origins of the psychological problems which affect a large minority of adolescents. But the primary school classroom may also provide us with clues to some of the puzzles surrounding intellectual development in adolescence, particularly the gap which opens up between boys and girls in mathematical and scientific achievement.

From their earliest days at school, children are intrigued by the fact that some of them are girls and some boys, and keen to work out exactly what the difference is. Their attitude towards sex role stereotyping, i.e. how they think males and females ought to behave, veers between hardline biological determinism (Mummies have to stay at home, while Daddies have to go out to work) and the more liberal position that individuals ought to be free to do their own thing, depending upon what stage of development they have reached. Before they get to school, children are given surprisingly little direct instruction from their parents in how boys and girls are expected to behave, and most teachers nowadays claim that they try to treat the two sexes the same. And yet children are extremely conscious of their gender. At primary school, boys and girls not only play separately but also have strong ideas about what the two sexes are like and about what life is likely to have in store for them. Some of these beliefs seem quite irrational. For example, a boy may tell you that boys are cleverer than girls, even though girls occupy all the top positions in his class, while a girl will state with solemn conviction that all doctors are men when her own mother is actually a GP! Many of these ideas must come from books and from TV, where heroes outnumber heroines by at least three to one, but research shows that teachers are also a powerful force in perpetuating the traditional sex stereotypes, however much they may deny this and however anxious they may be to avoid it.

For a start, they allow boys to talk and interrupt them more in lessons. This not only encourages boys to be more assertive than girls but also ensures that more of a teacher's time is devoted to resolving their problems. This may be justified on the grounds that girls, being more advanced developmentally. are less likely to need individual attention. But close scrutiny of what goes on in a mixed classroom reveals a subtler form of sexual discrimination by teachers which is less easy to excuse. Boys are more often punished than girls, but usually for non-academic faults such as untidiness or misbehaviour. When girls are reprimanded it is usually for academic mistakes. You might think that this would benefit a girl by focussing her attention on her work, but the problem is that praise is generally given to a girl not for work but for her appearance or conduct. So the lesson a girl learns is that what she is good at is being ladylike, while academic work is something which brings her criticism, when her efforts are noticed at all.

Teachers are even more at fault in the way in which they encourage children to react to their own mistakes. In studies of classroom behaviour, observers have noticed that when a boy gives the wrong answer, particularly in a 'masculine' subject like maths, his teacher is likely to keep at him, suggesting he tries new approaches to the problem until eventually he gets it right. He therefore learns to expect to get sums right, so long as he works at them hard enough. More generally, he will come to regard initial failure as a challenge to be overcome by trying again. But when a girl gets a sum wrong, the teacher's response is rather different. She is more likely to be told not to worry, and less likely to be encouraged to try again. The implication is that no one really expects girls to be able to do sums, and the more general lesson a girl will learn is that failure, especially in this area, is beyond her control and not really her fault. This attitude is known as *learned helplessness*. It is not of course confined to girls but it seems to affect them more than boys, and it may go some way towards explaining why they take against maths and science when they get to secondary school. It may also affect a girl's attitude towards life outside the classroom, leaving her with a life-long conviction that she will never be able to understand the complexities of a hire-purchase agreement or what goes on under the bonnet of a car. More seriously, the fact that a girl can form the impression at an early age that her life is governed by forces beyond her control (including the accident of birth which made her female) is thought by some psychiatrists to explain why the condition of clinical depression – which is accompanied by a feeling of complete helplessness – is much more common in adulthood among women than among men.

The reason why girls at secondary school react particularly badly to maths and science is not that they are naturally bad at these subjects, but rather a reflection of the way they are taught. Whereas in languages or history progress is made by building up more of the same sort of information while developing more sophisticated ways of handling it, most maths and science teachers in secondary schools present their subjects as a succession of quite different problems, each of which demands that a new technique be mastered. We inevitably make mistakes when first trying out new techniques, so it is not difficult to understand why boys, who have been taught to respond more constructively to their own mistakes, come to occupy most of the desks in science and maths classes in a mixed school.

Talk of mixed schools brings us to the final, and perhaps most important reason for girls' disappointing performance at maths and the hard sciences (in biology, which is thought to be a 'softer' science than physics and chemistry, girls do just as well as boys). This has to do with the importance adolescents attach to the notion of gender, and the fact that science and maths are seen as 'masculine' subjects. Even at primary school, when children are asked what they think about science and scientists, both sexes agree that science is a man's subject, and that scientists are grey-haired, scruffy and invariably male. Since they will have had little formal science education at this stage, their attitude is presumably shaped by comics and TV. The early years of secondary school are crucial in deciding a child's academic future, because this is when they decide which subjects they are good at, and their attitudes towards school and academic work in general begin to harden. But it is also the time when girls – but not yet boys – are beginning to be troubled by the doubts and uncertainty which mark the adolescent identity crisis, and are particularly anxious to establish their femininity. While the boys around her are still in the world of late childhood, cheerfully accepting things as they come and undisturbed by psychological concerns, the newly adolescent girl is eager to 'find' herself and to develop a consistent and pleasing personality.

Many of the problems of young adolescents stem from their newly acquired capacity for abstract and symbolic thought. So far as school-work is concerned, this is of great benefit because it allows them to handle formal logic and to think scientifically. You can see young adolescents revelling in their newly acquired talent for symbolic thought in the excessive use they make of irony, and their delight in puns and *double-entendres*. It also greatly assists in their psychological development by leading them – eventually – towards a clearer sense of their own identity and an adult system of values. They stop investing other people with their own personalities, and the ability to recognize and be fascinated by other people's idiosyncrasies marks the final demise of egocentricity and allows them to forge realistic and lasting friendships.

As a final bonus, abstract thought allows adolescents to immerse themselves in hobbies and interests in which growing expertise gives them a pleasant – and justified – belief in their own competence. Despite what you may think, studies show that our opinion of our own worth rises steadily between eleven and seventeen.

But the ability to entertain several hypotheses at the same time and to understand that there can be many different ways of seeing things is a double-edged sword. As children, we are bigots in the sense that we rarely bother to question the assumptions on which our lives are based. One of the great attractions of childhood is its certainty.

To take just one example, children usually accept that the way their parents treat them is the right way because it simply doesn't occur to them that there might be any other way, despite the fact that they must come across different child-rearing practices when they visit their friends' homes. Children have a powerful sense of fantasy but their powers of imagination do not lead them to question the way their own lives are organized.

Adolescence, on the other hand, is a period of maximum uncertainty. Here is how a fourteen-year-old girl described her soul-searching to us:

> I sometimes sit and think, What am I doing here, why was I born on this earth, why not on Jupiter or Mars or somewhere?' And I wonder how my Mum and Dad got here, and their ancestors, and I think, 'What are we doing here, why bother at all?'

Intelligent adolescents are overwhelmed by their ability to see all the alternatives, and many of them feel compelled to question assumptions they have previously accepted without question. Much of the anger of adolescence seems to come from realizing that we have hitherto been operating with a second-hand model of the world, handed down from parents and teachers. Once we begin to question it, it is as if Pandora's box has been opened, and every one of our old attitudes has to be re-thought. Given the enormity of the tasks, it is no wonder that young adolescents, especially those of an enquiring and reflective disposition, sometimes seem downcast. Here is how a seventeen-year-old recalled the period:

> When I was thirteen I found it quite a stormy age really with my parents, because as my mind developed I began to question what my parents would say. Before, everything they said was right. We used to have quite a few arguments in the house, because you used to question your parents more as you began to learn about the world around you.

How does all this affect a twelve-year-old girl's attitude towards her school work? Confronted by the need to work things out for herself, her first concern will probably be herself. 'My parents have always said I was a chip off the old block, and the teachers tell me I'm clever, but what am I really like, and what sort of person can I expect to become?' A girl's reaction to these first stirrings of adult self-awareness is to look desperately for some aspect of herself she is sure about, and the chances are that this search will lead her to her femininity. She may not know what sort of person she is yet, but every month her body reminds her that she can be certain of one thing: she is a girl and will become a woman. Adolescent girls cling to their femininity as a life-raft in an ocean of uncertainty, and it often becomes inordinately important to them that they should behave in a feminine way. Boys, too, enter a macho phase when they reach adolescence, and it is easy to understand why this is the period of life when we are most conservative about sex roles, and most intolerant of unladylike behaviour in females or cissyness in males.

Girls in particular scan the pages of magazines and observe the adult world to see how a woman is expected to behave, and adjust their own behaviour to fit what they see. The first thing that must strike them is that they have had the misfortune to be born second-class citizens. Wherever they look they cannot fail to notice that men give the orders while women tend to defer to them. A young adolescent girl may not understand why this should be so, but she does not yet question it. She is too concerned about her own performance to ask whether the role she is being asked to play is one which really suits her. But of course there is one glaring discrepancy between her own world and the adult world which she cannot ignore. In the classroom, she and her girlfriends are at least equal to and probably ahead of their male counterparts in most subjects, and it goes against the grain to defer to people when you know that they are your intellectual inferiors, even though you may accept that this is how you will be expected to behave later.

So girls of this age in mixed sex schools are in a quandary. They want to please their parents and teachers by doing as well as they can academically, but they are unhappy about doing better than boys in exams. This is partly for fear of being thought pushy and unfeminine but also because girls of this age are becoming interested in boys (sadly, their interest is unlikely to be returned), and they already know that being more successful than him is not the way to a man's heart. But of course there is a way out of this dilemma which has the double advantage of allowing a girl to reassert her femininity while reducing the ambivalence she feels about being in competition with boys. The solution many girls adopt is to abandon masculine subjects like physics and maths as soon as they can and concentrate their efforts on safe 'feminine' subjects such as languages or biology, where boys are thinner on the ground and less likely to be offended by a girl who does well. Girls are much less aware of this problem if there are no boys around, which explains why they do significantly better at maths and science in single-sex schools, whereas boys do equally well in single-sex and mixed schools.

We have now placed adolescence in an historical context, described the physical changes of puberty which herald its arrival, assessed the significance of being an early or a late developer, and explained how the ability to think abstractly forces adolescents to revaluate the world around them and turns their thoughts inwards. But I have emphasized that there is no universal experience of adolescence, and the time has come to establish just how typical what we think of as 'typically' adolescent behaviour really is.

How awkward is the awkward age

As with childhood, it turns out that some of our most cherished beliefs about adolescence are either untrue or else apply only to a minority of adolescents. The Generation Gap, for example, is actually a minute fissure rather than the yawning chasm it is sometimes made out to be. Many large-scale surveys of adolescents' attitudes have been carried out in Europe and America over the last twenty years and their results show a remarkable degree of uniformity. Whatever parents may think – and two-thirds of the adults we interviewed in Colchester were convinced that the younger generation had an approach to life very different from their own – adolescents are more worried about incurring their parents' disapproval than about falling out with their friends. Moreover, on the big issues like moral or political beliefs, adolescents are more in tune with their parents than with their peers. This is what a fourteen-year-old girl had to say on the subject:

I don't think I'm that far apart from my parents. We're pretty casual. It's not as if they were from 1898 or something – they're pretty close. I don't think they're a different generation at all.

But her next remark shows that things can be different:

I know a girl whose Mum's fifty-nine, because she's the

last, the youngest daughter. Her Mum seems so old, you know. Completely different to my Mum - a different generation.

It is ironic to find so many teenagers speaking of the merits of capital punishment, an opinion they must have picked up from their parents, since hanging was abolished in this country before they were born. Interestingly, there is closer agreement on the really important issues between today's teenagers and their parents than between the parents and *their* parents (i.e. the present generation of grandparents), which suggests that if anything the generation gap is closing. The great majority of adolescents say that they are satisfied and happy at home (three-quarters of them even express general approval of their parents' approach to discipline), and most of them name their parents when asked whom they admire most in the world. Moreover, two of the fears most frequently expressed by adolescents are of their parents dying and of moving away from home.

This is not to deny that adolescents are influenced by the approval of their friends, but most researchers agree that the influence of peers is stronger than that of parents only when it comes to such matters as clothes, records and what is the most profitable way to spend a Saturday evening.

A sixteen-year-old apprentice describes a typical quarrel:

When I talked about getting a motor bike, my Dad really annoyed me, saying he used to go to work for twenty years on a bicycle. Now I'm after a car, he's still going on about it. I don't suppose cars were even invented in his day.

Of course, there are times when such things seem far more important to an adolescent than whether he votes Labour or believes in God, but parents should know better than to allow disagreements over what are essentially trivial matters to obscure the fact that their teenage children probably agree with them about the things that really matter.

According to the results of a recent British survey, only a quarter of parents have serious reservations about their children's choice of friends. When they do so, it is usually because they are worried about their children being led astray (the 'bad influence' syndrome). There are two things to be said about this. The first is that if we forget about official crime statistics and actually ask children what they get up to, we find that a majority of boys (though not girls), have broken the law at least once by the time they are fifteen. Acts of delinquency peak at fifteen for boys and fourteen for girls (as always, girls get there first), remain quite common throughout adolescence, but then become much less frequent in early adulthood. So whatever view you take of adolescent' misdemeanours, they are not abnormal, and the passage of time is probably the most effective agent in suppressing them.

In many cases, children may well be egged on to perform some act of delinquency that they would not have committed had they been alone. But my second point is that when it comes to one of the most common forms of adolescent law-breaking – under-age drinking – it is parents rather than friends who are the bad influence. Researchers have found that virtually all teenage drinkers started at home, encouraged by their parents. They may go into pubs with their friends but it is hardly fair to lay the blame on them. Indeed, it is very hard to justify to adolescents – or to anyone else, for that matter – a law which forbids them to do in a public house something which their parents permit at home. A boy's first illicit visit to the pub, like his first cigarette, can be a very significant event, as we can see from the comment made by a thirty-six-year-old Colchester man:

> When I was fourteen, somebody said, 'Come down to the pub for a drink.' I said, 'No, I'm not eighteen.' 'Oh, you look it.' So I went. That changed my life.

So far as family life is concerned, the presence of an adolescent child does not seem to be the disruptive influence it is made out to be. According to the results of a survey of fourteen- to fifteen-year-olds in the Isle of Wight, only 12 per cent of boys and 7 per cent of girls ever express alienation by going off to their rooms, staying out of the house or refusing to do things with the rest of the family. Since half of those who did so used to behave in this way before they reached adolescence, we clearly cannot regard this as 'typical' adolescent behaviour. Nearly a quarter of the parents in this survey reported that they had difficulties in communicating with their sons (though only one in ten had any problems with girls), but here again the problem had usually been there before adolescence. When children are questioned, almost 90 per cent of sixteen-year-olds say that they get on well with their mothers, and three-quarters of them say the same about their fathers. (As a general rule, teenagers feel closer to their mothers than to their fathers, whom they see much less and often treat as little more than a source of cash.) When college students are asked to look back over their adolescence, only a quarter of them describe it as a period of rebelliousness.

So how did the idea that teenagers and their parents are constantly at war arise? I think it has several sources. The first is my own profession. Some of the most influential writers about adolescence have been psychologists and psychiatrists whose views on the period may have been distorted by the fact that most of the adolescents who came their way only did so because they had problems. Not surprisingly, parent-adolescent alienation is three times as common among adolescents who suffer from psychiatric disorders as it is among those who do not, and it would not be the first time that the public have been sold an over-pessimistic view of human behaviour by jaundiced mental health professionals.

The experts may be largely responsible for creating

the myth of the generation gap, but I think the blame has to be shared by the media, parents and teachers, and adolescents themselves. They way in which the media report on youth movements and youthful misdemeanours suggests that editors have a vendetta against young people. But of course the first law of the media is that success comes from telling people what they want to hear, and parents and educationalists have only themselves to blame if they accept the lurid account of adolescence offered by magazines and newspapers and ignore the evidence of their own experience with children. Of course, they don't totally ignore the evidence of their own eyes. But they see what they want – or expect – to see, instantly alert to signs of adolescent troublesomeness but blind to the long periods of calm. The contradiction between teachers' views of adolescence and what adolescents are really like emerges only too clearly from the results of two recent surveys. In one of them, 80 per cent of American high-school teachers questioned stated their conviction that adolescence is a time of great emotional disturbance. In the other, some 60 per cent of a large sample of fourteen to fifteen-year-olds denied that they ever felt very miserable or depressed.

In the same study, less than 10 per cent said that they had ever contemplated suicide (though it must be noted that suicide is the third most common cause of death among American adolescents and young adults), 20 per cent sometimes felt he or she didn't matter very much, and about a quarter of them said they sometimes got the feeling that other people were talking about or laughing at them. All these symptoms of emotional malaise were more common among adolescents than among their parents or among younger children, and feelings of depression, for example, are much more frequent among fourteen- to fifteen-year-olds who have reached puberty than among those who have not. So the high-school teachers were right in the sense that adolescence is the period in life when we are most likely to feel miserable and unsure of ourselves. It is also interesting to find evidence for a connection between these feelings and the physical changes of puberty. But it is patently false to say that all, or even most, adolescents suffer in this way. The majority of teenagers remain happy and confident throughout adolescence, for all the real difficulties they have to cope with and despite the fact that their teachers, parents and the magazines they read all tell them that they ought to be feeling miserable and making difficulties. Many of them, like this eighteen-year-old, cannot see what all the fuss is about:

When I was thirteen I was just in my little world, and I didn't really worry about things outside me, up to the age of seventeen. I'm nearly eighteen now, it's just been smooth running all the way through as far as I can remember. The only really traumatic time for me was when I left junior school and came to a secondary school for the first time.

The fact that what we think of as 'typical' adolescent behaviour actually isn't is the most surprising finding to emerge from research into adolescence. But I think we must accept it, because it appears so clearly in so many different studies, without a single discordant voice – a state of affairs almost unique in the behavioural sciences. Despite the link between the physical changes of puberty and a feeling of depression, the fact that only a minority of adolescents get depressed means that what we have to explain is not why some don't, but why a minority do. On this point, the comments of adolescents themselves are very revealing. Many of them spontaneously say that they are very aware that adults expect them to be difficult, and some even admit that they occasionally make a conscious effort to fall in with these expectations, behaving badly not because they want to but simply because they feel it is expected of them!

Some perceptive parents are on to this. As one of them put it to us:

I wouldn't say that they go out of their way to be like that but they know that teenagers are supposed to be difficult and perhaps they act a bit accordingly.

There is a rich irony here, but nothing that should surprise us. We know that adolescence is a period of great psychological awareness, when we are actively searching for a consistent personality and trying to decide how we ought to be behaving. Adolescents may sometimes appear to be rebelling against the adult world, especially in their determination to create their own fashions and to establish their independence. But in interviews they make it perfectly plain that they know they will shortly join the adult community and that they are acutely aware of its concerns, particularly those which will affect them. Surveys show that they are avid watchers of TV news programmes at home and worry about the country's economic situation. (No one follows the unemployment figures with more interest than a teenager.) At school, they appreciate the need for qualifications and are scornful of teachers who allow them to waste time. As one teenager put it in an interview recently: 'No one's impressed by a teacher who tells you about her lovers but doesn't mark your homework'! So adolescents are looking for adult models and anxious to behave as adults expect them to, which suggests that a great deal of adolescent misery is caused by parents' and teachers' ill-informed attitudes, rather than the physical and mental changes we all go through between childhood and adulthood. In short, one important reason why some adolescents have problems is simply that their parents and teachers expect them to have problems.

There is another popular belief about adolescence which scientific investigation knocks firmly on the head.

Many parents complain that their children change out of all recognition during adolescence, and cite this as another reason why they cannot get on with them. But the evidence of longitudinal studies, in which groups of people have been studied at regular intervals over a period of fifty years, suggests otherwise. There are some changes in personality during the years of adolescence: for example, both sexes become more interested in the opposite sex and inclined to eroticize situations, while boys become more straightforward, but girls less so! In most aspects of personality, however, we remain remarkably consistent between twelve and fifty, and where there are changes, these tend to take place in young adulthood or even later, so we shall consider them in later chapters.

Friends and lovers

Mention of the opposite sex brings us to two final aspects of adolescence where popular beliefs are much closer to the mark. Despite what I said earlier about the relative influence on an adolescent of his parents and his peers, friends are probably more important to us at this stage of life than at any other. I have discussed the psychological significance of friendship in my book *Habits: why you do what you do*, and pointed out there that one of the most important functions friends serve is to reassure us when we are in doubt of our own worth or about the value of our opinions. Although we saw earlier that only a minority of adolescents have serious doubts about their own worth, adolescence is the peak period for such feelings, as it is the time when we are most likely to question our view of the world. Earlier, we tend to accept other people's opinions without question. Later, we may have doubts from time to time, but generally feel that our way of looking at things has served us quite well so far, and will probably continue to do so.

Many - though not all - adolescents use their friends as sounding-boards for new ideas. When they are asked what they value most in friends, fifteen- to sixteen-year-olds reply that they must be able to trust and confide in them, as you can see from the comments one girl made to us:

I think friends are very important. You've got to have someone to turn to if there's a crisis, especially if you've had an argument at home. They feel the same – if they've had an argument, they come to me. If I didn't have them I'd scream, you know. There'd be nothing else to do . . . I talk to them about boy-friends – how you're getting on with them. You don't want to talk to your Mum and Dad about that. Friends understand. They have the same problems.

In the late teens, greater emphasis is placed on being able to talk to friends, and the need for a *confidant* seems to be greatly reduced by the early twenties, which presumably means that most people have worked out their identity crisis by then and no longer feel so strongly the need to discuss personal psychological issues. People who continue to need close *confidants* in their twenties tend to be those who are having difficulty in resolving the intimacy-versus-isolation psychosocial crisis which we shall discuss in the next chapter.

Although they get many of their attitudes from their parents or from magazines, what adolescents look like and how they spend their spare time is strongly influenced by their friends and the gangs or groups they belong to. But parents probably worry unnecessarily about the influence of 'bad' friends and attach too much significance to their son's or daughter's decision to become a Punk or a Mod. They should understand that the fickleness they complain about in their children works to their advantage in this respect. An adolescent changes his friends as rapidly as his opinion of himself, and the more 'difficult' a teenager is, the less likely it is that he or she will remain constant to a friend parents consider to be a bad influence.

Similarly, the adolescents we interviewed in Colchester left us in no doubt that they regarded their attachment to groups like the Mods as strictly experimental. Today's Punk may well be tomorrow's Rockabilly, because finding out what each group has to offer may play an important part in a teenager's search for his own personality. It is also worth remembering that only a small minority of teenagers bothers to join any of these cults, though a lot more of them opt for a sort of associate membership by going through spells of buying only records which carry the Mod or Punk seal of approval. One fourteen-year-old girl we spoke to added a new dimension to the so-called generation gap:

> I became a Mod because Mum wanted me to, really. She'd seen Mods in the street and thought they'd looked smart. And she said, 'Why don't you turn Mod?' So I said, 'Yeah, if you'll buy me the clothes.' So she bought me them. I'm glad I'm a Mod.

History suggests that adolescents have always formed gangs when given the opportunity. Not all adolescents feel attracted to them (some prefer the company of people of a different age altogether), but they have existed for more than two thousand years without posing a serious threat to the fabric of society, and I suspect that the experience of adolescence would be less pleasant and more difficult if they did not exist. The crucial psychological task of adolescence is to find an identity, and it may even be better for a teenager to form an identity as a delinquent than to have no clear identity at all, so far as his future psychological development is concerned.

Friends are no less important. Researchers have found interesting differences between the sexes in adolescent friendship girl's friendships are more fervent and demanding, boys' looser and less intense but in both sexes an inability to establish friendships puts adolescents at risk and is associated with psychiatric disorders. We cannot say that being bad at making friends *causes* psychiatric disturbance it may just be that teenagers who seem odd are not attractive to their peers – but parents have less reason to get worried if their children make what seem to be unsuitable friends than if they have no friends at all.

Most of what I have said so far applies to friendships between children of the same sex, because young adolescents tend to follow the childhood pattern of spending most of their time with others of their own sex. Given the difficulties they may be having in understanding themselves and their own sex, it's not surprising that they are hesitant about breaking new ground. But eventually their curiosity and the desire to conform get the better of them (genuine heterosexual lust is not often a major influence at this stage), and as always it's girls who get there first. In the Isle of Wight survey of fourteen- to fifteen-year-olds, 29 per cent of the girls but only 14 per cent of the boys said that they had a special friend of the opposite sex, and other studies in Europe and America confirm that throughout adolescence girls are more interested in boys than vice versa. Indeed, interviews with adolescent boys suggest that their feelings about girls are at best ambivalent and often downright hostile. Many boys resent the fact that they cannot seem to get away from girls: as one of them put it despairingly – 'they even play football these days!'

Since girls become interested in the opposite sex earlier than boys, a girl's romantic attachment is usually with a boy older than herself. Most girls complain that boys of their own age are too young to be taken seriously, and of course they are right in the sense that boys do indeed tend to lag behind girls throughout the whole period of growing up. The fact that women tend to marry men older than themselves is sometimes explained by saying that they want someone to look up to or even by the suggestion that they need a father figure. However, it seems just as likely that what they are after is an equal rather than a superior, and that they have learned at an early age that males of their own age rarely match up to their own level of emotional maturity.

Where sex is concerned, the popular view about adolescence is at least partly correct. There *has* been a revolution in adolescent sexual behaviour over the past couple of decades, though things may not be quite as 'bad' as some parents fear. According to the results of a national survey carried out in Britain in 1974–5, one in five older teenagers had broken the law by having sexual intercourse before the age of sixteen (though three times more boys than girls), and just over a half of them lost their virginity during their teens (55 per cent of the boys and 46 per cent of the girls). All these figures are significantly higher than those obtained in a comparable survey undertaken in 1964, and very much higher than those in studies carried out in the 1950s. Part of the difference could be accounted for by the fact that teenagers are now more willing to admit to being sexually experienced. But the fact that teenage pregnancy has become very much more common despite the greater efficiency and availability of contraceptives seems convincing proof that full sexual activity has become a feature of normal teenage life where once it was confined to the delinquent and the precocious.

At this point I must make an important qualification. I have talked about behaviour being 'typical' of the Teenager as if all teenagers were the same, but of course they are not. There are enormous variations in the way in which different people experience adolescence and in the way in which different teenagers live their lives. Some of these can be traced to biological facts, like the age of reaching puberty, but others have to do with the environment in which a person grows up. The influence of biological factors is sometimes overestimated. Being a late developer can have certain psychological consequences but it is a mistake to link physical growth with the *social* maturity of an individual too closely. For example, some fourteen-year-old girls go out with boys regularly while others don't, but whether a particular girl has started menstruating or not is a very poor predictor of which category she will come into. She is much more influenced by what the rest of the girls in her year at school are doing. If boys play an important part in their lives, the chances are that they will in hers too, even though most of her friends will have begun to have periods while she has not. So simple chronological age is a much more powerful influence on adolescent psychological development than physical maturity.

This leads us to the importance of experience and cultural and geographical factors. National surveys show how dangerous it is to generalize about what teenagers are like. For example, a survey completed in 1980 shows enormous differences between fourteen- to fifteen-year-olds living in London and those living in Leeds, especially in their experience of violence. Whereas five out of six randomly selected London girls reported that they had been physically attacked in a sexual context at least once, none of a comparable group of girls in Leeds had experienced this. The Leeds girls were also much more reluctant to talk about sex, and the researchers formed the impression that it probably played a less central role in their lives than in those of their London counterparts. If there are significant differences between the experiences of teenagers living in two large cities, how much greater must the difference be between urban teenagers generally and those brought up in small towns and in rural areas?

Nevertheless, there does seem to have been a change in the age at which teenagers reach the various rungs on the ladder leading from the first shy encounter to a full-blown sexual relationship. The 1964 survey showed that by sixteen, more than 70 per cent of boys and over 85 per cent of girls had experienced dating and kissing. Between fifteen and eighteen the ladder rises steeply, with deep kissing, fondling of breasts and genitals becoming increasingly common: whereas at fifteen less than a fifth of boys had touched a girl's genitals, nearly half had done so by the time they reached seventeen. Today's teenager probably goes through all these stages slightly earlier (we do not have accurate information on this), and the fact that contraceptives are now more easily available – and more frequently used – has presumably reduced one of the teenager's major worries about sex. Less than one in ten sexually experienced teenagers in the 1974–5 survey said that they had never used contraceptives, though only a third of them claimed always to use them.

The availability of the pill must have contributed to the fact that teenagers are now more sexually active, but it has not led to an increase in promiscuity. The majority of sexually active teenagers are sleeping with partners they have been going out with for more than six months, and this tendency is more marked among girls who are on the pill than among those who are not. Boys tend to have more sexual partners (which implies that there must be a small core of promiscuous girls), but although fewer girls than boys lose their virginity as teenagers, they are more sexually active once they start and are more likely to have sexual relationships which last for some time. So far as social class is concerned, the revolution in adolescent sexual activity seems to have swept away any differences there may once have been. Working-class boys are slightly more likely to be sexually experienced than their middle-class counterparts, but there is no difference in this respect between middle- and working-class girls.

Two other myths about the revolution in teenage sexual mores can be easily dismissed. The first is that it has changed adolescents' attitudes towards marriage. This is not so.

Nine out of ten teenagers still say they want to get married, regardless of whether they are sexually experienced or not. Interestingly, a majority of them still expect sexual fidelity within marriage. Nor is there any evidence to support the complaint that sex education has caused either the increase in sexual activity or a trend towards more promiscuity. A recent American survey found that sexually experienced girls were less likely than virgins to have had adequate sex education, while the 1974–5 British survey confirms that both boys and girls who learn about sex from friends rather than from adults are more likely to become sexually active as teenagers. Since teenagers who are not given adequate sex education by adults say that they regret that they had to rely on the often inaccurate information they got from other children, it's quite likely that they make an early start to their sex lives at least partly in a desperate attempt to compensate for their ignorance. So those who argue against sex education in schools may actually be promoting the very thing they want to discourage.

Although teenagers themselves say when interviewed that the classroom is the right place to be told about sex and birth control, at present in this country less than half of them receive adequate instruction, and for many of these the lessons come when they are already sexually experienced. Without such information, teenagers are obliged to believe what they read in newspapers and hear in the playground, and so can form the false impression that teenage pregnancy, abortion and promiscuity are commonplace rather than exceptional problems. We have already seen how eager teenagers are to conform with what seems to be expected of them, so there may well be a sad footnote to be added to our account of the teenage sexual revolution. Many teenagers today may embark on their first sexual encounters not because they really want to or feel ready for them, but because they don't want to be the odd man or woman out.

After School

Adolescense as I have defined it comes to an end when a teenager leaves school or college and joins the job market. There has not been space here to devote special attention to the select group of students whose education continues into their twenties, but in many respects the significance of someone's first job – or the first experience of looking for one – is similar whether they are sixteen or twenty-one. When Freud was once asked what he thought a normal person should be able to do well, he replied simply, '*Lieben und arbeiten*' ('to love and to work'). We have seen how adolescents' burgeoning sexuality prompts them to take the first steps in the journey which, if they are lucky, will end in loving, adult relationships, and I shall have a lot more to say on this score later in the book. But before leaving adolescence, we must see how the adolescent is affected by his first experience of the other great concern of our adult lives – work.

Until very recently, this would have involved me in writing two different sections, one applying to women and the other to men. Now, however, women form half the workforce in this country, and the results of our survey in Colchester leave no doubt that although few women can pursue their careers with the single-minded determination that some men manage, many women now regard their job as a central concern in their lives, rather than as a peripheral means of filling in the day which brings in a little extra cash. This is not to deny that men attach more importance to their jobs than women do. Our survey confirms that they do, especially after women have become mothers. But the significance of the first job, as a marker of official entry into the adult world and the end of the economic dependence of childhood and adolescence, is probably very similar for the two sexes.

Getting a job may bring economic independence but

it does not usually involve a change in domestic arrangements. Most young people continue to live with their parents until they get married, and the conflicts between parents and children may actually become more acute once parents have lost their ultimate weapon – financial sanctions. Nor is their first full-time job the first experience most adolescents have of paid work. More than half of the fourteen- to fifteen-year-old boys in the Isle of Wight survey had a paid part-time job during school terms. This proportion was much lower for girls (27 per cent), but by the age of sixteen almost two-thirds of girls in this country have experience of paid work as baby-sitters.

From the point of view of our psychological development, starting a career can have enormous implications. It offers a solution to the identity crisis of adolescence by finally providing a clear answer to the question, who (and what) am I? An adolescent may not like his or her first job, and may even be determined to quit it as soon as anything better turns up, but few would deny that they find it more reassuring to be able to say I am a secretary, salesman or whatever, rather than I'm at school. Throughout our adult lives we use our jobs in this way to bolster up our self-image and to explain ourselves to other people. It is a major psychological bonus for working, which explains many of the difficulties people experience on retirement, as we shall see in the final chapter of the book. This aspect of work gives an even blacker hue to the already dark cloud of youth unemployment, because it implies that school-leavers who cannot get jobs may not only lose confidence in themselves but also fail to mature psychologically since they are deprived of a prop essential for normal development.

Boys are probably more at risk than girls in this respect, not only because work plays a more central role in men's lives but as another consequence of the fact that girls seem to be more mature than boys throughout the entire process of growing up. As part of a wider study into the effects of unemployment in an isolated community with one of the highest levels of unemployment in south-east England, sixteen-year-olds about to leave school were asked to write essays about how they thought their lives would develop. Both sexes anticipated that a job would play a key role in their lives and both were pessimistic about their employment prospects – justifiably so. But the girls anticipated an interest in a much wider range of concerns, and generally showed a maturer and more realistic appreciation of what life might have in store. Boys who feared unemployment saw themselves as being destroyed by it; for a girl to despair, it seemed that she would have to despair of life itself. Girls seemed to find satisfaction in contemplating the whole of life's tapestry, rents and all, and interviews with the children's parents, who were themselves often unemployed, tended to support the view that unemployment is a much greater psychological threat to men than it is to women. More generally, the survey we conducted in Colchester of adults between the ages of twenty-nine and fifty-nine showed that, throughout this period, women consider themselves significantly happier and more secure than men do.

Even in a time of high unemployment, we have some choice in the jobs we do, though the decision is often less rational than we would like to think. Research shows that, to some extent, we try to choose a job to fit our personality, though there is more evidence to suggest that our personalities are shaped by our jobs than the reverse. Interests and qualifications also come into it, and many adolescents opt for the career of their father, mother or some other adult they admire. Background factors like class, race, sex and intelligence also operate in a complex – and often illegal – fashion. Whatever the law may say, some professions are dominated by certain ethnic groups or by one sex rather than the other. But perhaps the single most striking finding to emerge from all the research industrial psychologists have done to try and work out how we end up in one job rather than another is the enormous part played by pure luck, good and bad.

Whether you have arrived in it by accident or by design, the first taste of a new job is usually slightly bitter. There is the excitement of novelty – especially in your first job – but the reality is never quite what you expected it to be, and some disappointment is inevitable. Most jobs involve a brief training period to allow the new recruit to become acclimatized. Some organizations favour a gradual immersion, while others – the army is notorious here – believe in a more robust approach, as if determined to show just how unpleasant working life can be. But whatever the organization, the problems facing new recruits are the same. There is a specific job to be mastered, the structure of the organization has to be understood, and you have to work out what role you are expected to play in it and how you are expected to behave.

Once the initial shock has worn off, adolescents should find that they are quite well equipped to perform these tasks. There may be times when they miss the security of school or college life, and feel ambivalent about the responsibilities their new independence brings. But they are aware of the advantages of working and will be eager to fit in. A sixteen-year-old boy we interviewed was in no doubt as to which he preferred:

> I think they treat you more realistically at work than at school. In fact if you do something wrong they are more free. They'll tell you, but at school you had to write out a hundred lines or something. At work they just get you to do it again, put it right.

Learning a new skill should be no hardship for them since this is what their education has been all about. Nor are they strangers to the delicate art of identifying and trying out new roles. It's just a matter of applying the techniques they will have acquired throughout the adolescent search for self-knowledge in a new context. Coming to grips with the structure of the organization may present them with more problems, which is why it is often an advantage to get your first job in a large organization with a clearly defined hierarchy and structure, only later risking a move to smaller, more fluid outfits where the hierarchy is more subtle, and personal relationships more intricate.

So we come to the end of adolescence, a period of less turmoil and conflict than it is sometimes made out to be, but one which a significant minority of us find it difficult to negotiate. At its end, most seventeen-year-olds have a job and most will have some experience of what it feels like to share a close emotional involvement with someone outside their family. They are allowed to drive and will soon be able to vote. Some will have taken the decision to improve their future prospects by staying in full-time education, and others will already have started a family. But most arrive at adulthood with their options open, and even those who have already chosen a job or a spouse may find that their choice is less irrevocable than they imagine, as we shall see in the next chapter.

CHAPTER 3

Getting It Together

'If youth is a fault, one soon gets rid of it.'

GOETHE

When do we become adult? It's a perplexing question, and one to which different people give an astonishing variety of answers. When we put it directly to the 461 twenty-nine to fifty-nine-year-olds whose views about aging we canvassed in Colchester, their estimates ranged from fourteen to forty! Clearly 'becoming adult' meant different things to the different people we talked to, but their confusion is merely an illustration of the fact that we don't have an agreed criterion for the beginning of adulthood.

A few years ago, you got the 'key to the door' at twenty-one. This must seem a very quaint old custom to today's 'latch-key children', but the notion of 'coming of age' was a convenient symbol. The celebrations associated with it may have been intended as a *rite de passage* to emphasize the new responsibilities which reaching adulthood brings, though in fact only one in eight of the adults we interviewed gave twenty-one as the age at which they considered they became adult and only 3 per cent referred to coming of age as a significant event. Similarly, although the age of majority was lowered by three years in 1970 and eighteen now marks the end of most juvenile legal restrictions, not many of the younger people we talked to attached special importance to this age. Eighteen *was* a popular choice for the age at which adulthood begins, but only among the older generation, because it used to be the age at which National Service began. You can argue the pros and cons of compulsory military service on all sorts of grounds, but there can be no doubt that those who went through it see it very clearly as the event which turned them from boys into men. The post-conscription generation is less certain, but most men judge that they became adult some time between eighteen and twenty-one, while women give more varied answers, with a significant proportion of them opting for the mid- to late-twenties.

As you might expect, people associate reaching adulthood with a specific event in their lives. But it is not always the same event, which explains the variations in their answers. For most people, it doesn't happen overnight, though it did to one young Colchester man we spoke to:

> When I left college clutching my A-levels in my hand I decided that I didn't know what I wanted to do. So I thought about going to sea, and I phoned up a company and said, 'What have you got going?' and he said, 'What about a photographer on a Russian ship?' and I said, 'Fine, book me on.' . . . I realized I was the only crew member who was English. I thought, 'Jeez, boy, you're on your own!' And, you know, I had to make it work or die, so that was it. I grew up very suddenly that Saturday as we sailed to Leningrad.

For men over forty, joining the services is by far the most common marker-event. For women of all ages, and for younger men, it is getting married or the birth of their first child. As one woman put it to us:

> I just suddenly thought, 'I'm a mum — I must be old.' I didn't feel it, but I suddenly felt, 'Blimey, do I look like a mum? I wasn't a mum yesterday, but I'm a mum today. Do I look any different?' And I think I suddenly thought, 'Oh, I'm a different person in a way.'

For some people, like this thirty-two-year-old Colchester

woman, it is surviving a crisis which finally convinces them that they have reached adulthood:

> Well, I think I've grown up in the last couple of years. Last year I had a rotten year. Well I wanted this baby, and I fell for her, and the day I found out I was expecting this one I found out that my mother was dying. I had a real year of it last year, having had a threatened miscarriage and then the German measles scare – I would never have thought I could cope with all that lot in one go but I did. And in a way since then I've felt a lot calmer. It was a hard time because mum died six weeks after that.

A number of younger men and women also give starting work as the beginning of adulthood, but surprisingly few people of any age or either sex mention leaving home in this context. Interestingly, although the people in our survey had different ideas about when adulthood begins, they found the question a much easier one to answer than the related question: When does old age begin? One reason why they found this question more difficult must have been that virtually none of them felt that they had yet reached old age (none were over sixty). But other surveys of older people suggest that old age is a more difficult concept to come to grips with than adulthood, and many of the people in their forties and fifties in our sample found it just as hard to say when middle age begins.

Although a sizeable minority (10 per cent) of our sample felt that they had not really become adult until after the age of thirty, most people leave adolescence behind and come to think of themselves as young adults some time in the period we shall be discussing in this chapter – from the late teens to the mid-twenties. Some have adult responsibilities thrust on them early, for example by a shot-gun teenage marriage. Others seem to make a conscious decision to cling to the privileges of youth for as long as they possibly can, avoiding the commitment of a deep emotional relationship or a steady job until long after most of their contemporaries have settled down. And of course some of us never grow up. As one forty-eight-year-old man truculently told us:

> People say to me, 'Why don't you grow up?' when I'm enjoying myself. So I'm not sure what growing up is really. You get married and father children, but it doesn't necessarily mean you have grown up, does it?

For one group of young adults, the transition from adolescence to adulthood is peculiarly blurred. Students spend the years between eighteen and twenty-one in a very ambiguous position, with half a job and having half left home. In term-time, the hours a student is expected to work are not very different from those of his or her contemporary who has a regular job. By tradition, students are free to decide for themselves when to put in the hours (the flexitime principle runs riot in student digs) but the penalty for not working getting the sack is the same as in the outside world, and is if anything more rigorously applied, since a student's performance is more regularly assessed.

However, the financial provision made for students in Britain during term-time nicely illustrates our inability to decide whether or not they are adults. It seems to be accepted that they do a job, and the government lays down a rate for the job which should allow them to support themselves. While this calculation is being made, the student is treated as an independent adult who is working for the state. But when it actually comes to paying them, the state suddenly draws back, as if horrified by the implications of such an admission, and makes them dependent on the good will of their parents to ensure that they receive in full what it has been decided they deserve. The proportion of parents who pay their full share of the student grant is shamefully low (almost three-quarters fail to do so), so those who complain of the 'childishness' of some of the things students get up to should remember that it is adults who refuse to grant them proper financial independence, and so discourage them from assuming the responsibilities of adulthood.

Never better

Students make only fleeting appearances on the job market (during their vacations) before the age of twenty-one, and in this sense are untypical of their age group. In many respects however their interests and concerns are quite similar to those of their contemporaries who left school at sixteen. But what are young adults like? Dangerous though it is to make generalizations about people at any age, we can identify a number of characteristics which distinguish this period of life from those which precede and follow it. For example, although some functions, notably the performance of our hearts and circulatory systems, reach a peak slightly earlier, the years between twenty and twenty-five can be described as the pinnacle of our biological development. Physically and intellectually, we have never been so good before and never will be again. Our muscles continue to develop throughout the twenties, but where vision, hearing and the ability to react swiftly is concerned, a slight decline has already begun by the age of twenty-five.

Unfortunately, many young adults do not take advantage of the fact that they are at their physical peak; indeed, there are at least two ways in which they may hasten its end. When we asked people in Colchester about their participation in sport, we found that twenty to twenty-four is the period when men are most likely to give up such strenuous sports as football, athletics and even table tennis. Almost half of the women who had given up playing tennis since leaving school abandoned it at this age too. Of course, it's easy to understand how the major concerns of young adults – work, personal relationships and, for some, family commitments – make it increasingly difficult for them to find time for more peripheral interests. Perhaps they also think that playing games they enjoyed at school or college is incompatible with their newly acquired adult status. But it's sad to see them ignoring a major asset, and they often make things worse by continuing with the eating habits they developed in adolescence. A young adult with a sedentary job who no longer takes regular exercise doesn't need the high calorie diet he or she was accustomed to. Failure to realize this causes a lot of young adults to run to fat, and it may also speed up the decline in general bodily functioning which occurs throughout the whole of our adult lives, affecting the typical person at the rate of about 1 per cent every year.

So far as intelligence is concerned, a person's IQ score usually remains pretty constant over the whole of adulthood. But this does not mean that his intellectual powers are unaffected by the passing of the years, because IQ is simply a measure of a person's intelligence in relation to other people of the same age. We can get round this problem by using a different measure known as an efficiency quotient (EQ), which assesses your intellectual ability in relation to that of an average twenty-year-old. Using this measure, we find that most people achieve their maximum intellectual capacity between the ages of sixteen and twenty, after which there is a steady decline in some aspects of intelligence. Surprisingly, as much as a third of the total drop in EQ between the ages of twenty and sixty seems to occur in the young adult period.

However, the picture is less black than I have painted it. The main reason why our EQ drops as we get older is not that we become more stupid, but rather that we get slower. When intelligence tests are given without a time limit, age differences virtually disappear. Two other points should be borne in mind. The first is that IQ tests were invented for use with children, and most adult tests are merely souped-up versions of those used in schools. The knowledge and skills they tap are closely related to what children are taught at school, and although they are quite an effective way of predicting academic achievement, the further we get from the classroom the less likely it is that a measure based on IQ tests will tell us anything very useful about how good someone is at their job. The second point is that many aspects of intelligence do not drop off over the years. As we shall see later in the book, our reasoning ability holds up very well throughout most of adulthood, and there are some tests in which sixty-year-olds can outperform twenty-year-olds. Nor should we underestimate the importance of experience and the knack we have of finding new ways to perform both physical and intellectual tasks which can often cancel out the effects of any deterioration which occurs as we get older.

However, for young adults all this lies in the future. They are too busy establishing themselves in the adult world to worry about the physical and mental deterioration which is unlikely to affect them much until they have doubled their present age. Although the major part of the Colchester survey on aging consisted of interviewing a large sample of twenty-nine to fifty-nine-year-olds, we also held group discussions and much longer 'depth' interviews with a smaller number of nineteen to twenty-five-year-olds, which enabled us to form an impression of the interests and concerns of the young adult.

In most respects, our findings confirmed what the major development theorists have to say about this stage of life. On the negative side, we found young adults to be self-centred and still very naive in their views on what life is all about. In psychological terms it was clear that many of them were still in the throes of the identity crisis which had begun to disturb them in adolescence. Particularly among the unmarried, there seems to be an internal conflict between wanting to establish a position which commands respect and not wanting to get into a rut. Describing their attitude towards their jobs, young adults told us that they were afraid of slipping without noticing into the habits of their boss, for example by taking a briefcase of work home in the evenings. And yet at the same time many are anxious to carve out a niche for themselves at work and clearly enjoy the status and economic advantages of having a job. The contrast was nicely made by the different comments of two young adults in a group we were interviewing. One said:

> I know that if I want to spread and widen my horizons I've really got to get out now, so there's a niggling doubt at the back of my mind. Am I doing the right thing . . . ? From the point of security I'm absolutely fast, like being in an iron cage.

The other took a very different view:

> My choices seem to be enormous at the moment. It's really so vast, the things I could do after the next nine months . . . I think now I have more choice than ever before . . . there are hundreds of ways I can go from here, all of which are really exciting.

On the positive side, they also enjoy the feeling of 'no longer being a kid', and are quite scornful of the goals and expectations they had only a few years earlier. Now that they have had a taste of life, many say they feel more secure and have a clearer idea of where they are going. Some – particularly the married - take a positive pleasure in mapping out the future, though others complain that they are being made to take decisions which affect the whole course of their lives before they are ready to do so. Some already regret their educational shortcomings and lack of qualifications (this complaint was also very common among the older adults we studied), and say they're afraid that younger people are going to overtake them. Generally, the young adults we interviewed seemed convinced that they were being required to make once-and-for-all decisions, irrespective of whether this prospect gave them satisfaction or filled them with gloom. They felt that options were closing, and admitted that they were anxious about their ability to cope with the future.

These worries are all characteristic of the age, but there seems to be a difference between the social classes in who worries about what: specifically, we found that working-class young adults are more likely to have regrets about the past, while worries about the future seem to be more of a middle-class preoccupation. In keeping with this, when we asked older adults whether they had had a vision of how they would like their lives to develop when they were in their early twenties, we found that it was the middle classes – especially men – who were more likely to have had such a 'dream'. Not surprisingly, they were also much more likely when in their forties and fifties to say that they had fulfilled their youthful hopes.

The price of freedom

These often contradictory feelings illustrate the central psychological problem which faces the young adult. We saw in the last chapter that the development of abstract thought, which opens up new vistas for young adolescents, can also involve them in a painful examination of their entire value system. In the same way, the economic independence which marks the beginning of adulthood is not an unmixed blessing. Young adults may not leave home immediately (most people live with their parents until they get married), but the change in their status is likely to affect their relationship with their parents in a way which may not be entirely to their liking. As we shall see in Chapter 5, most parents, far from wanting to hang on to their children for as long as possible, seem only too glad to shed their parental responsibilities. For the young adult it often comes as a shock to discover that his parents are delighted to give him the freedom he has been demanding, especially when he discovers that they take the not unreasonable view that if he is now a free agent, then so are they.

So freedom is a double-edged sword for the young adult. To be able to take your own decisions is a long-awaited pleasure. But it's also a potential source of insecurity to realize that your parents no longer feel the same degree of responsibility for you, even though they may be willing to accept the lesser role of consultants. For some young adults, particularly those who have yet to resolve the identity crisis, the feeling of emotional insecurity far outweighs the self-confidence which comes from standing on their own two feet. Psychiatrists consider that many marriages of the early twenties are 'take-care-of-me-contracts', entered into in a spirit of panic rather than out of conviction that one has found the ideal partner for life. We shall consider the problems of such marriages later.

But this is only one of the dangers presented by the freedom of young adulthood. For some people, freedom becomes an obsession, to be guarded at all costs from the assaults – real or imagined – of employers or other predators. As one example of this, many young adults we spoke to in Colchester were strongly opposed to the idea of having children, partly because they looked back on their own childhood without much pleasure, but mainly because of the restrictions they felt it would impose on their sense of freedom. As one of them put it:

Probably the minute you have children you're fairly stuck, you know – and also if you get a mortgage. I have this phobia about mortgages.

If they valued this freedom so highly, they were surely right to want to avoid parenthood, at least for the time being, but we became rather sceptical about the notion of freedom which kept emerging in our discussions with groups in their early twenties. When older adults mentioned it, they seemed to be genuinely interested in increased personal liberty: for example, when asked what they thought middle age would be like, many people in their thirties replied that they were looking forward to the extra freedom they would have to spend on other interests when their children were off their hands. The young adults we talked to were greatly pre-occupied with freedom, but they were often very unclear exactly what it was they wanted to be free to do. It would be uncharitable to describe their sense of freedom as aimlessness, but it's difficult to resist the suspicion that one of the main risks a young adult runs is of depriving himself of the opportunity to have a good time, by refusing to commit himself on the grounds that he values his freedom too much to do so. In short, young adulthood is the period of life when you're most in danger of cutting off your nose to spite your face!

Despite this, people tend to look back on their early twenties with pleasure. When we asked our sample what age they would most like to be if they had the choice, the twenties proved to be a very popular decade. The reasons given for choosing it were interesting, too. Those who favoured the late twenties described it as the time when they had achieved the best balance between experience and opportunity, but the most popular reason for choosing young adulthood was that this was the time when life had been most enjoyable. (A sizeable minority chose it for the less cheerful reason that they wanted to start their adult life all over again!) However, the early twenties have their darker side. When older adults are asked if they have found any age since adolescence to be particularly difficult to live through, most reply that they have not.

No one age seems to be any worse than the others. But among those who answer this question in the affirmative, it is the early twenties that are most often identified as an awkward age. Men in particular say they were disturbed by the decisions they had to take at that time, and both sexes often remember finding it difficult to adjust to marriage, especially if they started their family at this age. It would be unwise to attach too much significance to people's often hazy recollections of how they felt in the past, but it's surely significant that three times as many of the adults in our sample would choose to be in their twenties again as wanted to be back in their teens.

Togetherness

You might expect that after all the effort which went into solving the adolescent identity crisis we would want to relax for a while and give ourselves a chance to become more familiar with the *persona* we have finally uncovered. But this does not seem to be the case. It's not that we lose interest in ourselves; I have already remarked on the fact that young adults tend to be fairly self-centred. But young adulthood is a period of unparalleled social activity, set in motion by a mixture of circumstances, many of which we have already discussed in this and the previous chapter.

The uncertainty we feel as a result of arriving in the adult world can be greatly reduced by meeting others in the same position. Hearing what they make of their new jobs, for example, can be very useful in helping us to cope with our own, though researchers who have studied the nature of friendship tell us that young adults no longer feel the adolescent need to discuss intimate psychological concerns with their friends. Indeed, the drive towards independence is often so strong at this period of life that many young adults seem to have little time left to devote to sorting out their own emotional problems. Internal problems tend to be pushed to one side, as the young adult struggles to get to grips with the demands of the external world. This explains why psychoanalysis is on the whole easier in the thirties than in the twenties. But it's certainly not the case that young adults don't need friends. In fact, young adulthood is the time when we are most likely to make close friends, and there is a good chance that the friends a young adult acquires will last him or her a lifetime. When we asked people in Colchester about their friends, one of the most striking findings to emerge was that even among people in their fifties, more close friendships dated from the early twenties than from any other period of life.

Above all else, young adulthood is a time for experimentation and role playing, when we try on a variety of caps in the hope of finding one that fits. It's also the time for final flings, when the mousey girl who's been a model of propriety all her life suddenly cuts loose and has affairs with wonderfully degenerate older men, and the young man who in a few years' time will be the pillar of his local tennis club now sits nodding mindlessly on the beach at Ibiza, in a haze of pot-smoke. In ten years' time, it will be PTA meetings and bridge; now it's strip poker, the Truth Game, and even the occasional orgy. Up to the age of about twenty, we want time to go faster so that we can enjoy the fruits of adulthood. But once we get there, the calender suddenly starts speeding up, and the days are now too short for us to cram in all the things we want to do.

One reason why young adults spend so much time with people of their own age is that this atmosphere of 'let's pretend' can be very irritating to older adults who have forgotten its purpose and think it's simply childish. It is very common for older adults to sneer at students for 'playing at politics'. Similarly, parents often express astonishment at the elaborate dinner parties their children organize for their friends; and how often have you overheard a pair of middle-age businessmen complaining in a wine bar that their lunch is being ruined by the antics of a tableful of young execs? The trouble is that we are not very good at remembering how we felt when we were younger, and the hostility many older adults feel towards people in their twenties suggests that we are no better at understanding the world of the young adult than we are at recreating the feelings of a child or an adolescent. But there are two other reasons why little love is lost between the middle-aged and young adults. In the first place, as we shall soon see, it is in our forties that we first receive intimations of our own mortality, and we cannot be expected to feel particularly warm towards those who are eventually going to replace us or surpass us. As one man in his forties put it:

> A younger man in the office, finding out what you do – there's so many of these young people behind you, they are going to be the top people. I am too old to be the top people now – I wanted to be the person.

And there is an even more galling thought for a reasonably thoughtful forty-year-old. Of course it's absurd the way these young people carry on, braying in restaurants and serving ridiculously extravagant meals in their flats. They're obviously play-acting, when they ought to realize that life is real and in earnest. But wait a minute. Where have these ghastly caricatures come from? Whom are they imitating? Why, us, of course!

So one reason why young adults spend so much of their time with people of their own age is that they are a mystery or even a threat to their parents' generation. Relations with those in their fifties or sixties are somewhat better (it's very common for young adults to be more at ease with their grand-parents than with their parents), but the young adult is anxious to find models, and it is very unlikely that he or she will want to imitate people who seem to be past it. So far as younger people are concerned, we have already seen that unmarried young adults show little interest in children. And although they may be flattered by the obvious admiration of younger brothers or sisters, they are too close to their own adolescence and too concerned with being taken seriously as adults to have much time for the generation they have just left. This only leaves them with their own generation and that immediately above them. Where the latter is concerned, American psychiatrist Daniel Levinson has claimed that most young adults have at least one mentor figure in their lives, someone about ten years older than themselves – usually a non-relative – to whom they look for guidance and whose approval they seek eagerly. Levinson's book *The Seasons of a Man's Life* is the bible of the new theory of adult development that I discussed in the introduction to this book, but we found very little support for this aspect of his theory among adults in Colchester. More than 40 per cent of the people we interviewed denied that they had ever had such a figure in their lives, and in the great majority of cases where a mentor had been important the mentor turned out to have been a parent or relative, rather than a senior colleague or ex-teacher, and so failed to match the definition of a mentor provided by Levinson.

Perhaps the most striking feature of young adulthood is its exclusiveness with regard to age. At no other time of life do we spend less time in the company of people older or younger than ourselves; and it may well be that never again are we so sensitive to the difference even a year can make. As with so many other aspects of young adulthood, it is students who make the point best. To their teachers, the differences between a first- and a third-year student are not that great. Of course there are some. It would be very surprising if an eighteen-year-old leaving home for the first time were to be unaffected by the experience of living almost exclusively in the company of his or her peers for three years. But when you examine their social networks, it is astonishing how little mixing there is between students in different years of the same course, given that their interests and the organization of their daily life are objectively so similar. Even though girls tend to follow the pattern laid down in adolescence of choosing boyfriends older than themselves, most of their close friends are in their own year. Indeed, students who spend too much of their time mixing with people in the years above or below them run the risk of being rejected by their contemporaries, who accuse them either of being pushy or else of being guilty of cradle-snatching!

Part of the explanation for this state of affairs presumably lies in the organization of timetables and in the fact that at most colleges students tend to live in halls of residence at certain points in their career and in digs at others. But it is difficult to resist the suspicion that the young adult's extreme sensitivity to age is at least partly responsible for the fact that students in the same year of a course knit so tightly together and express so little interest in the years above and below them. Each year develops its own flavour and ethos. Rival cliques may develop – the dedicated workers, the hard-drinking philosophers and the glamour-pusses whose flightiness is a front to disguise the fact that they are really secret workers – but there is still a strong sense of belonging to the class of '80, and the feeling that there is something special about *their* year.

Pairing and sharing

We keep coming up against a paradox which can make young adulthood an uncomfortable period. On the one hand we want to come in from the cold and give up the lonely adolescent hunt for self-understanding in favour of the cosy fraternity of the adult world. On the other, we want to enjoy our hard-won independence, keep our options open and avoid commitments which would trap us in a cage before we have had time to spread our wings, sow our wild oats or discover the meaning of any of the other metaphors writers have used to describe this period of our lives. It's a dilemma which affects every aspect of the young adult's life, but it appears in a particularly acute form in his or her emotional and sexual attachments.

As we saw in the last chapter, people who reach young adulthood without having had any sexual experience are now in a minority (though only just). Since most adolescents say that they are opposed to casual sex, and seem to feel quite strongly that sex ought to occur only in the context of an established loving relationship, it may well be that many of today's teenagers experience at least one such relationship before they reach young adulthood. We can't be sure that this is the case – it is not easy to assess the quality of a relationship – and there are many experts who claim that only a very exceptional adolescent is capable of the self-sacrifice involved in a successful intimate relationship. These experts base their argument on the assumptions that the psychological hallmark of the adolescent is isolation, and that isolation is a force diametrically opposed to intimacy.

We have already identified several tricky problems young adults have to cope with – accepting that their parents no longer feel responsible for them and finding a role for themselves in the adult world, for example. But psychiatrists consider that the most difficult of all the psychological tasks which confront us at this stage of our lives is finding a solution to what they call the intimacy-versus-isolation crisis. Given the amount of time adolescents spend thinking about themselves, it's easy to understand why when they reach young adulthood they sometimes have an almost unhealthy interest in themselves. 'Intimacy' is a more ambiguous concept, so we need to look quite carefully at how the psychiatrists use it. In the present context, intimacy implies the ability for mutual empathy (i.e. being aware of and affected by someone else's feelings) and for mutual regulation of needs (i.e. acting in a way calculated to please someone other than yourself). It involves taking pleasure not only in understanding and pleasing someone else, but also in being understood and pleased by them.

So the young adult has to make the transition from adolescent isolationism to adult intimacy, and the further he is

from resolving the earlier identity crisis, the ha
will be. Intimacy involves commitment, and the
fident you are about your own identity, the more re
you will be to share part of yourself with someone else.
young adult who is still struggling to find himself feels threatened when other people try to get too close to him. He erects
barriers to make them keep their distance, fearful of what the
close proximity of a more robust ego might do to the sickly
infant he is nursing. On this occasion, my tendency to write
as if all young adults were male is more than a stylistic convenience because it is men who seem to have more difficulty
in resolving the intimacy-versus-isolation crisis. There is
nothing surprising about this. Up to this point in development, they have consistently lagged behind women.

I said earlier that it's not easy to assess the quality of an
intimate relationship. But although no two relationships are
identical, most of the experts seem to agree that *self-disclosure* – the exchange of personal information – lies at the
heart of an intimate relationship, and is the yardstick by
which its depth should be measured. But young adults soon
learn that just blurting out everything they can think of to say
about themselves is not the passport to a successful relationship. Disclosures have to come from both sides, and they must
occur at an appropriate rate. It used to be thought that being
reluctant to talk about yourself was the main reason why
some people seem unable ever to get a relationship off the
ground, but recent research shows that talking too much (or
too soon) is just as often at the root of the problem. In fact,
when people are divided up into high, moderate and low
disclosers, it turns out that it's the moderate self-disclosers
who seem to have the most satisfying relationships.

If you're intending to base your relationship on sound
social psychological principles, you should also bear in mind
that revealing too much about yourself seems to be found a
particularly unattractive characteristic in men, whereas
women are more often damned for being too discreet about

...tion of a high-disclosing man and a
...nakes for the least promising re-
...erts tell us. If you're the sort of man
... himself talking in the presence of
...close to, it seems that your best hope
...ning other than yourself, since pre-
...only a real turn-off when they concern
the pe... ...person who is making them!

Studies of young adults in America suggest that there may
be four basic types of intimate relationship, involving intellectual discussion and exchange, physical closeness,
emotional communication, or a social context that supports
the relationship through similarity and the approval of
family and friends. Of course the ideal relationship involves
all these ingredients, but different people vary in how much
store they set by them, and one way of predicting the likely
outcome of a particular relationship is to assess how well
matched the partners are in their needs for each ingredient.
The recipe for success remains elusive. It includes such social
skills as self-disclosure and reciprocity (the ability to respond
in kind), but also more mundane considerations like similarity and compatibility. The attraction of opposites, for all
its romantic appeal, turns out to be a flimsy basis for a lasting
relationship, as can be seen from the success of computer dating agencies. They attempt to find their clients partners as
similar to them as possible, and their success rate is surprisingly high.

Studies of marriage confirm that couples who stay together tend to be more like each other than those who split
up, though this finding could be interpreted in two different
ways. It might confirm that fundamental similarity is the best
recipe for a successful long-term relationship. But it could
just mean that people who live together tend to become more
alike and that a couple that fails to adapt to one another in
this way are not likely to stay together.

In some respects, the intimate relationships young adults

try to form are quite similar to earlier relationships with their parents and friends. They may well have loved their parents and felt deeply committed to best friends. Nor will they need to be told how important it is to reveal themselves and establish common friends and interests with someone they want to stay close to. The new dimension is being in love, and the problem which has taxed young adults since time began is how to distinguish between being in love with someone and liking, admiring, depending on, or being infatuated with them. Until recently, psychologists and psychiatrists were uncharacteristically reticent on this point. In the last decade, however, they have taken their courage in both hands and ventured into the territory where, according to the songwriter, angels fear to tread.

When people are asked what being in love means to them they mention notions like trust, commitment, affection, self-disclosure and other qualities which characterize intimate relationships in general, rather than just those which involve being in love. Sadly, the extra ingredient which the young adult needs to identify in order to make sure he ends up with the 'right' partner seems so far to have eluded all social scientists' attempts to pin it down, though they say that lovers speak of an intense physical need to be in the presence of their loved ones and show a degree of possessiveness which is rare – though not unknown – between friends. However, I doubt whether this 'discovery' greatly advances our understanding of the phenomenon of being in love, and until the experts come up with something better, young adults are going to have to carry on as they always have done, trusting to their own intuitions and the advice of their friends to tell them when they have found the real thing.

Till death us do part

For all the changes which may have taken place in the pattern of our sexual and emotional relationships over the last twenty years, for the huge majority of us the quest for intimacy ends in marriage and parenthood. For example, only 2 per cent of our adult sample (aged twenty-nine to fifty-nine) in Colchester had never been married, and more than 90 per cent of them had children. Similarly, the new freedom to have sexual relationships outside marriage seems to have had surprisingly little effect on the number of people who choose to live together before getting married (still less than 20 per cent), nor is it causing people to get married later. Parenthood belongs in the stage of life we shall be discussing in the next chapter, but twenty to twenty-four is currently the most popular age for getting married. It wasn't always so. A hundred years ago it would have been exceptional for a couple to get married as early as this. But since the end of the Second World War about three-quarters of women and more than half of all men have become married by the age of twenty-four. The Colchester sample was typical in this respect. Eighty-two per cent of the women and fifty-eight per cent of the men had married before they were twenty-five, and when we looked at the pattern for different age groups, there was a definite tendency for younger people to get married earlier. Among adults in the fifty to fifty-nine age group, 47 per cent of the men and 71 per cent of the women had married before the age of twenty-five; among the twenty-nine to thirty-nine-year-olds, the comparable figures were 66 and 83 per cent. Even more dramatically, the proportion of people who got married after the age of thirty was twice as high among fifty to fifty-nine-year-olds as it was among the forty to forty-nine-year-olds.

According to some experts, these figures are misleading. They believe that the overall drop in the age at which people get married hides two very different trends – a very marked swing towards getting married younger among working-class couples, and a much less striking trend towards getting married later among the middle classes. In America, the proportion of women between the ages of twenty and twenty-four who were unmarried rose from 28 to 40 per cent between 1960 and 1975, which seems clear evidence of a tendency to postpone marriage until after young adulthood. However, we found no comparable trend in Colchester, and although there was a tendency for working-class couples to get married earlier than middle-class couples, this difference arose as much from the greater incidence of teenage marriages among the working classes as from any tendency for the middle classes to get married after young adulthood. Marriage between twenty-five and thirty *was* commoner among middle-class couples, but this was outweighed by the fact that marriage after the age of thirty was twice as common among working-class couples as it was among the middle classes.

There are at least two reasons why we get married younger now than we did a hundred years ago. The first is a simple matter of economics. It would have been very unusual for a Victorian servant or apprentice to have assembled a nest-egg large enough to support matrimony – let alone parenthood – before the age of thirty. Nor would a young man training for one of the middle-class professions have been in a much stronger position. So far as blue-collar jobs are concerned, today's young adults are no longer penalized for being young – an hourly rate is an hourly rate whatever your age – and although students and others training for the professions are not generously paid, they can afford to get married and a significant number of them do so. Nor can we ignore the fact that over the last century each generation has reached physical and sexual maturity earlier than its predecessor. There is a link between age of reaching puberty and age of marriage – early maturers tend to get married younger – and it could be that the ideal age for a woman to have children has also fallen.

I don't think we can prove that either or both of these factors have actually *caused* the drop in the age at which people get married. But both must have affected the general feeling we have about the suitable age for getting married, and this is probably the most important single factor of all. Opinions have certainly changed over the years, but there has been very little change in our conviction that people ought to be mature enough to know their own minds and to accept the extra responsibility before committing themselves to marriage. We still disapprove strongly of couples who get married 'too young', and the consequences of this disapproval make it very difficult to interpret the fact that more than half of teenage marriages (i.e. marriages where both partners are under twenty) end in divorce or separation. We tend to assume that teenage marriages fail simply because the couple are too young to choose the right partner or take on the responsibility, and that all might have been well if they had only waited for the greater maturity which comes with adulthood before taking the plunge. But closer examination of teenage marriages suggests that it is not just their youth which is against these young-marrieds. Their marriages often seem to be undermined by the disapproval and continued opposition of their respective sets of parents, particularly when the teenage wife becomes a mother and receives no support from her parents as a punishment for getting married against their wishes.

Of course, it's not just teenage marriages which founder, as we shall see in the next chapter. Some commentators believe that the whole institution of marriage is on the rocks and that young adults are wasting their time looking for Mr or Miss Right. But it is hard to defend this position because there is absolutely no evidence that marriage is losing its popularity. Not only are people now tending to get married earlier but fewer are choosing to remain unmarried. And if the divorce rate is going up, so is the number of second marriages. But there *has* been a change in the nature of marriage, which is closely linked to the matters we have been discussing in this chapter.

I have presented marriage in a psychological context, as an

instrument many young adults use to resolve the intimacy-versus-isolation crisis. I have also implied that being in love is an important ingredient in making a successful match. But the view that there should be any connection between romantic love and marriage is far from being universal. In fact, it seems to be peculiar to the United States, parts of north-eastern Europe, Polynesia, and to European nobility of the eleventh and twelfth centuries! Elsewhere and at other times, marriage has been seen as a business contract or an outlet for sexual desire rather than as a source of emotional gratification, and it's only since the age of getting married dropped to young adulthood that anyone started to describe it as an important step in a person's psychological development.

Instead of trying to understand how other societies manage with such an unromantic view of marriage, it is salutary to recall what George Bernard Shaw said about the institution as we know it:

> When two people are under the influence of the most violent, most insane, most delusive and most transient of passions, they are required to swear that they will remain in that excited, abnormal and exhausting condition continuously until death do them part.

This is an extreme view of the situation, and I doubt whether many couples today have quite such a starry-eyed approach to marriage. In a survey carried out in Britain in 1977, 60 per cent of unmarried young adults were prepared to admit that divorce was something that might happen to them. But it's true that marriage evolved to meet demands that have nothing to do with intimacy, and this may have profound implications for our experience of young adulthood.

We have seen that young adulthood is the time when we have to establish ourselves in the adult world, learn to function as independent beings, and form intimate relationships to replace the childhood bond with our parents. It is a period of paradoxes and conflicting urges, and one in which many people change. According to the study of personality development over the years which I referred to in Chapter 2, the changes which take place during this relatively short period of our lives are at least as great as those which occur at any other time. We tend to become more giving and productive, less gregarious (once we have found a partner), less prone to fantasize and better able to cope with frustration.

For the great majority of people, the period of independence is a brief one. Even before the links which bind us to the family home have been loosened most of us are actively searching for a single partner to whom we can make a lifetime commitment. This hunt can take several years, but it usually comes to an end before we leave young adulthood. Marriage may be an anachronism, but if so it is one we embrace with almost indecent eagerness. It has become the central event of young adulthood, and the context in which most of us try to resolve the intimacy-versus-isolation crisis and the other psychological problems which characterize this period of our lives. However, this state of affairs is a very recent development, and a significant number of people – especially men – still choose to put off getting married until the next stage of life. Whether or not they are wise to do so is something we cannot judge before viewing the next instalment in the longest-running soap-opera of them all.

CHAPTER 4

Life Assurance

'All the advantages that youth and old age possess separately, those in the prime of life possess combined.'

ARISTOTLE

Although children are very different creatures from young adults, and adolescents occasionally seem to be a different species altogether, it's tempting to lump together the three ages we have discussed so far and describe them as an extended training period for the real business of living. Of course they feel real enough when you are living through them, but to the outside observer they have an atmosphere of make-believe. You can see this very clearly when you watch children playing, but it's no less apparent in the studied formality of a young couple playing at being host and hostess. Of course, we don't – or certainly shouldn't – ever lose our love of fantasy and games-playing. William Hazlitt describes man as a make-believe animal who is never so truly himself as when he is acting a part. But it's in the first three ages, and perhaps the last of all, that we have most freedom to indulge this side of our nature.

However, this is not the only thing which unites the first three ages and distinguishes them from those which follow. Up to the point where we left them at the end of the last chapter, men and women have on the whole led fairly similar lives. Of course girls have had to contend with society's view that they are in some sense members of an inferior sex, and boys may have suffered from their tendency to lag behind girls in many aspects of development throughout the whole period of growing up. There *are* differences in the way boys and girls are treated, and I have tried to point these out when they seemed to be important. But given the way our education system is organized and the state of the law regarding job opportunities, there is no reason why a woman in her middle twenties who has not yet had children should find herself in a very different position from that occupied by a man of the same age. The figures tell us that she will be earning slightly less than he does, though many women of this age are paid more than most of their male contemporaries. But up to this point in life, the average man and woman have had fairly similar opportunities and experiences, so that much of what I have had to say about the first three Ages of Man has applied to both sexes.

A parting of the ways

Once we get to the fourth stage of life, however, this changes. The years of full adulthood are usually assumed to begin with the birth of the first child which happens to the average couple in their mid- to late-twenties. This is not to deny adult status to couples who put off having children until their thirties or to those who never have children, nor does it imply that someone who has a child is automatically transformed into full adulthood overnight, regardless of their age. But for most people, it is the birth of their first child which forces them finally to shake off the attitudes of young adulthood.

For some people, full adulthood can span more than half a century, and it's usually divided into four stages. However, the distinctions between these are much less clear-cut than those between the first three ages. The reason for this is very simple. We can view development during the first twenty-five years of life from any one of three perspectives - biological, educational or psychological - but the important marker-events in each sphere quite often coincide, so it's comparatively easy to decide where

one stage ends and another begins. In adulthood, the
position is much more complicated. We do change physically
and psychologically over the years, but more gradually.
And although there are a few obvious marker-events like
the menopause or retirement from work, the landmarks
in the two great concerns of the adult years – family life and
work – often occur at different times and are unrelated. So
the points at which an individual's life changes significantly
will vary according to how much importance he or she
attaches to each of these sometimes conflicting interests.

If we decide that work is the most important thing in an
adult's life, we can use the idea of a career clock to identify
the stages. For example, in most white-collar jobs you have a
pretty good idea of whether or not you're a success by the
time you are forty. (Politics is one of the few professions
where someone of forty can still be described as promising.)
So the period between the late twenties and late thirties
becomes The Deadline Decade, and you would expect a
person's experience of it to be greatly affected by his progress up the professional ladder. However, I use the word
'his' deliberately here, because the career-clock approach
to the adult years is heavily slanted towards men, and
North American men at that. For all the changes which
have taken place in our thinking about the role of women
in society, the huge majority (over 90 per cent) of women
in their thirties have children. And although most women
now regard motherhood as only a break in their careers, all
the evidence suggests that they give their children a much
higher priority than their jobs. So the limitation of the
career-clock description of adulthood is that it only applies
to people whose overriding concern is with their work.
American researchers consider that a significant number of
men and some women fall into this category, but the
Colchester survey suggests that this is not the case, at
least in Britain. When we asked adults to rank various
aspects of life in order of importance, both men and women

of all ages placed their marriage and family far above their jobs. As you would expect, the men attached more importance to their work than the women did (it came third and sixth in their respective lists of life priorities). But we would clearly get a very restricted view of adult development if we treated it simply from the point of view of a person's working life.

There are two other ways of describing the first stage of full adulthood. It is sometimes called the prime of life, and it's certainly tempting to follow Aristotle's description of the thirties as the period of our lives when we achieve the best blend of youthful strength and the wisdom which comes with maturity. But once again the results of our survey on age show how much more complicated the human life-cycle becomes after the unisex preparatory period of the first three ages has come to an end. When we asked adults between twenty-nine and fifty-nine to identify the prime of life, men and women gave very different answers. Nearly half of the men, but only 29 per cent of the women, placed it in the thirties. And when we interviewed people in their early forties, we discovered that one woman in three, but only one man in twenty-five, shared Miss Jean Brodie's view that the prime of life still lay ahead of them.

We decided to explore this striking discrepancy between men's and women's attitudes by asking them to explain why they had chosen one period rather than another as the prime of life. Their answers leave no doubt that the thirties and forties are the period of life when the two sexes have least in common, and they suggest that it's parenthood rather than marriage or work which makes the lives of men and women so different. For women of all ages, the most frequently mentioned marker-event of the prime of life was freedom from the responsibility of looking after children. For men, this was rarely a consideration. Men in their thirties (and some in their forties and fifties) simply say it's 'how I feel now', but they also associated the prime of life with being at the peak of their careers, understanding how the world works and being at their physical peak. We shall return to the different preoccupations of the two sexes during the thirties and forties at various points in this and the next chapter. But I hope I have said enough to convince you that when people describe the thirties as the prime of life, they are really only talking about men. Similarly, when we come to evaluate the suggestion that the forties are a particularly difficult period of adult life (the idea of the Mid-life Crisis), we shall have to remember that this is the age which many women (and some men) think of as their prime.

The fact that men and women have different views of when they are in the prime of life illustrates how difficult it is to identify and describe the different stages of the life-cycle in adulthood. But it's not impossible, because although many women are primarily concerned with their children while their husband's attention is divided between his family and his job, husbands and wives usually live together and must inevitably be affected by each other's interests and preoccupations. Most women with children have jobs of their own, and even those who don't must be affected by what is happening to their husbands at work. Similarly, very few husbands today follow Oscar Wilde's prescription for fatherhood ('Fathers should be neither seen nor heard, that is the only proper basis for family life'), and even a man who does can hardly expect his relations with his wife to be unaffected by her dealings with their children. In fact, if we give due weight to men's and women's different interests and allow for the fact that their perceptions of life at any given time may not be identical, we can divide the adult years into four stages, each marked by distinctive events and feelings which affect men and women alike, though also by some concerns which affect one sex more than the other.

Making it

In this chapter we shall be concerned with the period which runs from the mid-twenties to the late thirties. For most people it begins with the birth of their first child, which means that women – as always – tend to reach it earlier than men, and by the time it ends, their youngest child will probably be at school and its mother back at work. For most women at least, I think we can legitimately dub this the Age of Parenthood, even though more than half of them now combine looking after their children with a full- or part-time job. Coincidentally, these are critical years in most middle-class careers, at the end of which the 'fliers' are easily recognizable. When men and women enter these professions in young adulthood, they do so with similar qualifications and in theory have the same opportunities for advancement. But by the time they reach forty, the fact that most women have devoted a significant proportion of their time and energy over the last decade to rearing a family has taken its toll. Not many of them will be described as 'fliers', and even fewer will go on to reach the highest jobs in their professions.

For some people, men and women, the consuming interest in this period of life is becoming a professional success. For them, it is the Making It or Deadline Decade. Others, especially men, feel that this is the Prime of Life. As we saw in the last chapter, our real biological peak actually comes earlier. But we don't usually become aware of any significant decline in our physical powers before the mid-fifties: for example, your ability to climb up a flight of stairs remains much the same until you're about thirty-five, as does your hand strength and capacity to work flat out without becoming tired. So, physically speaking, it's not just wishful thinking to imagine that you can still be somewhere near your peak, at least till the early thirties.

Of course, you won't be able to sprint as fast as you once could, but some of the greatest long-distance runners have been in their thirties, and, besides, it's not often we want to sprint. However, there are signs that the rot has started to set in, as you can see from the following comment made by a thirty-four-year-old man:

> If I've had late nights during the week I need to have more sleep. Before we used to stay up till about two o'clock every night. Now I just couldn't cope.

Looking back from his mid-forties, another man conjures up a more vivid image:

> When I was thirty I used to play a lot of tennis, and having turned thirty I did notice that the return balls from the other side of the net seemed to be coming back a little faster.

Men in their thirties may also find that they can't read the small print as well as they used to because the lenses of their eyes have become less elastic and so less able to focus. There's also a loss of elasticity in a woman's pelvic tissue after the age of thirty which can make childbirth more difficult, especially if she has not yet had a child (if her birth-canal has been widened by having a child, this effect of aging is much less important). Blood pressure also rises slowly but steadily from thirty to forty even in perfectly healthy men, as the aorta becomes less elastic too. It's important to know that this process is exaggerated by being overweight, and that this can lead not only to abnormally high blood pressure at the time, but also to trouble much later. So the first steps towards ensuring a healthy old age need to be taken as early as your thirties, by eating sensibly and taking enough exercise to avoid getting a weight problem which can otherwise dog you for the rest of your life. Most of the adults in their thirties we talked to were aware of this, and many of them – especially middle-class men – had recently taken up jogging.

The fact that we can give this age so many different names reflects the great diversity of people's interests during the first stage of full adulthood. As we shall shortly see, it's when most people finally settle down and achieve the identity they will wear for the rest of their lives. For some, however, this period is marked by the discovery that the choices they made in early adulthood were not after all, irrevocable. It is not considered eccentric to embark on a new career in your thirties, and divorce is relatively common-place. But as it approaches its end, even the most dedicated procrastinator has to recognize that certain options which opened up as long ago as adolescence become closed once and for all when this era is over. The novelist Anthony Powell has compared this stage in our lives to the moment in a game of bar-billiards when the bar falls. Few professions welcome raw recruits who are over forty, and for women who have put off having children to pursue their careers, the mid-thirties can be a period of great internal conflict, which is apparent in the comment made by a thirty-eight-year-old teacher we interviewed:

> Well, to tell the honest, honest truth I would like to get married and have children. I would give up my teaching to get married and have children. I would actually do that - and teaching is everything to me.

For women like this, as for the ambitious young professional or executive who feels that he is a round peg in a square hole, this is certainly a Deadline Decade.

Before turning to the major events of the period, we must establish what it feels like to be in your thirties. Given that so much happens during these years - in many respects, it is the most decisive decade of our lives - it's not surprising that people of this age (and older people, as they look back over it) seem to have very mixed feelings. However, on the basis of our interviews with more than 250 people in the twenty-nine to thirty-nine age range in Colchester, we can identify at least some of the distinguishing characteristics of our fourth age.

Since nine out of ten of the people we talked to had children, it came as no surprise to find that they were the dominant influence, not only on people's present lives but on how they viewed the future and even on their feelings about the past. We saw in the last chapter that young adults are often very doubtful about having children for fear of the effect it will have on their freedom. But the reality of parenthood seems to produce a *volte-face* in the thirties. Even though our earlier fears are confirmed - few people deny that having children severely affects their social lives and general freedom of manoeuvre - it seems that people in their thirties feel that the loss of freedom is more than compensated for by the feeling they have of responsibility and being needed. For all the forebodings they might have had ten years earlier, virtually none of the parents we talked to regretted having children.

People in their early thirties are unanimous that the arrival of children was the major turning-point in their lives, and a much more significant step than getting married. With the benefit of hindsight, they are now almost scornful of the importance they once attached to getting married, and are generally blasé about the marriages of their friends which have ended in divorce. The tendency to play down the significance of marriage seems to be only a passing phase, however. It is most marked in the early thirties when the impact of parenthood is at its greatest, and by the late thirties getting married is once again perceived as a very significant milestone. This ties in with the results of other surveys which have identified the early thirties as the time when people (especially women) are least satisfied with their marriages (the syndrome of The Seven-year Itch). So whatever else parenthood may do for people, it doesn't seem to improve their marriages, at least in the short-term.

Throughout life, we have a tendency to sneer at what we were like a decade earlier. This is very marked in the early thirties, as you can see from the following comment made by a thirty-four-year-old man:

> You talk about the good times; my God, the number of times when Saturday night was going to be our big night – it was invariably nothing. We would sit around and argue where we were going, and perhaps end up by sitting in a pub or something.

Our thirty-year-olds felt very strongly that they had only really reached adulthood when they became parents, and they made a point of emphasizing how much more responsible and considerate they were now that they had children. But despite this, many people freely admit that they are already looking forward to the time when their children leave home. So although they may have successfully suppressed the young adult demand for freedom, it clearly isn't dead; indeed, many of the people we talked to were already planning what they would do with the extra leisure they would have when their children had gone. Sometimes their plans involve their children. As one woman put it:

> I think the time when I'm going to enjoy myself is when the children are grown up, and I can start going out with my children, and then go back to my teens.

For other women, the great attraction of the empty nest is the opportunity it will give them to expand their interests:

> My children will be leaving home, so I think my life should be easier. More time for leisure then ... do

something in regard to myself – things I have been wanting to do for a long time. I always wanted to take up art
again.

For all our protestations that only people with children
can know what life is really about, our attitude towards
parenthood is ambivalent. Not surprisingly, this is particularly true for women. Although virtually every woman we
spoke to left us in no doubt that her children were the
most important thing in her life, when we asked them to
tell us what they thought of as their special treats, the
second most popular choice of women at this age (after
'holidays in the sun') was getting away from their children
for a while. As an interesting aside on the discrepancy
between men's and women's lives in the thirties, we found
that a similar proportion of men answered this question
by saying that their idea of a treat was being *with* their
children!

Another indication of the way in which this period
of life is dominated by parenthood is the almost obsessive
tendency people in their thirties have of evaluating themselves as parents. They constantly compare their children
with those of their friends, and are even more interested
in the comparison between the way in which they bring
their children up and the way in which they themselves
were treated by their own parents. The adults in Colchester
are convinced that they were doing a better job in this
respect than their parents had, largely because they were
adopting a more liberal approach. Interestingly, their
ambition as parents is not so much to produce respectful
or successful children as to end up as friends of their children when they have grown up. For the most part, they do
not think of their own parents as friends, but, like every
generation before them, they are confident that the child-
rearing methods they are using will produce the desired
results. As one young father put it:

I would like to think that because I came from the 1960s I would be more understanding towards my children . . . your parents just didn't seem to understand the music, the way you dressed . . . that's what made me rebellious ... and it makes me think I'm more relaxed with my child.

However, young parenthood also has its darker side. Although children clearly give their parents a sense of self-assurance and responsibility, they are also a major source of worry, especially for women. (Throughout the whole period of life covered by the Colchester survey, twenty-nine to fifty-nine, women are three to four times more likely than men to mention children when asked what they worry about.) We found that women worry most about their children when they are under five or between eleven and nineteen. But although it was women in the thirty-six to forty-five age bracket who expressed the most concern on this score (they were most likely to have teenage children), we were struck by the number of mothers in their thirties who are already worrying about how they will cope when their children reach adolescence. Here is how one young mother described her feelings:

I think, 'if he's swaggering around with his school shirt undone, no vest underneath and so on at six, what on earth is he going to want to do when he reaches his teens?' It horrifies me at times.

Mothers also worry to a lesser extent about their children's long-term future. Will there be jobs for them and what sort of society are they going to have to bring up *their* children in?

The thirties bring other problems. For both sexes, money is a greater worry at this age than at any point subsequently, and the number of Colchester men who admitted that they were worried about their jobs was twice as high in the twenty-nine to thirty-five age bracket as it was among thirty-six to forty-five-year-olds. So far as psychological feelings are concerned, both men and women in their thirties tend to describe themselves as less tolerant than they were ten years earlier. We also found that women of this age are more irritable and less tranquil than those in their forties and fifties, presumably as a consequence of having to spend so much of their time with young children. But only one woman in three considers that she is less physically attractive than she was ten years earlier. Only 15 per cent of men admit to this worry about themselves, and just as many reckon that they have become more attractive. Only one woman in ten shares this optimistic view about herself. However, the majority of men and women in their thirties seem to think that they are neither more nor less physically attractive than they were a decade earlier. They also say that there has been very little change in their sex-life. Where there has been a change, it's towards more rather than less sexual activity, and both sexes – but especially women – disagree strongly with the statement that sexual relationships are more important to younger than to older people.

A good time of life

Despite the worries about young children, money and work, the thirties may well be the most agreeable period of life to live through. Some of the men we interviewed in their early thirties expressed a wish to be five years younger, while a surprisingly large number of men in their late thirties (but very few women) said they would like to be teenagers again. But more than a third of men and half of women of this age say they would prefer to be their present age than any other, and it is also the most popular choice amongst older adults when they are asked what age they would most like to be. Furthermore, when older adults are asked if any period of their life since adolescence has seemed a particularly awkward age, only 3 per cent mention the thirties, whereas 8 and 6 per cent mention the early and late twenties respectively. When they look back on their thirties, many older people share the sentiments expressed in the following quote from a man in his fifties:

> I think I would have liked to have stopped aging at about thirty-five. I did say at the time to my wife, you know, this seems to be a wonderful age for us, everything's going right - this is how I would like it for evermore.

When we asked people in their thirties to list the ways in which they thought they had changed over the last ten years, almost all their replies suggested that life has improved. Some I have already mentioned: they feel more mature and responsible, and although they have money worries, they feel more financially secure than they did earlier. Both sexes are also more assured, especially in their ability to deal with other people. As one thirty-five-year-old woman put it to us:

> I'm more confident now. A prize example would perhaps be going into shops and buying something when I was younger, getting it home and not liking it, and having to keep it because I didn't have the confidence to go and change it. Whereas now, anything that's wrong goes back immediately.

People now find it easier to make friends and are much less worried about what other people think of them than they were as young adults. Despite this, 44 per cent of the men we spoke to said that they had no close friends, whereas only 17 per cent of the women were in this position. Most of the men's close friends seem to date back to school or college days, while women tend to have neighbours or work-mates as their friends. This difference between the sexes continues throughout adulthood, though the older men in our sample (those in their fifties) were less likely to see themselves as friendless than the younger. We were surprised by the number of men who claimed they had no close friends, but other surveys carried out in Britain and America confirm that friends play a much less important part in most men's lives than they do in women's.

People in their thirties also claim that they now find it easier to accept new ideas, and say they are more in control of their lives. This is a significant finding because it confirms the psychologist's view that the most important distinguishing characteristic of this period of our lives is that we are willing and able to take responsibility for our own actions and decisions. Of course, all the findings I have been describing are based on how people see themselves. The Colchester survey does not prove that people in their thirties really are more responsible, mature, self-confident and so on than they were in their twenties, just that they think they are. The people we spoke to may have been very bad judges of themselves or perhaps they gave a misleadingly favourable impression of themselves to interviewers. But there is no obvious reason why this should apply more to people in their thirties than to those in their forties and fifties, and the fact that older adults tend to look back on the thirties with pleasure supports the view that although only men may describe it as the prime of life, the era of parenthood is for most people a pleasant and satisfying time.

Where jobs are concerned, the Colchester sample confirmed that the thirties is a period of mobility, generally upwards. Thirty-eight per cent of those in the twenty-nine to thirty-five age group had had more than three different employers in the last ten years. Women were generally more mobile than men, and working-class men tended to change their jobs more often than their middle-class counterparts. When we asked them to compare their present jobs with those they had had five years earlier, 57 per cent of the men and 31 per cent of the women said they were now in a better job, 8 per cent of the men and 23 per cent of the women that they were now working at a lower level, while the remainder said they were either in the same job or one that was roughly comparable.

There is an interesting class difference among the men in the hours they work. We found that middle-class men in their thirties tend to put in more hours of overtime than their elders, whereas the opposite is true for working-class men. For them, overtime seems to be the prerogative of older workers. So although there is very little difference between the classes when men are asked what priority they give to their work – both agree that it is less important than their health and much less important than their families – it's the middle-class thirty-year-old who is more likely to sacrifice on the altar of professional advancement time he might otherwise be spending with his family. Since it is also middle-class women who are more likely to put off having children until their thirties, it seems that to call the thirties the Deadline Decade is to take a strictly middle-class view of the matter.

There is one other aspect of the fourth age which has considerable practical and theoretical importance. In Chapter 1 we examined the significance of what happens to us in childhood as a predictor of what sort of adults we turn into, and in Chapter 2 I suggested that while some aspects of adolescence seem to follow on from childhood experiences, others anticipate developments in adulthood. We tried to tackle the question of when someone's personality really settles down by asking all the adults in our sample, 'At what age would you say you became the sort of person you are today?' Their replies were illuminating. No more than 6 per cent thought it had happened before the age of twenty, which suggests that very few of us believe that development stops before we reach adulthood. The most popular choice of age was the first half of the thirties. Interestingly, this applied to all age groups except the twenty-nine to thirty-four year olds, i.e. those who were actually at this age when they answered the question. They tended to opt for the mid or late twenties, which perhaps implies that we don't like to admit that our personality is too recent an acquisition!

But the tendency, even for people in their late fifties, to say that they became the people they are today as long ago as their early thirties strongly suggests that the feeling twenty-nine to thirty-four-year-olds have of reaching maturity and settling down is a realistic one. The early thirties seems to be the time when we finally resolve the identity crisis which has been with us since adolescence, and at last settle down with the personality we shall have for the rest of our lives.

Of course, life in the fourth age isn't all a bed of roses. Most people regard their thirtieth birthday as a watershed, as you can see from the following comments made by a group of twenty-nine to thirty-four-year olds:

I cried. I didn't want to be thirty. I don't mind, but I didn't want to be thirty . . . I shall probably feel the same when I'm forty and when I'm fifty – I don't know why.

It's half a pension.

My husband's a year younger than me. He offered to escort me for my pension . . . and he was going to treat me to a walking stick for my birthday . . . I mean, you don't feel any different from one morning to the next, obviously, but it did seem to be a milestone.

But once we have survived the shock of reaching the milestone, the thirties is a time for waxing philosophical about the phenomenon of getting older. As one woman put it:

When you look forward you think, 'Oh dear, what's it like to be forty? Oh dear, dreading getting to that.' But of course it never happens, because you creep up on it very, very slowly and you don't notice it. But suddenly to project yourself forward like that, it isn't acceptable, I think . . . I mean, when you're twenty, if somebody said, 'Oh, you're thirty-four,' I would most probably have died of shock and started worrying. Oh, it certainly looks different in advance, but the way I feel now that I am thirty-four, I am no different to how I was when I was twenty.

A thirty-two-year-old woman was less philosophical when she told us of a recent experience she had had:

I got a shock when my children pulled out some slides they'd found in a cupboard. There I was, a sweet and innocent seventeen. I was absolutely horrified at how fresh and young I looked in those photographs, but I didn't *feel* fifteen years older. But I looked at them, and there was the truth, facing me.

To the young, thirty marks the end of youth – it was no accident that the youth movement of the late 1960s adopted as one of its slogans, 'Never trust anyone over thirty!' A thirty-one-year-old man we talked to describes how thirty looked to him from the other side of it:

At twenty, thirty feels an old man. Thirty, you think that's a long way off. It's getting old, that. Start wearing suits and ties, and having your hair cut short all the time.

According to Gail Sheehy in her book *Passages*, some people are galvanized by the realization that they are now thirty into reviewing their lives and taking stock of how successful they have been in turning the dreams of their early twenties into reality. But there are two reasons for doubting that this early thirties' unease is very widespread. The first is that only a minority of the adults we talked to had had any clear idea of what they wanted out of life when they were in their early twenties, and the vast majority of those in their early thirties who had had such a dream ten years earlier felt it had been almost completely fulfilled. The second reason I have already mentioned: less than one adult in twenty-five describes their early thirties as an awkward age. So it looks as though people who complain about the Catch 30 syndrome are very much in a minority.

Nevertheless, we cannot ignore the exceptions. People who are still unmarried and women who have not yet had children may be increasingly disturbed by worries about becoming an old maid or being on the shelf, while couples who had children very young can face a difficult period of readjustment. Just as a husband is becoming reconciled to the prospect of finally settling down, his wife may be eager to break out of the domestic rut and to find new interests outside the home, now that her children are at school all day. Some women become resentful when the consequences of their break from work are brought home to them. Their male contemporaries have forged ahead, and a woman may not find it easy to sympathize with the dilemma of female contemporaries who are trying to decide whether to take the plunge into maternity if they have moved up the ladder while she has been away. The women we spoke to in Colchester described some of the problems they had faced when rejoining the work force. They had found it difficult to establish a routine which suited both employers and young children, and it had taken them as much as a year to regain their professional competence and confidence. Some also find it disconcerting to have to work alongside much younger people, and a few are disconcerted to discover how much things have moved on technically since they last worked.

Here is what a rather older woman had to say about her return to nursing, after a long period away from it:

> I was petrified for about three months . . . I really used to dread going to work . . . When I was there before, the theatres were split into two, and now we've got the theatre suites, so the whole place was a lot bigger, many more people about, and I felt really lost . . . I did get lost several times, and I couldn't tell who was who . . . I had no one to talk to about it until another staff nurse came along, and then two or three more came, and they were all as new as I had been; they'd all come back like I had come, and were finding it just as hard as me . . . It doesn't worry me now, I'll take it as I find it now, and feel quite happy to do so.

But despite the problems some people have at this age, most of those we interviewed radiated an aura of satisfaction with their lives, which tended to grow rather than recede throughout the period. For the 'typical' man or woman, thirty-five seems to be a better age than twenty-five. Part of the reason for this must lie in the reservoir of financial and emotional security which seems to fill up over the decade. As one thirty-eight-year-old woman put it to us:

> I think that within the last five years I've grown up incredibly, you know. I mean, really grown up, from being a not-knowing-what-to-do sort of person.

But I suspect that much of the satisfaction (and, especially, self-satisfaction) of the mid-thirties comes from knowing that you have survived what many people consider to be the most harrowing experience of their lives – the birth and early years of their children. A great deal has been written about the relationship between parents and their children, but it's almost all concerned with the effect parents have on their children. Here I want to look at the other side of the coin, and see how adults' lives are affected by the great marker-event of the fourth age of man – parenthood.

Happy families

There is a school of thought which believes that motherhood comes naturally to women, and claims that when a woman becomes pregnant she is gripped by a primeval instinct which ensures that she will love, cherish and instinctively recognize the needs of her child after it is born. According to this theory, there is a 'natural fit' between what a child wants and how its parents will behave, which suggests that we ought to adapt to parenthood as easily as ducks take to water. Many contemporary child-rearing manuals follow this line, urging their readers to 'trust to their instincts' rather than worrying too much about what the experts tell them.

No doubt the authors of these books mean well, but I'm afraid they may have the opposite effect to that intended, because there are good reasons for doubting whether there is any such thing as a maternal instinct. I have discussed this very controversial subject at length in my book *A Question of Sex*, and will not repeat all the arguments here. But mothers who have been made to feel guilty and even 'unnatural' by the discovery that they didn't experience love at the first sight of their babies will be reassured to learn that they are not alone. Recent surveys show that only about a half of all women feel an immediate sense of love for their babies. And those who believe in the notion of a maternal instinct should ponder on the fact that while male philosophers and psychologists have spent two thousand years trying to convince women that they ought to breastfeed their babies, a significant number of mothers have always firmly rejected this idea. So even in as basic an aspect of behaviour as this, there seems to be little sign of a maternal instinct.

Although some people do appear to take parenthood in their stride without any obvious signs of distress, I think we have to take seriously the very different school of thought which describes it as a developmental crisis, especially if we accept the psychologist's definition of a crisis as a set of circumstances or events for which one's existing behavioural patterns are inadequate.

On the face of it, it seems strange to suggest that people should be unprepared for and so surprised by what happens when they first become parents. Even if we don't believe in a maternal (or paternal) instinct, we usually know that we are going to become parents well in advance, and have many months in which to adjust to the idea and make the necessary practical arrangements. But although the practical consequences of becoming a parent are spelled out very clearly in the baby-books, first-time parents are adamant that reading about the sleepless nights, the worries about illness and all the other negative aspects of parenthood is a totally inadequate preparation for the reality. Conscientious first-time parents may know intellectually what to expect, but emotionally they can still be knocked flat when what they have read about starts actually happening to them. We must also bear in mind that many first-time parents refuse to read baby-books until after their baby has been born, for reasons we shall discuss shortly.

Another problem is that many of us have very little to do with babies before we have our own. The modern family tends to be small and closely spaced, so it's quite unusual for there to be babies around by the time the older children reach adolescence. We saw in Chapter 2 that many adolescent girls have experience as baby-sitters, which must give them some idea of what to expect. But the results of a national survey carried out in Britain in 1979 into women's attitudes and feelings towards motherhood leave no doubt that the vast majority of first-time mothers consider that they are quite unprepared for the reality of motherhood, and frequently describe it as a major crisis in their lives. On this evidence alone, I think we can rule out the suggestion that women have a natural instinct for mothering, and instead accept that for most people, full adulthood begins with a major crisis.

Paradoxically, however, the distress caused by this crisis may well be responsible for the feeling of general contentment and self-satisfaction which we found to be the dominant mood of people in their thirties. The more traumatic the first year of parenthood, the greater the satisfaction that comes from realizing you have survived it, and the more you can congratulate yourself on being so much more mature, as you observe how much more relaxed you are in coping with later children. Like anything else, looking after young children is something we get better at with experience, and the pleasure we get from becoming more competent may go a long way towards explaining why some people choose to have unfashionably large families.

The pregnancy which precedes the birth of a woman's first child has several puzzling features. However, these begin to make sense if we think of this period as a transition between young and full adulthood. The survey into motherhood I mentioned earlier investigated the attitudes and feelings of three groups of women: pregnant women, first-time mothers with babies under two, and experienced mothers. One of the most striking features of women pregnant for the first time is that a third of them say they would prefer not to have children, thus reflecting the young adults' distaste for parenthood we discussed in the last chapter. Only 3 per cent of women who actually have babies feel the same way.

Many women pregnant for the first time also seem

very reluctant to make more than the most rudimentary preparations for the arrival of their child. It is difficult to know what to make of their unwillingness to think of the 'lump' they are carrying as a person, or their lack of enthusiasm for articles and books on such useful subjects as the mother-child relationship. They are avid readers of advertising material about baby-products, but this doesn't seem to have the effect the advertisers must hope for of encouraging them to go out and buy the products they know their baby will need. Of course, you could argue that a panic-buying spree is exactly what a new father needs to divert his attention from the enormity of what he has let himself in for. But it may not do much for a new mother's peace of mind to reflect, as she lies in hospital, that she has failed to make adequate preparations herself for the arrival of the child she will shortly be taking home for the first time.

However, women know that there are still risks attached to childbirth, and it is perfectly reasonable for a woman to justify her behaviour on the grounds that if by any chance her child does not survive, the last thing she will want is a heap of poignant mementoes of the child that never was. But many of the pregnant women interviewed freely admitted to a superstitious fear that they would be tempting providence if they bought things before their child was born. It may not be too unkind to regard this ostrich-like behaviour as a final manifestation of the young adult's penchant for make-believe, and a sign of their reluctance to face up to the responsibility of parenthood until they are certain there's no way of avoiding it. However, it would be difficult to prove that women behave in this irrational way during their first pregnancies simply because they have not yet shaken off the attitudes of young adulthood. Women *are* more pragmatic during subsequent pregnancies, when they are full adults, but they now have the enormous advantage of knowing what to expect. So we cannot be sure to what extent the differences in the way a woman behaves during her first and subsequent pregnancies are a reflection of the differences between the attitudes of young and full adulthood, and to what extent they are simply the result of her previous experience of parenthood, which will be helpful regardless of age.

The 1979 national survey into motherhood provides other insights into the impact which parenthood has on women. So far as pregnancy is concerned, the message is reassuring because it suggests that many of the symptoms we associate with pregnancy are much less common than we are led to believe. Only three symptoms were experienced by more than half the women interviewed – tiredness, heartburn and frequent urination. Morning sickness and general nausea are the next most commonly reported symptoms but, like painful breasts, cravings for certain foods and depression, they only affect a minority of women. Women pregnant for the first time mention three symptoms – painful breasts, irritability and depression – more frequently than new or established mothers, but overall the results of the survey present a much less unpleasant picture of pregnancy than that conveyed by magazines and even by some doctors. Only one woman in three says that she feels less well during pregnancy; just as many say they feel fitter than usual, while the remainder say they haven't noticed any significant difference.

But of course there are problems. Most of the pregnant women interviewed complained that their husbands were over-solicitous. They obviously take great pride in remaining active until the last possible moment, occupying themselves during the tedious weeks between leaving work and giving birth with such demanding tasks as decorating the house. On the psychological side, they find it increasingly difficult to maintain their ideal concept of themselves as active, independent and attractive people, and they express great anxiety about the prospect of their personal identity being swamped.

Few pregnant women find fatness easy to accept; they think the 'lump' has made them ugly, greatly dislike maternity clothes, and say that their ideal is to get back into jeans as soon as possible! In the final weeks before birth, their major concern is that their child should be born normal, and their main fear is that they will reject it. As another sign of their superstitiousness, they are very unwilling to discuss what life after birth is going to be like, though they are quite prepared to talk about what the child may be like in ten years' time, and even to discuss what sort of problems may arise when it becomes a teenager! Generally speaking, the mood of a woman in the final weeks of pregnancy is one neither of great distress nor of joyful anticipation. She just wants to get it over with.

But the evidence this survey provides on how women experience birth and the early stages of motherhood is less reassuring. We saw earlier that adults with children of school-age derive enormous satisfaction from the feeling that they are responsible for their children. However, the initial impact of this feeling of responsibility is very different. Most young mothers say they are overwhelmed by it, and describe themselves as being in a state of perpetual crisis throughout the first weeks of the baby's life. Many of them also suffer from postnatal depression, or the 'four-day blues' as it's sometimes called. Some doctors believe that this is caused by the hormonal changes which take place in a woman's body after her child is born, but they are probably wrong. They have yet to come up with a convincing account of which hormones might be involved, nor can they explain why postnatal depression is unknown in many non-industrial-ized societies, even though women in such cultures are presumably affected by exactly the same hormonal changes as elsewhere. It's more likely that postnatal depression is a psychological rather than a physiological phenomenon, though its effects are nonetheless disturbing.

It may well be the price women have to pay for having

so much freedom of choice about how to bring up their children. In societies where child-rearing techniques are laid down by tradition and common consent, mothers are spared the anxiety of trying to decide what is best for their children. Moreover, the elaborate ceremonies surrounding birth in these cultures emphasize that the whole society feels involved in the upbringing of an individual child, which must lessen the burden of responsibility mothers feel. Western industrialized societies are unique in the extent to which they expect a mother to be responsible for her children, and this probably explains why, for all the sophistication of our medical and social services, we seem to find parenthood, at least in its early stages, so traumatic.

It is universally accepted that the birth of her first child is one of the most profound emotional experiences of a woman's life. Since we know that deep emotional experiences often leave people feeling rather vulnerable and prone to exaggerate the significance of what is happening to them, it's hardly surprising to find a new mother behaving rather oddly. The motherhood survey has pin-pointed six major sources of stress in her life. The most important of these is the woman's fear that she will not be up to the task of motherhood, which is reinforced by the frustration she feels when she cannot work out what her child wants. There is also the dread of accidentally hurting or even killing her child as a result of her inexperience. Many mothers find this prospect literally too intolerable to contemplate, as can be seen from the fact that two-thirds of the mothers in the motherhood survey flatly refused to discuss the subject. One who did talk about it said:

> I'm awake but my mind is asleep and part of my mind knows she's in her bed next door, but I'm afraid she's been suffocated in the duvet. I used to have horrible daydreams just as I was going to bed. I'd think she was choking or something.

Although women who have babies in hospital are more prone to postnatal depression than those who have them at home – perhaps because having to cope with the frightening institutional world of a hospital makes them more vulnerable – there is a third source of stress which only becomes acute when a woman returns home. This is the feeling of physical and psychological isolation and lack of mobility. In hospital, a woman is surrounded by others in the same position with whom she can discuss her new feelings frankly and without any fear of boring her audience. At home, she may feel that there is nobody who understands her predicament. This explains why new mothers prefer the company of others in their position, and why they set great store by their visits to postnatal clinics.

These worries can be compounded by two other factors. The first is a lack of sleep, the second the woman's unsettling discovery that she no longer has any time to herself, which is made worse by the fact that she feels ashamed of herself for minding about this. Guilt is an emotion very familiar to the young mother. It stems most often from usually unjustified worries about her shortcomings as a mother, but also from the resentment she may feel at how much her life is dominated by her child, or from the fact that she finds herself spending so much less time than before on housework, her own appearance, and her relationship with her husband.

There is one other problem which can face the shell-shocked new mother and her husband. It will come as no surprise to them to discover that they are effectively housebound, but they may not be prepared for the extent to which their private emotional life is disrupted by the regular stream of relatives and other well-wishers who want to inspect the baby. The most persistent visitors are usually the child's grandparents, and we shall see in Chapter 6 that their devotion to him, though easy to understand and touching to witness, contains the elements of a potentially explosive confrontation between the two generations of adults which will not make the young mother's life any easier.

Fortunately, the initial traumas of parenthood do not last for long. It is surprising how soon a young mother stops questioning her own competence. Anxiety may be her dominant emotion for the first four months, but it recedes rapidly as the baby becomes more responsive and starts to take an obvious interest in her. Virtually all mothers come to value their relationship with their children, though a surprising number of them freely admit that they never altogether stop resenting the price they have to pay in terms of their emotional commitment. The ambivalence of a woman's attitude is brought home to her sharply when her child becomes old enough to go to nursery or play-school. She suddenly realizes how important he now is to her, and she may feel guilty about entrusting her child to the care of strangers, especially if she has read articles which tell her that a child's mother is the only person capable of looking after him properly.

Such worries are probably exaggerated. There is no evidence that young childen are adversely affected by going to nursery school. On the contrary, the social benefits which a child gains from an early opportunity to mix with his peers can still be seen in adolescence, and any effect on intellectual development is likely to be for the better. The influence of child-minders is a more controversial subject. Until very recently, the experts gave their approval to mothers who entrusted their children to competent child-minders, but the results of a large-scale investigation carried out in Oxford in the late 1970s are far from reassuring. These researchers found that one in three children who were being looked after by child-minders seemed to be very depressed. Unfortunately, they do not tell us how many children who are looked after by their mothers become equally depressed, so we cannot be certain that it is being looked after by a child-minder which depressed the children.

Further research is needed to resolve the controversy surrounding the influence of child-minders, but I think mothers need have no qualms about sending their children to nursery schools. So at least in this respect, parenthood may be a slightly less awesome responsibility than we have been led to believe.

Odd man out

I have written about parenthood at some length because for seven out of eight people it is a concern beside which all others pale into insignificance during this, the fourth age of our lives. But we must not forget the eighth person, who may be homosexual, as yet unmarried, married but separated or divorced, or married but without children. These groups form a significant minority of the population, but unfortunately we should have to rely on guesswork if we wanted to incorporate their experience into the present book. The reason for this is very simple. Most of the evidence we have been discussing is derived from surveys based on interviews with people carefully selected to be representative of the general population. Since single people, whether homosexual or heterosexual, form only a very small proportion of the adult population, the number of them who take part in general surveys is far too small to allow us to draw any statistically reliable conclusions about them. Of course, some surveys have dealt exclusively with homosexuals or single people, but such surveys have not been concerned with the experience of age. Since this is the central theme of *Seven Ages*, homosexuals and adults who remain unmarried will receive no more than the occasional passing mention here. This is not because I believe we are all married heterosexuals, but simply because the dearth of relevant information leaves me with no choice but to write as if this were the case!

We do however have quite a lot of information about divorce and the divorced, and I think we should conclude our survey of the fourth age of life by returning to the institution of marriage, both to see how well it stands up to the ordeal by parenthood and to investigate how people in their thirties are affected by successful and unsuccessful marriages. So far as the former is concerned, we have already seen that the early thirties tends to be a rocky period for the first marriages, but that those which survive the trials of young parenthood seem to have become stronger again by the end of the period.

Marriages can be divided into five categories. The first, *conflict* marriage, is characterized by constant arguments and bickering which both partners find a perfectly acceptable basis for staying together. It is often said of such couples that they deserve each other, but so long as each gives as good as he or she gets, these marriages can be surprisingly resilient. The second sort of marriage is called *devitalized*. These couples may seem disenchanted and get little out of their relationship, but they see their marriage as a good one, despite their boredom, and this may be enough to keep them together. The third variety of marriage is called *passive-congenial*, where life is comfortable and responsibilities are shared so as to minimize conflict, though the couple are not much involved with each other. Such couples conjure up Samuel Johnson's description of the sleepy-souled woman's view of marriage – it is like 'playing at cards for nothing: no passion is excited, and the time is filled up.' These first three types of marriage are known collectively as *institutional* matches. It is estimated that about 90 per cent of all marriages fall into one or other of these categories, and their success seems to depend at least as much on the husband's performance as a bread-winner as on the quality of the couple's relationship with each other. This is not the case, however, for *companionship* marriages, which are called either *vital*, where both partners are highly involved in all common aspects of family life, or *total*, where they are so involved in every aspect of each other's lives that to the outside world they sometimes look like a two-person neurosis!

But whatever sort of marriage you have, several things remain true. The first is that if you want to stay together, money helps. The connection between marital stability and affluence seems to be stronger in America than in Britain, but shortage of cash is a major precipitating factor in the break-up of marriages involving very young couples in both countries. The second common factor is that marriage seems to be a much more advantageous arrangement for men than for women. Compared to single men, married men live longer and have more successful careers, less mental illness and a lower suicide rate. Married women enjoy none of these advantages over unmarried women, and in fact are more prone to neurosis and depression than either single women or married men. Finally, the success or failure of a marriage seems to depend much more on the personality of a husband than on that of his wife.

But why do some marriages end in divorce while others survive? This question was the subject of a large survey carried out in Britain in the 1970s, in which 570 people in apparently stable marriages were compared with 520 divorcees. Although there is no single pattern of divorce, any more than there is a single pattern of marriage, one thing is clear. The fact that the divorce rate has risen steadily over the last 25 years (at least one in five marriages in Britain today, and a third of American marriages, will end in divorce within fifteen years) is not simply due to changes in the law which make divorce easier. The change in divorce rates is virtually identical in all European countries, irrespective of their different laws and dominant religions, and it is just one aspect of a much more general set of social changes which have been going on throughout the twentieth century, but especially since 1945. Only two of these need concern us here. The first is the reshaping of the human life-cycle which I have remarked on at various points in the book. More of us now live to old age, and the fact that we are getting married earlier means that most couples still have twenty or so years of their lives ahead of them when their last child leaves home. This post-parenthood phase of life hardly existed for our ancestors, and it has transformed our experience of the last two ages we live through.

People are very aware of this difference, as you can see from the comments made by one of the women in her thirties to whom we talked:

> My mum was forty-three when she had me, and by the time I got married she was sixty-two . . . She never had a life of her own, and that's terrible . . . I think I look forward to the time when the children will be old enough to fend for themselves, because I'll still be young enough to go out and do something, and go places and still be young and fit enough to do it, rather than a pensioner hobbling about, with a wheelchair.

Even more important are the changes which have taken place in the institution of marriage itself. Where once it was primarily a business arrangement in which the husband contracted to be the provider in return for his wife's services as child-rearer and household-manager, we are now led to expect something more out of marriage than a simple exchange of services. We look for emotional fulfilment and personal satisfaction, and judge a marriage as much by the quality of the relationship between the two partners as by how successfully each fulfils their part of the traditional bargain. Despite the fact that the great majority of marriages today still fall into one or other of the categories of institutional marriage I described earlier, there is no guarantee that either or both partners will be satisfied with this state of affairs. Perhaps the real change has not been in marriage itself but in what we expect to get out of it. Asking yourself the question, 'surely there must be more to marriage than this!' is often the first step on the road which ends in the divorce courts, and one of the most important differences between a married couple today and their predecessors is that it's a question the latter very rarely seem to have asked themselves.

The high incidence of divorce amongst people in their early thirties may seem to imply that The Seven-year Itch is more than just a film title. But the timing of divorce actually tells us very little about when marriages tend to break down, because divorce is usually preceded by a fairly long period of separation. In fact, there are two different types of divorce – aborted marriages that never really get off the ground because the partners are incompatible from the start, and those which fail because the partners grow apart and become incompatible. Since more than half of the people who get divorced say that their marital problems started before their second wedding anniversary, it looks as though the first pattern is more common. In fact the majority of divorced couples separate between their first and fourth anniversaries, and divorce itself follows on average two years later. So the Seven-year Itch can only apply to the second category of divorce – the slow growing apart – and it may be linked with the fact that many women nowadays return to work while their children are still very young. Going back to work presents a woman with problems, as we saw earlier, but it also gives her a chance to discover new qualities in herself and hence to change, as well as many more opportunities for meeting new men.

There has been a sharp increase in the proportion of divorce petitions filed by women in recent years. According to one researcher, the most common chain of events goes as follows. It is the wife who first mentions the possibility of divorce, but the husband who first decides that he actually wants it to happen. He then behaves in such a way that she is the one who asks for a divorce. But what sort of people get divorced? It is widely believed that people whose parents' marriage was unhappy are themselves divorce-prone, but the connection has probably been exaggerated. There is quite good evidence that children suffer more often as a consequence of their parents' getting remarried than as a result of the original divorce, and three-quarters of the divorcees in the survey we are discussing grew up in stable homes with happily married parents. Women who prefer their father to their mother are slightly more prone to divorce, while those who prefer their mothers seem more likely to have stable marriages, an effect which is particularly marked among working-class women. Women who are only children and men who have no sisters are two other groups over-represented among divorcees. So far as social class is concerned, we have already seen that divorce is more common among the lower than the higher socio-economic status groups. More highly educated men are also less likely to get divorced, though the most striking connection between education and divorce is that divorced people more often say they don't know anything about their ex-spouse's education than those who are happily married!

As we saw in the last chapter, marriages which take place against a background of parental opposition are also particularly likely to run into trouble. This may be because of the extra strain imposed on young parents by sulking grandparents who refuse to help out, for example by baby-sitting, or the tensions caused by having to take sides, or simply because the parents were right to oppose what was basically an unsuitable match. Two other features of couples who get divorced are that they're more likely to have had break-ups before they got married, and to have had a shorter period of courtship than those who remain happily married. Rather touchingly, couples who take a proper honeymoon are also significantly less likely to get divorced than those who do not, though this probably has more to do with the relative affluence of the two groups than with anything else.

Shot-gun marriages also have a rather poor prognosis. Whereas a third of the divorcees in the survey had conceived children before getting married, only a fifth of those in stable marriages had been in this position. There are several possible explanations of this connection. It may be the effect of having to rush through the preparations for marriage and the lack of time the couple have to get to know each other properly, or it could be a result of financial difficulties caused by the absence of savings and the fact that the wife is unable to work at a time when every penny is vital for the couple to set themselves up.

Divorced couples are twice as likely to be childless as those who stay happily married, but they are also more likely to have had children very early in marriage. So both infertility and precocious fertility seem to make divorce more probable. Of course, the fact that divorced couples are less likely to have children may imply one of two different things. It could mean that they have made a conscious decision not to have children because they already doubt the stability of their marriage. But it may also mean that they have sexual problems, as a result of which they rarely have intercourse and so don't give themselves many opportunities to become parents. There *is* a connection between a couple's sex life and the stability of their marriage, and it's apparent from the very beginning. When asked about their early sex lives, divorcees are twice as likely as people whose marriages have remained intact to say that they derived no pleasure whatever from sex when they got married. But it's not just that people who get divorced don't like sex, because they admit to more extramarital and premarital affairs than those whose marriages survive.

Although there are many different patterns of divorce, the key to successful marriage seems to lie in effective communication between partners. This is what we might have expected to find, given that marriage is now seen as a source of personal satisfaction rather than merely a business arrangement. The main threats to effective communication include physical separation, being unwilling to talk about yourself or bad at interpreting your partner's needs, and the lack of a common language – in a metaphorical rather than a literal sense – or shared culture. However, effective communication alone is no guarantee of a successful marriage. A couple may understand each other only too well, but this will merely bring their marriage to a speedier close if they realize that they cannot or will not meet each other's needs. But perhaps the most significant aspect of Divorce 1980s-style is that it has become an option that women are turning to with increasing frequency. Although both sexes now expect more out of marriage than formerly, we have already seen that men derive more benefits from the married state, and also that they have more alternative sources of gratification and interest to turn to if their marriage turns out to be a disappointment.

These, then, are the reasons for divorce. But it is the *consequences* of splitting up which are of more concern to a significant minority of us during the fourth age of life. Of course, some people get divorced very much earlier, and are most affected by the financial aspects of divorce. But the major problem of the newly single man or woman in their thirties is that he or she is a good deal older than the majority of the single population. They will have lost their taste for many of the things young adults enjoy, and may have grave doubts about their ability to make out in the mating and dating game. Divorcees are also a notorious embarrassment to their married friends, who are terrified of being accused either of taking sides or of match-making. They often solve the problem by avoiding the separated couple altogether, as a result of which new divorcees are denied support at the time they need it most. This explains the popularity of divorcees' clubs, and it also accounts for the most striking fact about divorcees – the speed with which they remarry. About a half of all divorcees marry again within a year of their divorce, and three-quarters of them find a new spouse within three years.

On the face of it, it seems rather surprising that they are so eager to take a second sip from a chalice they could be forgiven for thinking was poisoned. But of course many people decide to end their first marriage because they have met someone else they think they would rather be married to, and although divorcees need no one to tell them of the drawbacks of marriage, they will also be aware of its advantages. Whatever reservations we may have about monogamy, the married state still seems the most convenient arrangement for the vast majority of us, and it is actually quite rare to find even the messiest divorces producing a lasting aversion to matrimony. The final reason why most divorcees embrace matrimony again with such alacrity is a negative one. They may not look back on their experience of marriage with much enthusiasm, but it is very unlikely that they will find the state of being divorced any more to their taste.

The stigma attached to divorce has declined as its frequency has risen (it's risky taking too sanctimonious a line on broken marriages when you know yours has at least a one in five chance of going the same way), but many of the emotional and practical problems remain. Divorcees are more prone to both physical and mental illness than married people, and they also have a higher suicide rate. But although there is a wealth of evidence which confirms that the short-term consequences of getting divorced can affect virtually every aspect of our lives, most divorcees actually recover surprisingly quickly. The first year seems to be the worst, especially for men. As we know, they get more out of marriage, and so they presumably have more to lose from divorce. However, studies show that two years after getting divorced, only a quarter of women and even fewer men say they now feel that their divorce was a mistake.

Although I have struck a sombre note by introducing the topic of divorce, I don't think there is any doubt that the prevailing mood of the fourth of our seven ages is one of optimism. As they approach the end of their thirties, most people can look back with a justified sense of achievement over a decade in which they have finally established an identity and a role for themselves in the adult world. You could say that people in their thirties are *too* aware of their own achievements, and it may well be their smugness which is most likely to annoy those older or younger than themselves most. I doubt, for example, whether the thirty-three-year-old William Pitt endeared himself to the elderly Parliamentarians around him when he said:

> The atrocious crime of being a young man . . . I shall neither attempt to palliate or deny!

But it is understandable if thirty-five-year-olds feel pleased with themselves, and if they choose to take a loftier view of things, they can also congratulate themselves on having contributed to the survival of the species. By reproducing ourselves and nurturing children we ensure that our name will live on, even if nothing else we do is sufficiently note-worthy to earn us a place in the history of the times. There may have been false starts and unexpected dead-ends, but I think we can summarize our progress in life up to the end of the fourth age by saying that the future has not yet become an enemy. Generally speaking, changes which have occurred have been for the better at least as often as for the worse. How long we can console ourselves with this thought will emerge from the remaining chapters of the book.

CHAPTER 5

Taking Stock

'One of the pleasures of middle age is to find out that one *was* right, and that one was much righter than one knew at say seventeen or twenty three.'

EZRA POUND

If we accept the biblical estimate of the life-span as three score years and ten, then 35 is the mid-point. But very few thirty-five-year-olds would describe themselves as middle-aged, whatever younger people may think of them. In fact, the consensus is that most people don't reach middle age before their late forties. So I think we should treat the fifth age of life, which runs from about thirty-nine to forty-eight, as a period in which we gradually come to terms with the idea that we are about to become middle-aged, rather than as middle age itself. For most of us, the forties are a decade in which we are more aware of our age than at any other time of life, which makes it a particularly interesting one for this book. Of course, it's not that age doesn't affect us before this – there is ample evidence that it does – but it is only now that it becomes a real concern in our lives.

There are two reasons for this, the first of which is obvious: how can we avoid thinking about age when it draws itself to our attention every time we look in a mirror or run for a bus? But it's not just the unmistakable physical changes in himself which cause the thoughts of a forty-two-year-old to turn to the concept of age. At this point, we are also uniquely aware of our position in the life-cycle, and of the notion of generations. For children and adolescents, it's very much a case of Us and Them, 'They' being everyone older than themselves. For the young adult, it's really only

Us, and to hell with Them, whoever they may be! In the thirties, we're involved with our own and our children's generations, but we have very little time left for older people, including our parents. In fact, as we shall see in Chapter 6, many young parents allow their relations with their parents to deteriorate, and postpone the task of repairing the damage until they no longer have young children on their hands. Much later, as we approach the end of life, many of us revert to the young adult pattern of age exclusiveness, either because we feel that only the old can understand the old, or else because we feel that we have done enough, and that it's about time other people started putting themselves out to adjust to our idiosyncrasies rather than the other way round!

As a result, people in their forties are sandwiched between two demanding and often – in their eyes - unreasonable generations, both of whom rely on them for psychological and practical support. At no other stage in our lives do so many people depend on us, and it's the realization that they are now the lynch-pin of the whole system which causes people in their forties to brood darkly on the cyclicity of life and the passing of time, as well as asking themselves more mundane questions like should a woman/man of my age really be wearing slit-skirts/jeans? So although the forties may not be middle age, they are a uniquely age-conscious decade, as you can see from the following observation made by an American woman in her forties to the gerontologist Bernice Neugarten:

> It is as if there are two mirrors before me, each held at a partial angle. I see part of myself in my mother who is growing old and part of her in me. In the other mirror I see part of myself in my daughter. I have some dramatic insights from looking in those mirrors . . . a set of revelations that I suppose can come only when you are in the middle of three generations.

Layer by layer

When people talk about the effects of aging, they sometimes distinguish between different layers of themselves, which age at different speeds. The outer layer is the surface varnish, the way we look to the rest of the world, and it's here that the changes appear first. In fact, worries on this score start in the mid-thirties, as you can see from the comment a thirty-four-year-old man made to us:

> It suddenly struck me, probably last summer, I hadn't got quite as much hair as I had. It hadn't gone overnight, but suddenly I thought, 'It's going.' I thought, 'Crikey'. It suddenly struck me.

And sometimes it's other people's reactions, or, in the case of this forty-seven-year-old woman, their lack of reaction, which brings it home to us:

> You walk along a street and pass a couple of workmen, and whereas a few years back they would whistle at you, now they don't. 'What's wrong, they're not whistling?' – and you realize you're getting old.

Our appearance does begin to change in the forties. For example, everywhere in the body, fat starts to be redistributed. As part of a process which continues for the rest of our lives, fatty tissue begins to disappear from our lips, breasts, eyelids and the orbits of our eyes. The upper lip in particular starts to look thinner, and breasts to sag. Eyelids come to look wrinkled and transparent, and the eyes take on a sunken appearance. The full effects of these changes aren't seen until later, but we realize that we are beginning to look different in the forties. The skin on parts of our bodies usually covered by clothes changes very little in thickness between the ages of twenty-five and seventy-five, but where it's constantly exposed to the elements – particularly on our faces, hands and forearms – it becomes thinner and flatter. Since most of the damage is done by the ultraviolet rays of the sun, sun-worshippers might as well resign themselves to the fact that their complexions will be the first to go. However, the darker your complexion, the less it will be affected, and it's blue- or green-eyed blondes and redheads who should ask themselves the most searching questions when the time comes to book the annual holiday!

The next layer to be affected by aging houses the mechanical functions of our bodies. The balance between physical improvement and physical degeneration wavers during the thirties, but in the forties it tips towards degeneration, and tilts more and more firmly in this direction for the rest of our lives. Your skeleton actually starts to shrink after about forty-five, and the strength of a man's back muscles, for example, declines from 96 to 92 per cent of its maximum value between the ages of forty-five and fifty. We get slower in our movements throughout the forties and fifties, not because muscles and joints can't move as fast as they used to, but because the brain needs longer to organize the activity. This decline in sensori-motor activity not only makes you slower at carrying out tricky jobs with your hands, but also means that you will be slower to respond in an emergency. Many of our physical capacities fall away in the forties – for example, lung capacity, grip strength, eye-sight and hearing. In some cases, the process started earlier, and all the effects are most noticeable later. But even though we are definitely slower workers and have less energy at forty-eight than at thirty-eight, there are very few jobs in which we need be any less effective at the end of the decade than we were at the beginning, because our greater experience and, if necessary, greater effort, usually makes up for any physical decline which has taken place.

But the fact that workers in some jobs have to make

more effort to keep up during their forties puts them under strain. This may have some bearing on the fact that the forties are a decade of generally worsening physical health, though there is some consolation in the fact that our chances of suffering from mental illness are less between the ages of forty-five and sixty than they are between twenty-five and forty-four. But it's our physical health which concerns us more in the forties – the decade Don Marquis dubbed as 'the time when a man is always thinking that in a week or two he will feel as good as ever'! For men, health becomes a major concern during the fifth age. They may have taken up jogging ten years earlier as an antidote to an expanding waist-line, but that was a very different level of worry from the feeling they get when a friend drops dead from a heart attack. Cardio-vascular disease accounts for nearly 40 per cent of all deaths during the forties, and four out of five heart-attack victims are men. It therefore comes as no surprise to find that it's the men rather than the women in the thirty-six to forty age bracket in the Colchester survey who are more likely to admit to worries about their health. Women actually seem more worried about their health in their thirties and fifties, no doubt as a result of having children in the former and the menopause at the beginning of the latter.

When we asked people in their forties what was the worst thing about life now as compared with ten years ago, their main complaints were the feeling of being so much older and worries about their appearance and health. But it's very noticeable that when they are asked to describe how they have changed over the last decade, both men and women seem to think that most of the changes have been for the better. In many respects, we don't think we have changed at all. As in the thirties, most people of both sexes think they are neither more nor less physically attractive than they were ten years earlier, nor are they aware of any significant change in their sex life. Most of those we interviewed disagreed strongly with the suggestion that sexual relationships are more important to the young than to the old, though they were less confident about this than people in their thirties.

The fact that the brain needs more time to organize itself and respond as we get older might be expected to have some effect on the third layer of our existence – the ability to function intellectually. However, the people we talked to seemed to be more concerned about physical than mental decline, and they were right, because so far as this period of our lives is concerned, there's actually very little cause for alarm. Ten years ago, the picture looked more bleak. Researchers then were alarmed by the results of studies which seemed to show that intellectual functioning falls away dramatically as we get older, and that the process begins quite early in adulthood. But these studies used what is called a *cross-sectional* design: the researchers simply tested groups of people at different ages, and found that the older the group, the worse it performed. However, this approach may not tell us anything about the effects of aging *per se*, since seventy-year-olds might perform worse than twenty-year-olds not because of what fifty years of growing older has done to them, but simply because their education was inferior to that enjoyed by today's twenty-year-olds. The only way we can get an accurate picture of how aging affects our minds is to look at the same group of people at regular intervals over the years. When we do this, we find little or no sign that people get worse at using the skills and information they possess between the ages of forty and sixty. As we saw in Chapter 3, there *is* a decline in performance on timed IQ tests, but not everyone gets worse even on these. The cleverer and more highly educated you are, the less likely it is that your performance on IQ tests will deteriorate. All in all, I think we can safely conclude that whatever other worries people in their forties may have, any fears about declining mental faculties are more likely to be imaginary than real.

This is good news for anyone in their forties, but it's particularly significant for those who change jobs or even take up a new career altogether. Although older people are less likely than younger to change their jobs, we found that 26 per cent of the men in the thirty-six to forty-five-year-old age group, and 18 per cent of those between forty-six and fifty-eight had worked for more than three different employers during the last ten years. We don't have the information to say how many of these had made a real career change, but the fact that Colchester is a garrison town focussed our attention on the phenomenon of second careers, because the army - like the police force - operates an early retirement policy for most of its workers.

A mid-life career change can stem from a variety of factors. For some careers one simply gets too old. Soldiering and police-work are two examples, and more glamorous careers like modelling and professional football also fall into this category. But some people decide to change careers for the simple reason that they are not happy with what they are doing. Our attitude towards such people is curiously ambivalent. We admire their nerve, but feel that they are being irresponsible, especially if they have a family to provide for. Perhaps the old Puritan proverb, as you have made your bed so you must lie in it, lies at the root of our disapproval. If so, I think we should remember G.K. Chesterton's retort: if I have made my bed uncomfortably, please God I will make it again! But I suspect that jealousy also plays a part, because surveys suggest that a significant minority of us (perhaps a third of all blue-collar workers, though rather less white-collar) would change jobs more often, and even try our hands at something entirely different in mid-life, if we had the courage and the opportunity.

Of course there are problems, which include forfeiting seniority, the chance of promotion, and pension rights, and also the fact that, as one writer has put it, most jobs seem to be designed for twenty-five-year-old athletes! But there are at least two reasons for thinking that mid-life career changes can benefit those who make them, and also the organizations they leave and those they join. The first is that the malaise of a discontented worker can affect those who work around him, which is to no one's advantage. The second is that when we look at what sort of people actually change jobs later in life, we find that they aren't just footloose malcontents, desperately searching for something at which they can succeed. On the contrary, studies suggest that those who keep on the move tend to have higher than average intelligence and achievement motivation, and that many of them – especially craftsmen – find that the challenge of a new job stimulates them to greater productivity. The studies on which these observations are based were concerned with changing jobs rather than careers. But what little evidence there is suggests that we should reconsider our prejudice against those individuals brave enough to make a mid-life career change. If it works out, there's a good prospect of greater job satisfaction and the possibility that the psychological readjustments of the forties will be easier to make. If it doesn't, there's always the wry consolation offered by the nineteenth-century American writer, Washington Irving:

> There is a certain relief in change, even though it be from bad to worse: I have found in travelling in a stage-coach that it is often a comfort to shift one's position and be bruised in a new place!

An awkward age?

Given the domestic responsibilities we have to bear, the realization that change is in the offing, and the fact that men in particular are very conscious of their age and often worried about their health, we might expect the early forties to be a difficult time of life, for men if not for their wives. This is certainly the impression given by a number of books which have appeared recently, which suggest that men go through a mid-life crisis or a male menopause around their fortieth birthday. This is actually a very old idea. Ptolemy, for example, who derived a classification of the life-cycle from his study of astrology in the second century AD, claims that a man of forty is governed by Mars, who gives him 'some sense of passing his prime and urges him, before he approaches the end, by labour to accomplish something among his undertakings that is worthy of note.'

Some of the men we talked to certainly showed signs of this sort of attitude. This is a forty-two-year-old speaking:

> I suppose one regards life with possibly a bit more urgency. As one gets older one realizes that there isn't quite so much left as there was. I mean, when you're in your thirties you still feel very young and regard yourself as a young man. I think now I'm forty-two I don't regard myself as a young man any more. But I think one has a feeling that if you're going to do things there is slightly less time to get on and do them, so one looks at it with probably a bit more urgency than one did before.

There *is* some sense of urgency here, and a feeling that he hasn't as much time as he once had to do all the things he wants to do, but I think 'crisis' is much too strong a word to describe what this man is going through. In fact, when we analysed the answers people gave to the question in our survey which asked if any age since adolescence had seemed particularly difficult, we were astonished to find that not a single man or woman in the forty to forty-four age group described their present age in these terms. In the forty-five to forty-nine and fifty to fifty-eight age groups, 17 and 14 per cent of the women said that the forties had been awkward (almost invariably on account of the menopause), but only 8 and 3 per cent of the men identified this decade as a troublespot.

In view of all the publicity which has been given to the male menopause and mid-life crisis, this is a very striking finding. But it is by no means unique. In fact, the majority of large-scale American surveys and long-term studies of how the same group of people change over the years have found exactly the same thing. When given a questionnaire to fill in, people in their forties stubbornly refuse to show any signs of a mid-life crisis! Against this we have to set the opinion of some psychiatrists, based on their psychoanalytic sessions with men of about forty, that the early forties are a particularly difficult time of life. How can we explain this discrepancy? One suggestion is that there *is* a mid-life crisis, but that people tend to deny it or rationalize it away. Only a trained psychiatrist can penetrate their defences and get them to admit to the inner turmoil they are experiencing. But this explanation won't wash, because these same psychiatrists tell us that it's the young rather than the middle-aged who tend to deny and rationalize internal conflicts. They say that people in their forties are particularly good at recognizing and facing up to their problems. At present, the experts disagree violently among themselves about whether there really is a mid-life crisis. Our results clearly support those who deny its existence, and I think we must conclude that if there is such a thing as the male menopause, it affects only a very small proportion of the male population.

Following on from this, I think we might risk making a generalization: insofar as age-related life crises exist at all, they seem to be very much a minority taste, rather than something we must all expect to go through. I suggested in Chapter 2 that only a small minority – perhaps less than 20 per cent – of adolescents actually go through the horrors we think of as 'typical' of adolescence. The proportion of people who suffer at the other alleged crisis points – for example, the Catch 30 syndrome, the Mid-life Crisis and the adjustment to life without work – seems to be no greater, and it's tempting to suggest that the same small group of problem-prone individuals make up the numbers at each point. Only time and future research will be able to show whether or not this is so, though we shall return to the elusive mid-life crisis before the end of this chapter, to see what sort of people are most likely to be struck down by it.

Looking ahead

The forties are a time when we have to acknowledge that some changes are necessary. As Carl Jung put it, we have to realize that we cannot live in the afternoon of life according to the programme of the morning. There are at least four changes we have to make. First, we have to persuade ourselves that wisdom is at least as valuable a commodity as physical strength or attractiveness. If we fail here, we are bound to become increasingly bitter and depressed as we have to fall back on ever more desperate measures to counteract the inevitable effects of aging. What's called for is a change of body-image. It is usually assumed that when a man in his forties leaves his wife for a much younger woman, he is trying to reassure himself about his sexual potency. But it may also reflect the fact that he is suffering from a case of selective short-sightedness – he observes the effects of aging on his wife but not on himself. He sees her all too clearly as middle-aged, but retains a youthful body-image of himself. Of course, in the short term he may be right – men in their forties are often judged to be more youthful and attractive than their wives. But not even the most attentive twenty-two-year-old will be able to protect him from the consequences of aging for ever.

The consolation Nature offers us for losing our youthful physical appeal is the mellowness and understanding which can only come with experience, and the overwhelming feeling amongst adults in Colchester is that the exchange is one they are very happy to make. Here are a few typical comments:

> In the business world you cannot substitute for experience . . . Sometimes I think, 'I've handled forty decisions today' . . . but the thing that gets me by is that I've got the confidence in my experience and know that it is the right thing to do.

> In the words of the good book, I have learned in whatsoever state I am, there to be content . . . We have learned to be content with our lot.

> I don't worry about things, not now. When the children were younger, or had anything wrong with them, or the school report wasn't very good, you worried about it. Those sort of things don't worry me at all now. I think, 'Oh well, there's another day tomorrow – let's start afresh, and it will all sort itself out.'

One man of forty-eight left us in no doubt where he stood:

> Aging? It's a collection of experience of life. Maturing in your emotions. It's got nothing to do with grey hair, or growing old, or wrinkles in your hands. You mature with experience of life, contact with people, appreciation of people's problems.

Not many people would agree with his view that the physical aspects of aging are completely irrelevant, but his was only an extreme version of the feeling expressed by the vast majority of people we talked to, that the forties were nothing to worry about. So whatever the position may be in California, the mid-life crisis doesn't seem to have reached

Colchester yet, even though many of those we talked to knew all about it from magazines!

Their replies to the question, 'How have you changed in the last ten years?' were very much in line with what you might expect from what I have said. They felt more mature, responsible, settled, relaxed, confident, trusting and tolerant, and less critical, dependent (the women), and active (older men only). The major changes which had taken place in their lives also tended to be for the better: they felt more financially secure, more responsible at work (this applied to women only in their late forties), and also thought that their social lives had improved.

This last observation brings us neatly to the second adjustment which psychologists think we need to make in our personal lives as middle age approaches. Unless we decide to tear up the roots and start again, we have to alter the emphasis in our personal relationships from sexuality to sociability, and this applies particularly to marriage. We saw in the last chapter that people start, as early as the thirties, to dream about all the things they'll be able to do when their children have left home, even though most of them will be fifty by the time the last child has left. But it is in the forties that husbands and wives start sizing each other up surreptitiously, and wondering how they will adjust to living as a couple again, without the shared responsibility of parenthood to bind them together.

The results of this inspection often make people flinch because, as C. S. Lewis put it, 'when two human beings have lived together for many years, it usually happens that each has tones of voice and expressions of face that are almost unendurably irritating to the other.' During the thirties we are too busy to notice the aggravation building up, or, if we do, we usually manage to find something to take our minds off it. In the early forties, however, the chickens come home to roost, and we were not surprised to find that the people we interviewed in the thirty-six to forty-five bracket said they felt less close to their spouses than those in any other age group. The fact is that at this point in life most marriages seem to fit into one or other of the institutional categories we discussed in Chapter 4. The newlyweds' determination that they will never take each other for granted like their parents do has long since gone the way of all such good resolutions, a victim of demands of parenthood and careers. But most couples of this age realize that an enormous emotional vacuum is about to open up, and it is interesting to see how they prepare to deal with it. In Colchester, we found that more women had jobs in the thirty-five to forty-nine age bracket than in any other. The fact that fewer women in their fifties worked is probably just a generational effect. Women of this age are much less likely to have worked before starting their families, and so have no career to return to.

The return to work can be a very significant event in the life of a woman in her forties who decided earlier not to try and combine bringing up her children with a career. Just how significant this change is can be seen from the answers to another question posed in the Colchester survey. When we asked adults to rank different aspects of life in order of their importance, we were very struck by how little variation there was in the lists drawn up by people of different ages. For men, the order was marriage and family, health, job, money, friends, intimate relationships and hobbies, and it was identical for every age group. For women the order was slightly different. Up to the age of forty, it went as follows: marriage and family, health, friends, money, job and hobbies. But the importance of women's jobs rose steadily from one age group to the next. It overtook money as a priority at forty, and by the end of the fifties ranked almost equal with friends. The fact that this was the only change in life-priorities shown by either sex between the ages of twenty-nine and fifty-nine clearly shows that this is one of the most significant changes which occur in the forties.

And it's not just that women who have not been working for some years now go back to a job. Those who have been working all along, with only short breaks to have babies, also show an increased interest in their work as the time approaches when their children will abandon the nest. It would be tempting to link this increased interest which women show in their jobs with the fact that this is the period which many of them describe as the prime of life. But our survey doesn't support this suggestion. The prospect of freedom from family responsibilities, and the feeling of being wiser, are the two things women relish most about this period of their lives, and in fact virtually none of the women we interviewed mentioned professional success in connection with the prime of life. For some reason, women seem to find it much more difficult than men to identify the prime of life. Miss Jean Brodie, who of course was an expert on the subject, seems to have been speaking for her whole sex when she gave the following advice to her pupils:

> One's prime is elusive. You little girls, when you grow up, must be on the alert to recognize your prime at whatever time of your life it may occur. You must then live it to the full. (Muriel Spark, *The Prime of Miss Jean Brodie*)

The fact that women become more interested in work in their forties may well be a sign that they realize they're soon going to have time and emotional energy on their hands. But how do men prepare themselves for the future? Sociologists have suggested that many men in their forties take up new hobbies, or else return to earlier interests they have neglected since they got married. In keeping with this suggestion, a forty-three-year-old told us he had recently returned to his boyhood hobby of flying model aeroplanes:

> At my age, you've got a lot of pressures, work and so on. It takes my mind off it. Mind you, the wife thinks I'm a bit of a nutter.

Although we didn't find that the majority of men in their forties in Colchester were becoming more interested in hobbies, some clearly were prepared to run the gamut of their wives' and children's sneers, and were developing new interests, not only to take their minds off today's worries but also in preparation for the long days they know await them after retirement.

It may sound implausible to suggest that men in their forties find time to look as far ahead as retirement, given all the current concerns they have on their plates. But there is a curious feature of men's friendships at this age. Half of those we interviewed denied that they had any close friends – an even higher proportion than we found among men in their thirties. But now, unlike a decade earlier, the friends they do have are quite often ten years older than themselves, and so may alert them to the problem of retirement. However, spending time in the company of people approaching retirement doesn't seem to have the effect of making men in their forties gloomy about their own future. Quite the reverse. Replying to a question which asked if they were worried about the prospect of being ten years older, only one man in ten admitted to any concern whatever on this score!

So the forties is a time for looking ahead, and planning a life without children and – eventually – without work. More than half the people we talked to in the thirty-six to forty-five bracket had lost at least one of their parents, which seemed to cause some of them to look even further ahead, and make a preliminary effort to come to terms with the last developmental task of all – reconciling themselves to the fact that they too must die. But it would be quite wrong to see this as a time when we are thinking only of the future. The forties are sometimes called the Management decade, and the two remaining psychological adjustments we have to make at this age both reflect the fact that this is the generation which makes the whole system work.

Learning to manage

The qualities of a successful manager are the same whether you're managing a business or a family. But they are not necessarily the same as those which got you the job in the first place, which is why we have to adjust some of the attitudes which served us well in the Making It decade in order to flourish in the Management decade. In the thirties we need such attributes as drive, energy, ambition and single-mindedness. Some of these remain useful in the forties, but now they have to be augmented by other qualities like versatility, tolerance and patience. These generalizations are based on studies of the art of man-management at work, but I suspect they apply just as much to the running of a family. After all, who's to say that the difference between being a young executive and a manager is any greater than that between being the mother of primary-school and teenage children?

Psychologists describe the qualities we need to develop in the forties as cathected and mental flexibility. The first refers to the ability to broaden our emotional investment to include new people, activities and roles. We need to become more versatile, but also more responsive to the needs of others, and not just people we love or like. Mental flexibility involves being able to accept new ideas and solutions to problems. But how good are we at making these adjustments? Some surveys have found that people actually become *less* sociable, more dogmatic and less good at judging the feelings of both younger and older people at this stage of life. The explanation offered for this is that since forty-year-olds are in the driving seat, they get used to laying down the law and don't see why they should waste time trying to understand people who will do what they tell them anyway. The results of the Colchester survey offer a very different picture of people in their forties. As we have already seen, there seems to be an *increase* in sociability and emotional stability, and we tried to explore the flexibility issue by asking people how easy they found it to adapt to change and accept new ideas, and also about their ability to learn and remember new things. These are notoriously difficult qualities to assess in yourself, so perhaps we shouldn't attach too much significance to the fact that only one person in ten of those in their early forties said they found it more difficult than ten years ago to adapt to change or to accept new ideas, whereas three times this number said they actually found it *less* difficult.

But it is striking that women are if anything more likely than men to say that they have become more flexible, which confirms that this psychological adjustment is not just confined to industrial managers. However, women of this age are more than twice as likely as men to admit that they find it difficult to learn and remember new things. But this difference between the sexes seems to be confined to the forties, so it doesn't reflect a real difference between men's and women's abilities. The most likely explanation lies in something we discussed earlier in the chapter. Women in their forties go back to work in large numbers, and we have already seen that many of them are temporarily dismayed to discover how much technical progress has been made since they last had a job.

Talk of sex differences brings us to one of the most interesting aspects of the changes which take place in the forties. Rightly or wrongly, we tend to think of some human characteristics as masculine and others as feminine. Ambition, aggression, toughness and single-mindedness are perceived as predominantly masculine traits, and qualities like these are more highly valued than the so-called feminine virtues during the first half of our lives, particularly during the Making It decade of the thirties. To the extent that a woman is branded as unfeminine when she shows masculine qualities, she is clearly at a disadvantage so long as they are what's needed to be successful. But the skills required for management – flexibility, tolerance and the ability to handle people – all seem to involve qualities we think of as feminine. Indeed, you could describe the changes we have to make to adjust to life in the forties as a feminizing process. Success now depends on subduing the masculine side of our personality and fostering feminine qualities.

In my book *A Question of Sex*, I argued very strongly against the view that there is any biological reason why men should be more aggressive, ambitious and so on than women. But there can be no doubt that we do expect the two sexes to conform to traditional sexual stereotypes, which means that a woman in her forties will have much more practice than her husband at the skills which are valued at this age, and indeed throughout the rest of life. Some writers have gone so far as to suggest that whereas the first half of life belongs to men, the second very often belongs to women. However, if there is a shift in the balance of power between the sexes, I suspect it takes place rather later than the forties, and this is a theme we shall return to in the final two chapters of the book.

Where work is concerned, the early forties are often a critical period. Statistics show that your chances of being made redundant double once you pass forty, and I pointed out in Chapter 4 that there are very few professions where someone of this age can still be called promising. Such considerations were clearly in the forefront of a forty-three-year-old teacher's mind when she spoke to us:

Being a teacher means you have to plan your career very carefully if you want to go a long way in it. You have to have done certain things and moved to a better job at certain ages, and if you've passed these ages as I have, then there's not a lot of chance to really get much further . . . You just have to be content to stay as you are, or try and find another career.

Her sentiments seem to be widely held, as you can see from

the very striking differences we found when we asked people in the thirty-five to thirty-nine and forty to forty-four age brackets to assess their promotion prospects. In the former, 63 per cent of the men and 34 per cent of the women expected to get a better job in the next ten years. In the latter, the comparable figures were 38 and 29 per cent. Despite this, we found no sign that people in their forties are any less committed to their jobs, though we did find that they seem to respond very sensibly to the fact that their prospects are now less bright. You can see this from the answers they gave to another question we asked them, about how much importance they attached to being promoted. Whereas 60 per cent of the men in the thirty-five to thirty-nine age bracket say they think it is important for them to get a better job, only 26 per cent of those in their early forties say this.

The position seems to be rather different for women. There is a fall in expectations of promotion and in the importance attached to getting a better job among women in their early forties, but it is much less marked than among men. This is presumably another consequence of the fact that so many of them are returning to work at this point of their lives after a long break. It is quite likely that a woman's first job on re-entering the work-force will be more menial than her talents deserve, so it is reasonable for her to hope that her qualities will eventually be recognized. And although only 10 per cent of women in the forty-five to forty-nine age group in Colchester and 16 per cent of those in their fifties actually were in better jobs than they had been five years earlier, the fact that a woman now in her early forties is more likely than one in her fifties to have worked before starting a family means that we should not dismiss the hopes of the former as mere wishful thinking.

On the home front

But it is at home that the forty-year-old's newly acquired tolerance and flexibility are likely to face their sternest test. We saw earlier in the book that adolescents are only rarely the monsters they are made out to be, but also that parents of younger children are often less worried by their present responsibility than by the prospect of having to cope with the teenage years. So far as the reality is concerned, being the parent of teenage children seems to be every bit as difficult as we anticipate, though I strongly suspect that many of the problems are exaggerated, if not actually created, by the fact that we have spent so much time living through them in advance. According to one school of thought, adolescents only have the problems their parents wish on them. My own view is that teenagers are not entirely blameless for their parents' fears, but that we cannot ignore the evidence discussed in Chapter 2 which showed that adolescents take a much less apocalyptic view of the period they are living through than their parents do.

If you are at all doubtful about the impact teenage children have on their parents, consider just one statistic from the results of the Colchester survey. When we analysed all the answers to the item in which people were asked to list the things they worried about, we found that the concern people between the ages of thirty-six and forty-five expressed about their children was the largest single worry of either sex at any age. And when we re-analysed the data so that we could see how adult worries were affected by their children's rather than their own age, we discovered that it is oldest children between the ages of eleven and nineteen who cause their mothers most concern from day to day, and those between sixteen and nineteen whose future their mothers are most anxious about. No less than nine out of ten of the women we interviewed whose eldest child was between sixteen and nineteen said they were worried about their child's future. At every age, the men in our survey are much less likely than their wives to worry about their children, and the concern expressed by those in their forties on this score is neither more nor less than by those in their thirties or fifties. But even among men, children were the second most frequently mentioned source of worry by those in their forties (the first was money). Small wonder, then, that so many of the people we interviewed told us that they were counting the days until their last child left home!

But it would be quite wrong to conclude that teenage children are merely a source of worry to their parents, and equally wrong to suppose that parents look forward to their departure with nothing but glee. Some, like this woman in her early forties, do not relish the prospect at all:

> I don't look forward to it . . . because I do a lot with the children, and I'll miss them very much if they go.

Another woman pointed out that teenage children are rewarding as well as demanding:

> You move on from changing nappies to becoming chauffeurs really. But on the other hand they're far more company now. You know, they're like having adults about the house.

Then there are those, like this father, who, as a result of their children's widening interests, get a taste of what life will be like after they have gone:

> When we take Clare to music we tend to go together, and while Clare is having her lesson we finish up in the local pub. This is quite strange to us . . . it's something we haven't done for years and years and we find it's a most peculiar sensation to be on our own in a pub and com-

pletely free. But it's something we'll probably do more of, I should imagine, as time goes on.

The ambivalence some parents feel about the prospect of their children leaving is nicely captured in this woman's comments:

I think there's a lot of room yet for them to become more independent than they are at the moment . . . Before they leave home they'll want to go on their own holidays, so from that point of view we shall have a freedom we haven't had before. But I certainly don't *want* to see them go – there's no hurry as far as I'm concerned although we'd both like to see them go on their way.

The problems associated with teenage children not only cause their parents' thoughts to turn to the freedom the will soon have, but also have the effect of bringing them closer to *their* parents. Whereas the young parents we talked to were generally scornful of their own upbringing, and convinced that the more liberal approach they were adopting would produce better results, people in their forties are much less certain. They wonder whether permissiveness hasn't gone too far, and increasingly find themselves identifying with their own parents and defending their values rather than rebelling against them. Whereas people under forty we talked to stressed how different they were from their parents, those over forty were more inclined to see them as 'the people we're turning into'. So as middle age approaches, there seems to be a clear shift in our loyalties and attitudes, which is part of a growing awareness that we are about to join the older generation.

Generate or stagnate

The psychological adjustments we have to make in the middle part of our lives form part of a psychological process called *generativity*, the first flowerings of which can be seen in the early years of full adulthood. The idea is that we all have a deep-rooted wish to create something by which we'll be remembered, whether it is a child, a great work of art, a building named after us, or just an abiding memory that we were a pleasure to know. For this to happen, it is essential that society should continue and that there should be future generations to remember us. So we spend our adult years trying to achieve something of lasting value, nurturing the next generation, and bolstering up the established order as best we can.

We pursue all three tasks simultaneously throughout the years of our adult lives, but devote more time to one or other of them at different stages. As the years of active parenthood draw to a close, we have more time to spare for two other aspects of generativity – civic and social duties and a more general interest in the younger generation. The proportion of people involved in committee work rises steadily from one age group to the next in the Colchester survey, and both voluntary organizations and local interest groups benefit from the fact that most of us feel an increasing obligation to make a contribution to the community as we get older. A scoutmaster we spoke to described how his scouting activities provided him with a welcome relief from the pressures of work, but then went on to explain the satisfaction he got from working with the younger generation:

> The future generation is going to be helped by me because we're training boys to be leaders . . . I think that's where we're going to get the benefit of the time I've put in, in the next two decades . . . I can see boys who've been cubs

with me who have gone on to take responsible positions in the community, as opposed to the other lads who just don't take anything except perhaps things that aren't theirs.

The impulse to bring on the next generation can express itself in many different ways, and it's not just an escape from jobs which seem boring or over-taxing. The chief executive of a successful firm described to us how his horizons seem to be getting wider:

I think I've started becoming more interested in several things, particularly the world in general, the world situation ... I do many more things like chairing meetings ... You've got the experience now to be able to give something to other people ... One's family seems to grow in all respects as one gets older ... In your twenties you're very concerned with your immediate family ... As you get to the next stage, it widens to be your children and your close friends and your parents ... Now I feel very responsible and protective towards everybody who works in the company and all their families. And so one's family seems to grow wider and wider as one grows older.

Generativity seems to come naturally to most people, which is just as well, since society could hardly survive if the older generation refused to pass on the benefits of its experience to those who will eventually take over from them. But we saw earlier in the book that some people find it difficult to abandon their adolescent isolationism for the intimacy and give-and-take of young adult relationships, and that others are just as reluctant to leave the make-believe world of young adulthood for the more demanding and less forgiving world of full adulthood. In the same way, not everybody is at all eager to give up the ruthless and single-minded pursuit of their own interests, especially if this has brought them dividends in the first half of life. But there are risks attached to clinging to the old attitudes and failing to develop psychologically, at this as at the earlier transition points. People who refuse to look beyond their own needs and take no pleasure from taking care of others run the risk of becoming psychologically stagnant as middle age approaches.

Stagnation can take one of two forms, which are associated with two different types of personality flaw. The first is narcissism. Narcissists can carry on quite happily lining their own nests until the physical and psychological implications of getting old begin to make their impact, and this is unlikely to happen until long after their forties. As they move towards old age, such people are particularly susceptible to anxiety about dying, and it's not uncommon for them to experience a sort of 'conversion' after a serious illness or emotional crisis which brings home to them the limitations of a lifestyle devoted entirely to looking after Number One. But it may come too late, and it is difficult to suppress the uncharitable thought that they are getting no more than their just deserts if they have difficulty in finding anyone prepared to listen to them confessing the error of their former ways.

There is a second type of individual prone to mid-life stagnation for whom it is much easier to feel sympathy. Depressed individuals often feel no sense of achievement at this point of their lives, and so cannot believe that they have anything worth offering the younger generation or to society in general. A phenomenon quite common in the helping professions, but by no means unknown elsewhere, is the 'burn-out'. These are people whose day-to-day professional experience of other people's inability to cope eventually makes them cynical and callous to their clients' suffering, and convinces them there is nothing they can do to help others. This form of stagnation is similar to *learned helplessness*, which we discussed in Chapter 2, and it can only be overcome by finding something – however simple – you're good at, and using it to restore confidence in your own competence and ability to control events.

The mid-life crisis

For all the evidence that most people find the forties a re-rewarding decade to live through, the idea persists that there is a mid-life crisis. In Chapter 4, I gave the psychologist's definition of crisis as a set of circumstances or events for which one's existing behavioural patterns are inadequate. Everything I have said in this chapter makes it clear that, according to this definition, the forties *are* a crisis point in our life, because our existing attitudes have to be substantially modified between the first and second half of life if we are to avoid becoming stagnant. However, most of us don't seem to be put out by having to make these changes. We see it as a challenge, and are intrigued and often quite pleased to see a new 'me' emerging. But for a significant minority of us, things are not so easy, and it is these people whose struggles are described in *Passages* and other popular books about the Mid-life Crisis. (From here on, I shall use capital letters when referring to the malaise which afflicts some people, especially men, around the age of forty.)

But what are the symptoms of the Mid-life Crisis, and what causes it? The symptoms are a very mixed bag, consisting mainly of psychological feelings like emptiness and uncertainty, strain and boredom, hollowness and lack of enjoyment, and unfocussed melancholy and depression. They can also have a more physical flavour, since the early forties is a peak time for accidents, hypochondria, illness, drug addiction, alcoholism and suicide. But for most people who experience it, the Mid-life Crisis seems to manifest itself as a prolonged low-key emotional state. Writers on the subject have hazarded many guesses as to what causes it, some of which cover ground we are already familiar with. It may be set off by realizing the extent to which we have failed to fulfil our youthful ambitions, and the resurgence of the dreams of early adulthood. This could explain why we found so little sign of a Mid-life Crisis in Colchester, since less than half the men in their forties we talked to could remember having any clear idea of what they hoped to achieve when in their twenties, and only 6 per cent of them were in the position of having had a dream they had completely failed to fulfil. Other possible explanations include trouble in the family, having to come to terms with changes in social status and role, and the sudden awareness of one's own mortality.

All these problems do confront the forty-year-old, but why do some of us find them so oppressive when most people take them in their stride? There's some evidence that the roots of the Mid-life Crisis lie in childhood experience. The suggestion is that anxious children who are racked with doubts about their own ability compensate for this by becoming high achievers, and that their earlier anxieties re-emerge when their powers begin to wane, or as they come to realize that more is expected of them than just having a large bank balance and a plushly carpeted office. We still know tantalizingly little about the Mid-life Crisis, but what evidence there is suggests that it is more often brought on by work pressures than by what is happening at home or worries about one's own mortality. However, it's not clear whether people who are very successful at work are most likely to suffer from it. We might expect this to be the case, since they presumably have most to lose from the discovery that there's more to life than work. But very successful people in their early forties are actually less likely to say they would like to be in their twenties again than their less successful colleagues, according to the results of an American survey. So the Mid-life Crisis remains something of a mystery, and we don't even know the answer to the most interesting question of all: Does it strike everyone who is exposed to a particular combination of circumstances, or is it just something certain individuals are particularly likely to experience, because they are the people they are? Until we know the answer to this, there's very little constructive advice to be offered to people approaching this stage of their lives who want to make sure that they negotiate the mid-life crisis without suffering from the Mid-life Crisis.

But one thing we can be sure about. The Mid-life Crisis is *not* a universal experience no one can hope to avoid as they come up to forty. For most of us, the readjustments we find ourselves making in the forties are a source of pleasure, accompanied by the anticipation of freedom from family responsibilities and a feeling of relief that we shall be more our own men and women in the decades which lie ahead than we have been at any stage of our lives so far.

CHAPTER 6

Winding Down

'Middle age, in America, is considered a state only slightly more desirable than venereal disease.'

JUDITH MARTIN, in the *Washington Post*

Without knowing its author's age, it is impossible to tell whether the comment above is a tragic *cri de coeur* or just another example of the uncharitable way in which people of different ages sometimes think of each other! But whichever it is, I think she overstates her case, because although there are drawbacks to being middle-aged, our thinking about middle age has changed quite dramatically in recent years, and we no longer think of it as a social disease. What we *do* object to is the old-fashioned view of middle age that you see in saucy seaside postcards. Here the men are balding and beer-bellied, the women harassed and inadequately corseted, and the underlying assumption is that once we reach middle age, we lose all interest in our appearance and ask nothing more from life than a bit of peace and quiet, as we sit in our carpet-slippers in front of the fire to the soothing background accompaniment of *Match of the Day*. Such a picture holds little appeal in a society which is as health-conscious and achievement-orientated as ours. But it bears very little resemblance to what most people in their fifties are actually like today, and I doubt whether it was ever more than a crude caricature of life as we live it in this, the sixth age.

Adults who took part in the Colchester survey say that middle age begins some time between forty-five and fifty-five, with fifty itself the most popular choice. Since we located the beginning of the fifth age at the point where some men begin to display symptoms of a psychological malaise sometimes called the male menopause, it seems only fair that the female menopause should be the starting point of the sixth. The change of life lasts for more than two years in the average woman (it can take as many as ten), so it's difficult to say precisely when the sixth age begins. But this is a problem we have become very familiar with in *Seven Ages*, and I don't think we shall go far wrong if we think of it as beginning at fifty and running through to retirement. This, too, is not a fixed point. The age at which men become eligible for a state retirement pension in Britain is sixty-five, but according to the results of an official government survey published in 1980, nearly a third of men aged sixty-four have already retired. Similarly, although the 'official' retirement age for women is sixty, 36 per cent of them are retired a year earlier than this, and 10 per cent of both sexes are still employed at the age of seventy-two. Retirement is clearly a movable feast, but for most people the sixth age ends in the early or mid-sixties.

Life in the empty nest

The major events of this period of our lives are the menopause, becoming a grandparent and retirement, and I shall have more to say about all of these later in the chapter. But first we shall follow our usual practice of seeing how people feel at this stage of their lives, and identifying the physiological and behavioural changes which occur during it. Like every other stage of life, the fifties have their advantages and their drawbacks. On the positive side, people do seem to become happier in their marriages when their children have left home. One sign of this is that the divorce rate falls abruptly in the fifty to sixty age group to a mere 10 per cent of all divorces. No doubt there is a generational effect at work here: people of this age were brought up and got married at a time when far more stigma was attached to divorce than is now the case, so they are less likely than younger people to be able to overcome a deep-rooted prejudice and take advantage of the fact that divorces are now much easier to come by. It may also be that unhappily married women decide that their chances of finding a second husband are greatly reduced once they reach the menopause and can no longer offer the promise of children. Many women are also afraid that their sex appeal will disappear with the menopause, and this too could encourage them to make the best of a bad job, and dismiss any further thoughts of a divorce.

But there is quite strong evidence that we genuinely become more satisfied with our marriages during the fifties. In Colchester, both sexes – but especially men – in their fifties seem to be much closer to their spouses than those in their forties. As they anticipated, life in the empty nest seems to be an improvement. They have had plenty of time to get used to the idea, since children leave home one at a time over a period of years, and by the time the last bird has flown, the prevailing mood amongst their parents seems to be one of relief, albeit tinged with some sadness and nostalgia.

Many of the people we talked to have noticed that a lot of the arguments they have had with their spouses over the years no longer take place now that the children have gone. Here is how two of them describe the situation:

There's an advantage once the children are off your hands. Yourself and the wife, you find you're more compatible. There aren't the niggling little things . . . you tend to sit down and get closer, I think.

You've got used to one another's company and I think if you're used to one another's company you can make a life. Your children aren't there, you're on your own – back to two – you're there to more or less please each other, whereas when you have a family you find you don't please each other.

They have more time to please themselves and each other, and it's not surprising to find that women, who have borne the brunt of the traumas of child-rearing, have higher hopes than their husbands of their second honeymoon. As a result, they are more likely to be disappointed. According to a recent American survey, women in their early fifties are much less satisfied with their husbands than vice versa. And their husbands seem to realize that they are not coming up to scratch, since their replies to the question, 'Do you think your husband/wife is satisfied with you?' were much less confident than those their wives gave! However, this survey also found that these differences between husbands and their wives tend to disappear by the end of the fifties, when the two sexes seem to be equally satisfied with each other, and equally confident that they're giving satisfaction to their partner.

For one group of women, the empty nest brings particular relief. So-called 'independent' women, who can be identified from adolescence by their high need for achievement, and their intellectual, introspective approach to life, have a rougher ride through the years of parenthood than those who fit more easily into the traditional feminine role. In a study in which researchers divided adolescent girls into one or other of these categories, and then followed their progress for more than thirty years, two distinct patterns of development emerged. For traditional women, the forties, far from being a decade of crisis, are actually a period of increasing happiness and psychological well-being, in which their gregarious, nurturant qualities stand them in good stead. These women were sociable and popular as adolescents, and they have remained socially competent and liked. None of the women in this group showed any signs of a Mid-life Crisis, and all were happily married and firmly home-oriented at the age of fifty. Independent women, on the other hand, take less easily to motherhood. They have always derived more satisfaction from developing themselves than from their attachments to other people. A significant proportion of those in the study we are considering show symptoms of the Mid-life Crisis around the age of forty: they become depressed and irritable, their earlier originality increasingly turns into fantasy, and for them the forties are not a golden decade. However, such women revive as they reach the fifties and their children leave home. As their emotional life becomes more free, they return to their earlier intellectual interests and seem to become warmer and more sympathetic people.

Within marriage, the subtle shift in the balance of power which began in the forties is now much more apparent. Most men seem to be consciously reconciled to the greater control their wives now exercise over them, and so long as a wife takes care not to wound her husband's *amour-propre*, both partners are usually quite happy with this arrangement. We found little sign of people in their fifties hankering after their youth. As one woman put it:

> Quite frankly I wouldn't want to young again . . . I wouldn't want to be sixteen. I'd want to be at least thirty. I realize I've gained a certain amount of experience. I've learned an awful lot, and I can make judgments for myself, whereas before . . . .

As in the forties, experience is the great gain, and health a significant worry. We also find ourselves continuing to re-adjust our priorities. All these feelings can be seen in the comments made by one of our groups of fifty to sixty-year-olds:

> I'd like to be frozen in time about now – but with less aches and pains. I know what I'm doing now, so that I wouldn't make as many mistakes as I have in the past.

> I think I will be more useful in life . . . A chap at work, he had an awful lot of personal trouble he came to talk to me about.

I think at the stage I am now the job is quite responsible, but I've no ambition to go up the ladder any higher. I have a standard of living that is satisfactory . . . I've just been on holiday in North Wales, and that's the back end of nowhere really, but that's beautiful, because you've got all the time in the world to think – and when I came back I thought, the job isn't important any longer – it's living that's important.

People in their fifties are ambivalent about the passing of time and aging. On the one hand, they feel they now have more time to listen to other people's problems and for their own philosophical musings. There is a marked drop in this age group of the Colchester survey in the number of men who say they have no close friends, though the proportion of women in this position is actually higher than among those in their thirties and forties. The most likely explanation of the latter finding is that many of the women of this age whom we interviewed had left work some years before they were eligible for the state pension, and had lost an important source of friends by doing so.

We seem to become more tolerant of others in our fifties, and also less self-critical and demanding on ourselves. As one person put it, 'You don't run for a bus any more, because another one will come.' But there are sudden flashes of realization that it's not just your friends who are getting old:

It struck me that I was getting old when I saw someone I hadn't seen for thirty-one years . . . and I looked and I thought, 'God, thirty-one years have gone since I saw that boy,' and it's shattering. And I think now that when I realize I can look back on thirty-odd years it frightens me.

And just as we see our thirtieth and fortieth birthdays as landmarks, so the opening of the sixth decade is an event which cannot be ignored. Life may begin at fifty, but this wasn't how one man in his fifties saw it:

> On my fiftieth birthday I was having a quiet coffee on the patio in the cool of the evening, thinking about the lovely day I'd had, when I suddenly thought, 'God, half a century!' And then I thought, 'Three score years and ten – if you live that you've only got another twenty years,' and that really sobered me.

The other great worry in the fifties is that we are losing flexibility, becoming set in our ways, and unable to take in new ideas. Perhaps as a sign of their increasing self-confidence, more of the women than the men in this age group claimed that they actually found it easier to accept new ideas than they had ten years earlier, but we found a sharp increase in the proportion of people of both sexes who say they find it more difficult to learn and remember new things now than a decade ago. Whereas only 15 per cent of the men in thirty-six to forty-five age group were willing to make this admission more than half of those between the ages of forty-six and fifty-eight now find it more difficult to take in new information.

However, very few of the people we spoke to see the decline in mental flexibility as a symptom of the physical effects of aging. Most share this man's view that it is just an aspect of the way our personality changes over the years:

> One is getting to the stage where one is less adaptable to doing something fresh . . . whether it's because you lose a bit of confidence as you get older, or whether it's just the fact that you've got set in your ways to a degree . . . .

Although this is a decade of generally worsening health, we were struck by the fact that people are not significantly more concerned about their health than those in the age group beneath them. In fact, 42 per cent of the men and 28 per cent of the women in their fifties describe their health as excellent, as compared with 34 and 17 per cent of those in their forties. However, these statistics conceal a very marked class difference among men. The proportion of middle-class men worried about their health falls from 13 to 4 per cent between the thirty-six to forty-five and the forty-six to fifty-eight age groups, while that of working-class men actually rises from 20 to 31 per cent.

Many studies have shown that our self-perceived health bears very little relationship to our actual health, because our judgments are always relative – 'Well, I'm certainly healthier than old Fred' – and coloured by our expectations – 'Well, I'm not bad for a man of my age'. While a lot of the men we spoke to seemed content to let things take their natural course, this is the only age group where the women in our sample were more likely to be taking regular exercise than the men. Moreover, both men and women in their fifties are more philosophical than those in their forties about their appearance and, rather surprisingly, the prospect of dying. Forty-one per cent of the men and forty-five per cent of the women agree with the statement that you get less afraid of facing death as you get older, and less than one person in ten in their fifties say they are more afraid of dying than they were ten years ago. Women in their fifties are not only less worried about facing death than those in their forties, but also less concerned about the prospect of being lonely. Although in both cases the object of their fears is now ten years nearer, it's a sign of their increasing mellowness and philosophical outlook that they have become less rather than more frightened.

Unlike any of the younger age groups, a significant proportion of people in their fifties are aware of a decline in their sexual activity over the past decade. Forty per cent of the men and thirty-two per cent of the women describe themselves as less sexually active than they were ten years ago, although the majority of both sexes say there has been no change or even an improvement in their sex lives. Other changes in attitude and priorities are fairly predictable. The fifty to fifty-eight-year-old group in our survey is slightly more conservative in its outlook and more hostile towards the young than any of the younger groups. Less expectedly, they are also rather resentful towards those older than themselves, and envious of the special privileges the retired enjoy. They complain that they have nothing equivalent to old people's clubs, travel passes and so on, and sometimes say they feel in a kind of limbo, not being sure whether to think of themselves as young or old. Although they say they feel more secure, emotionally and financially, than they did ten years ago, the prospect of retirement causes money worries, especially among working-class people.

Our depth interviewers found a number of significant class differences in the way people feel in the period leading up to retirement. Among working-class men and women, they detected more signs of resentment and the feeling of being threatened and unwanted. This was less marked among women, partly because the job opportunities for unskilled women of this age compare quite favourably both with what they have been used to in the past and with those of unskilled men in their fifties. Here is how one woman described the position:

> I think employers like older people, really, because they get a job done properly . . . The youngsters today don't seem to put their minds to it.

For the middle classes, the fifties seem to be a noticeably easier period to negotiate. They feel more secure, are more philosophical about the future, and seem happy to capitalize on their experience and enjoy their memories. Fewer middle-than working-class women of this age are at work, for reasons we discussed earlier. Those who are at work do not have the advantage that working-class women have over their husbands, since the jobs they tend to do – for example, secretarial work or dental nursing – are harder to come by the older you are. Generally, class differences in people's attitude towards life are more marked in the fifties than earlier: where the middle classes think that on the whole things have got better over the years and are looking forward to the prospect of 'doing their own thing' after retirement, working-class people are more likely to say that things have got worse, and to view retirement as a time of financial hardship. Many of the lower-paid workers we talked to were worried about how they would manage on their pensions and were already cutting down on such luxuries as holidays and even fresh fruits and sweets. They find themselves wondering whether they are making major purchases for the last time, and it obviously takes a lot of the fun out of buying things like furniture if you have to ask yourself if it's going to last you until you die.

There is also a class difference in the reality of the empty-nest syndrome. Some children of all classes stubbornly refuse to leave home, preferring the security – and the financial benefits – of living with their parents to the problems of setting up on their own. Although mothers are sometimes accused of clinging to their children and refusing to cut the apron-strings, those we interviewed were more often disappointed than pleased by children who refused to stand on their own feet. They see it as a failure on their own part that their children are not living up to expectations in this respect. But even when children have left home, and have children of their own, a substantial proportion of women in their fifties still list their children among their worries. As one of them told us:

I think when you get to our age and you see your children married and you see their lives, you tend to worry about them more than when they were smaller and under your control.

Working-class women in particular, whose children are more likely to live near them, complain that they are less free of their children than they thought (and hoped) they would be. We shall have more to say about being a grandparent later, but it's worth noting here that not all grandparents are flattered to be called in as consultants – especially when there's no guarantee their advice will be followed – and some resent being exploited as baby-sitters.

As further evidence that the Generation Gap is less marked than some people think, there is no doubt that younger people are impressed by the wisdom of those in their fifties, and turn to them for some sorts of advice in preference to their own contemporaries. This emerges very clearly from the answers to an item in the Colchester survey in which people were asked whether they would choose a person in their thirties, forties or fifties to turn to for advice about a personal matter, for advice about buying a house or some other financial matter, to be their boss, or to be on the jury if they ever had the misfortune to be tried in a court of law. People of all ages said they would rather turn to someone in their fifties as a source of advice about both personal and financial matters. When it comes to a boss, they show only a slight preference for a person in his or her fifties over someone younger, and we seem to be even less inclined to throw ourselves on the mercies of fifty-year-olds as jurors. This suggests that although younger people are impressed by the wisdom of those who have reached the sixth age, they are not so sure of their tolerance and impartiality.

But these findings make it clear that being in your fifties has real consolations. You not only feel wiser, but also appear wiser to younger people. So the people who complained to our interviewers of being unwanted may have been under-estimating their own value. In terms of the psychological processes we discussed in the last chapter, they seem to have allowed themselves to become stagnant. Our finding that younger adults look to those in their fifties for advice, coupled with the results of other surveys which have found that both children and adolescents tend to have a high opinion of their grandparents' generation, suggests that there is ample scope for older adults to display their generativity, and no need for people in their fifties to feel that they no longer have a role to play.

Sound in mind and body

So far as physical changes are concerned, the fifties are a period of steady rather than dramatic deterioration. However, the process can be accelerated by ill-health – from this point onwards, we ought really to plot two different courses of development, one for the healthy and one for those with serious health problems – but there is no biological reason why healthy people should start to function significantly worse during this period of their lives. The contrast between the beginning of the fifth age and the end of the sixth is quite marked, however. For example, a man in his late fifties can only do hard physical work at about 60 per cent of the rate achieved by the average forty-year-old. Nevertheless, there are very few jobs where biological considerations make it essential to retire even at sixty-five because there are very few jobs where we have to operate at anything like our maximum physical potential. The older worker may be nearer to his maximum than younger colleagues, but this does not mean that he is in any danger, and as at every other stage of life, you have to balance the advantages of the raw physical energy of youth against the benefits which come from greater experience and the ability to find short-cuts and more efficient ways of doing things.

The main reason why our capacity for hard physical labour declines as we get older lies in the lungs, where a steady thickening of the air sac walls impedes the diffusion of gases which means that we need increasingly more air to provide the same amount of oxygen for the blood. So we get out of breath sooner, and anything which augments this – smoking is the obvious example – can speed up this aspect of our physical decline. And we don't only become less efficient at taking oxygen in; its passage from the blood to working muscles is hindered by a thickening of the sheaths of the connective tissues which surround the muscle fibres. It becomes increasingly difficult for oxygen to make its way out of the blood vessels which are buried in this tissue, and there is the additional problem that while the amount of oxygen carried in our blood remains near its peak until about the age of fifty, it then begins to decline.

These changes are significant indices of aging, but they don't have much effect on most people's everyday lives. Much the same applies to the changes which take place in our physical appearance during the fifties, though we're certainly aware of them, as you can see from the comment one man made to us:

> I started to get a middle-aged spread . . . Don't know what happened, but all of a sudden I found I couldn't get my trousers on . . . I've got a cycle and ride fifteen to twenty miles a day . . . It's getting harder, yes I get off and walk up hills now.

The idea that we consist of different layers which age at different speeds is as firmly held by people in their fifties as by those in their forties – yes, of course I look older, but it's still the same person inside! And we don't seem to blame biology for the fact that we look older or get ill more often. Some people just take a fatalistic approach, like this man:

> I don't think you dread it. You accept it if it comes along . .
> I don't think you think about illness unless you have it .
> it's just your hard luck if you get something.

Others, like a woman we talked to, put it down to the stresses
and strains of living:

> I feel, 'Christ, what is it that makes me look older?' If it's
> the hair I'd go and have a rinse. You try as best you can to
> rectify it, because obviously there's something wrong if you
> look older. It could be worry. I mean, let's face it, some
> people do have a lot of worries, and that does make them
> look old.

Most people would accept that worry can age you – there are
even reports of people's hair going white virtually overnight
after some particularly traumatic experience – and the
results of a recent American study suggest that it's not just
current psychological problems which affect the way we look
and the state of our health.

For almost forty years, the Harvard University Health
Service has been monitoring the physical and psychological
development of 188 men who were undergraduates in the
early 1940s. In 1975, when their average age was fifty-four,
one-hundred of them were in excellent physical health, fifty-
four were suffering from minor complaints, fourteen were
chronically ill, nine were disabled, and eleven were dead.
Eight years earlier, all had been given scores on a scale which
assessed how well they were adjusting psychologically to life
in the forties, and there is a striking relationship between these
scores and the state of their physical health almost a decade
later. Only two out of the thirty-one men who were dead,
disabled or chronically ill in 1975 had been well-adjusted
psychologically in 1967, while most of those in excellent
health or with only minor problems had had average or
better scores on the psychological adjustment scale eight
years earlier. Between 1969 and 1975, i.e. between the ages
of forty-eight and fifty-four, the health of the worst adjusted
men was two-and-a-half times more likely to deteriorate than
that of the best adjusted. We cannot say for certain that this

study proves that psychological maladjustment causes poor physical health, because it might just be that the same people are prone to both. But the researchers found that such signs of psychological trouble as frequent visits to a psychiatrist, job dissatisfaction, failed marriages, heavy use of drugs and a poor social life regularly preceded physical problems by a number of years. If future research confirms that the way we respond to the psychological adjustments of the forties is an accurate predictor of how well we resist the physical challenges of the fifties, then the Mid-life Crisis we discussed in Chapter 5 will take on a new significance.

So far as mental abilities are concerned, the fifties should not be a disturbing decade for most people. We are slowing up, mentally as well as physically, and our senses are becoming less acute, but in both cases the decline started much earlier and is unlikely to make a serious impact on our lives. The intellectual skills which may show a marked deterioration if we live to an advanced old age are rarely affected at this stage. Studies show that our vocabulary, for example, continues to grow until the mid-fifties, and it is unusual for short-term memory to be significantly worse now than it was earlier. However, some tasks do start becoming more formidable in the fifties, especially those where you have to handle new and difficult information at speed. For example, learning to drive a car or how to operate a complex new piece of machinery in a factory are both tasks which the fifty-five-year-old will probably find more difficult than he would have done when younger. On the other hand, skills already acquired hold up remarkably well. It's proverbial that we never forget how to swim or ride a bicycle, and it seems that 'knowing how' is almost immune to the effects of aging.

The fact that some types of ability are hit much harder than others by aging may account for the class differences mentioned earlier. Since established complex skills are least affected, it's understandable that middle-class workers are more complacent about life in the fifties. They don't have to learn how to work new machines, and they can even turn the physical symptoms of aging to their advantage. Since their professional status is based on the assumption that wisdom can only come from experience, greying hair or an elegant pair of half-moon spectacles may actually enhance their authority. For the manual worker, the position is very different. He is particularly vulnerable to technological progress, and his age can only be a handicap if he finds himself competing with younger men. Technological advance threatens him in two ways. He may suffer the indignity of being replaced by a machine, and if so will come up against the prejudice many employers have against hiring older workers. And even if he manages to hang on to his job, it may well be redesigned, and we have already seen that old dogs don't much relish having to learn new tricks. Since blue-collar jobs also tend to be more physically demanding than those done in an office, the manual worker is his fifties is doubly disadvantaged, and it's not difficult to understand why his outlook on life is gloomier than that of his middle-class counterpart.

The fact that the first serious burden imposed by aging falls on working-class men is a taste of things to come, as we shall see in the final chapter. But it's important to remember a point I made earlier in the book — not everyone's ability to master new skills falls away in the fifties. A significant minority of people continue to perform just as well as the typical twenty-year-old, which suggests that when deterioration does occur, it may not simply be the result of biological changes. Where biology is involved – for example, in the decline of vision and hearing – changes over the years are much more consistent and predictable, and there are very few exceptions. So why does a mental decline set in in some people but not in others? The answer seems to lie in a person's mental attitudes: if you expect to find it increasingly difficult to master new skills, there's a good chance that you will, even though there may be no obvious biological reason why you should. Since so many people now live longer, it's obviously important to find out why some of us are unnecessarily pessimistic about the mental consequences of getting older. At present we don't know the answer to this question, but we do know that the consequences of changing people's expectations about what the elderly and even the very old are capable of learning can be very dramatic indeed, as we shall see in Chapter 7.

The change of life

So far, the bogey-man of middle age looks very much like a paper tiger. We may look look older in the fifties, but our everyday lives are still largely untouched by the biological aspects of aging. The things we can no longer do are things few people of this age need to do, and most don't want to. But the fifty-year-old woman does get one reminder – perhaps the most dramatic since puberty – of the fact that our lives are at least partly shaped by biological forces beyond our control. For her, the beginning of the sixth age is marked by a series of biochemical and physiological changes which make it impossible to conceive any further children.

The word menopause refers to the fact that women stop having periods, usually some time between the ages of forty-five and fifty-four, but this, the official end of the reproductive era, is just one event in a sequence of changes in a woman's reproductive system which can be traced back to the beginning of full adulthood. Her ovaries, for example, have been shrinking since the age of about thirty. The number of eggs she produces starts to fall at the beginning of the forties, when her periods also start to become more irregular. The menopause is usually preceded by several years of both shorter cycles and missed periods. As a result, women get plenty of warning of the approach of the menopause and often have a number of false alarms. Another change which dates back to the early forties is a drop in the production of

Graffian follicles and *corpora lutea*. Since these are the major sources of oestrogen and progesterone respectively, there is a marked fall in the production of hormones between the ages of forty and sixty, the effects of which can be seen throughout the entire female genital tract and reproductive system. For example, the weight of the uterus falls by more than a half between the ages of thirty and fifty, the vaginal walls shrink and become thinner, and vaginal secretion is significantly reduced. Some of these changes can be reversed by oestrogen replacement therapy, but this can never be more than a delaying action, the long-term consequences of which are still unknown.

Although the timing varies greatly from one woman to another, we have a pretty clear understanding of the inevitable and universal chain of internal changes which leads to the end of a woman's reproductive life. But when it comes to the more interesting question of how women are affected by these internal changes, the certainty disappears, and we find ourselves in a perplexing tangle of old wives' tales, ill-formed medical opinion, and sexist prejudice. Perhaps we should dispose of these before trying to make sense of the scientific evidence on the subject. If the old wives are to be believed, the change of life is a very unpleasant period when all women must expect to suffer from a collection of distressing physical and psychological symptoms. Since old wives tend to be rather vague on biochemistry and physiology, I suspect that if we asked them why this happens, they would mutter darkly a woman's justification for existence disappearing once her child-bearing days are over. I doubt whether many women these days ever think of themselves simply as child-bearing machines, and most of them anyway call a voluntary halt to the proceedings long before Nature steps in, either by using contraceptives or, increasingly, by having themselves or their husbands sterilized. But the old wives' sexist prejudices are supported by biologists who take a strictly functional view of a woman's role in the world, and their opinion still seems to carry some weight with younger women, who, surveys show, are more frightened of the menopause than those who either are experiencing or have experienced it.

At the other extreme are those doctors – usually male – who stoutly maintain that normal women take the menopause in their stride, and that only neurotics complain of hot flushes, dizziness, depression or any of the other symptoms associated with the menopausal syndrome. They point to the fact that some women sail through the change of life without reporting any physical or psychological symptoms whatsoever, and justify their practice of 'treating' middle-aged female patients with a bracing pep-talk by saying that all the medical literature relating to the menopause is based on case histories of women under the care of gynaecologists or even psychiatrists. These doctors may get through their surgery hours faster, but they obviously don't spend the extra spare time reading medical journals, because this view of the menopause is out of date.

In the last decade or so, surveys have explored the symptomatology of the menopausal syndrome in large groups of women selected at random from the general population, and although they do not show perfect agreement as to how many women experience what symptom at each of the different stages of the change of life, they do give us a much clearer picture of what a woman can expect to go through during the sixth age of her life. Perhaps the most significant finding is that there are only two symptoms – hot flushes and night sweats – which the great majority of women must expect to experience at the climacteric. Neither of these is unique to the menopause (approximately one woman in five experiences either or both of them while she is still menstruating regularly), but they affect at least two-thirds of women during the year following their last periods, and they are still much more common six years after the menopause than they were the year before it. Moreover, whereas hot flushes before the menopause are generally felt only on the face and neck, afterwards they affect the whole body, and three women out of four find them embarrassing and uncomfortable, though only a fifth of them seek medical treatment.

So far as the other symptoms of the menopause are concerned – headaches, dizzy spells, palpitations, sleeplessness, depression and weight increase – it seems that although they affect a substantial minority of women during the change of life, they are not directly caused by the menopause. They do tend to occur together, but the 30 to 50 per cent of women who suffer from them did so before they reached the menopause and still do so ten years later. Finally, at the two extremes, about 10 per cent of women describe themselves as incapacitated by the menopause, while some – estimates vary between 5 and 25 per cent – report no symptoms at all.

Before leaving the symptoms and turning to the question of what effect they have on a woman's feelings, we have to ask two further questions: what causes them, and what sort of women are most affected by them? The first question is much easier to answer than the second. The symptoms seem to be closely related to the drop in oestrogen production, since postmenstrual women produce only a sixth of the amount of oestrogen produced premenstrually and administration of oestrogen to menopausal women usually alleviates the symptoms. But it is not at all easy to predict in advance how a woman is likely to be affected by the menopause. Social class is no guide, nor is there any convincing evidence that the severity of menopausal symptoms is significantly linked to a woman's personality. We might have expected that neurotic women would suffer most at the change of life, but in fact it seems that a woman who has hitherto been a tower of strength to all around her is just as likely to become depressed as one who has always been at the mercy of her nerves. Nor does it seem to make any difference whether a woman has had children or not, whether she has a job, what her domestic work-load is, or even whether she is married or not. The time may come when we can identify in advance who is going to be incapacitated by the menopause, and who will escape unscathed, but at present it appears to be a lottery.

This element of unpredictability, coupled with the finding that only one woman in ten seems to regret reaching the change of life, has led some researchers to suggest that we may have been barking up the wrong tree in trying to link the symptoms some women experience at this time of their lives with the physiological changes of the menopause. After all, other things happen to women in their fifties, many of which are stressful in the sense that they force them to adapt to change. Fifty itself is an age of triple significance for the 'typical' woman: not only is it the commonest age for the menopause, but it is also the age at which Mrs Average can expect her mother to die and her daughter to get married, since the former will be seventy-eight (currently the commonest age for death amongst once-married women), and the latter twenty-three (currently the average age of marriage in women). You may want to dismiss this as mere coincidence or statistical sleight of hand, but it makes the point that a woman who is experiencing the change of life has other things to think about than the state of her reproductive system, and it raises the possibility that what are sometimes thought of as symptoms of the menopause may actually be nothing of the sort.

This suggestion is strongly supported by the results of a very recent piece of research in which the severity of physical and psychological symptoms experienced by a group of normal middle-aged women were matched not only with their menopausal status (had they stopped menstruating, and if so how long ago?), but also with their chronological age and, more importantly, with how many stressful events they had experienced during recent months. Examples of such events are the death of their husband, divorce or separation, involvement in a law case, illness, being fired from work and financial difficulties. The major finding of this study is that so-called Life Stress seems to be a much more reliable predictor of what physical and psychological symptoms a particular woman displays in her fifties than whether or not she has actually reached the menopause or how old she is. The task of disentangling the effects of the menopause from the other events of a woman's life has only just begun, but the early signs are that even here the biological effects of growing older may be much less important during the sixth age than we thought.

There are four important points to be made before we leave the subject of the menopause. The first is that most perfectly normal women must expect to experience at least two distressing symptoms – hot flushes and night sweats – as a direct consequence of the changes taking place inside them during the change of life. However, my second point is that although they do suffer in this way, surveys show that menopausal women visit their doctors no more frequently than women of other ages, so doctors who grumble that their surgeries are clogged up with neurotic middle-aged women are doubly unjustified – there is nothing neurotic about getting hot flushes, and only one woman in five actually troubles her doctor with this perfectly legitimate complaint! It is also important to realize that only a tiny minority (about 10 per cent) of women are actually incapacitated by the change of life. Nine out of ten seem able to carry on with their lives perfectly efficiently, so there can be no excuse for employers discriminating against middle-aged women on the grounds that they are bound to be less efficient workers.

My final point ought to reassure women who have not yet reached the change of life. Quite simply, it will not be as bad as you expect! As we saw earlier, it is younger women who fear the menopause most, either because they are afraid they will lose their looks or their interest in sex, or because they think they will suddenly become old women and lose any purpose in life once their child-bearing days are over. Women who have been through it take a much more sanguine view of the change of life. They know that the symptoms are only temporary, some of them have discovered a new interest in sex (remember that only a third of the women in the fifty to sixty age group in Colchester reported that they were less sexually active than ten years earlier), and most of them feel a sense of relief and release from the obligations of motherhood. There are of course exceptions. A woman who has failed to develop a sense of generativity and still lives only through her children, or one who is terrified by the prospect of growing old, cannot relish the prospect of the menopause. But our survey, and others like it, leaves no doubt that such women are in the minority; most have had enough of motherhood, and are willing and eager to turn their energies elsewhere. As one fifty-two-year-old woman put it to us:

> I think you tend to live for your children while you are bringing them up, but once they become the age like mine are now, they're off your hands, and you start living for yourself.

Great grandparenthood

But of course the postmenopausal woman does not live only for herself. Almost a half of those in this age group in Colchester have jobs, a quarter of them are involved in committee work, and the great majority of them become grandparents at some point in their fifties. Grandparenthood seems to be the great bonus of life in the fifties, and certainly the event about which we have least mixed feelings. I have argued that most of us are quite relieved when our children leave home. But we also feel a sense of loss, and some people don't see it as a gain at all: one woman told us it was like losing an arm when one of her children moved away. Similarly, although most of us are pleased when our children get married, a significant proportion of parents – particularly women – are saddened, especially by their daughter's marriage, and there is some evidence that a woman's menopausal symptoms can be enhanced by the anticipation of her daughter's wedding – further proof of the fact that the events of a woman's life play an important part in her experience of the change of life. But becoming a grandparent is an event which offers great rewards, and has very few drawbacks.

On the negative side, the arrival of grandchildren calls for an immediate overhaul of the relationship between a middle-aged woman and her daughter. We saw in Chapter 4 that young parents tend to be scornful of the way their parents brought them up, and the survey on motherhood we discussed in that chapter shows that young mothers will turn to almost anyone – health visitors, other relatives and other young mothers rather than their own mothers for advice on how to treat their babies in the difficult weeks after birth. So these weeks can be very frustrating for a grandmother who is looking to give her daughter the benefit of her experience and is not at all accustomed to playing a deferential role. If she makes suggestions, she runs the risk of being called an interfering old busybody, since her daughter is far too busy with her own problems to worry about her mother's feelings, and is probably too anxious and short of sleep to notice that she is causing offence anyway. To make matters worse, on the occasions when a young mother does turn to her mother for advice, she expects her to know all the answers. If she does not – and why should she, since it may be twenty years since she last had to cope with a baby – the older woman is likely to receive a totally unwarranted blast of scorn and abuse!

But although her advice may not often be wanted, the new grandmother soon finds that she has a role to play: according to the results of the motherhood survey, she is likely to be the only person her daughter really trusts as a baby-sitter. Acting in this capacity, grandmothers can experience the joys of motherhood without the burden of ultimate responsibility. When asked to describe the best thing about being her age, one young grandmother replied:

Having grandchildren – especially when you have had enough, hand them back and say, 'bye bye'. You know you're not going to get woken at five a.m.

Two other comments illustrate the real pleasure people get from their grandchildren:

The grandchildren, they keep us young. My husband and I are thrilled with the children when they come up.

One of the pleasures of my stage in having grandchildren is that they like to come and stay with me. I go into a different world.

Many women find that they prefer grandmothering to mothering, and almost all agree that it is easier. Harassed young parents have mixed feelings about the enthusiasm with which their children greet the grandparents. They are delighted to have tame baby-sitters who allow them to get out of the house occasionally, but they sometimes commented to us resentfully on the fact that their children seemed to get on better with their grandparents than with them. They were in no doubt at all that grandparenting is easier than parenting, and this knowledge can often add to the friction between the two generations of adults. Fortunately, this seems to lessen as the years go by. There may still be arguments about how the children should be treated – it's ironic that although young parents tend to claim that their own childhood was too strict, they usually accuse their parents of being too soft on the grandchildren! – but the older woman learns to accept and even admire her daughter's new authority. A new, more equal, relationship between the two women is usually forged over the years, though they may never re-establish the intimacy they enjoyed earlier.

I have concentrated on the relationship between a young

mother and her mother, but of course there are four other adults involved: the younger woman's husband, her father, and his parents. According to popular mythology, in-laws are a major cause of marital disharmony, and every comedian has a father- and mother-in-law joke up his sleeve. The reality seems to be rather different. Research shows that most young marrieds actually like their in-laws, and spend more time visiting them than in the company of their friends or neighbours. Moreover, where there is trouble, it tends to be between wife and mother-in-law. There are two reasons for this. The first is that young couples spend more time with the wife's parents, so that the husband's mother is more likely to feel rejected as a result of the marriage. Not so with one woman we talked to:

> When my son was courting, I wasn't concerned with him –
> I was more concerned with the girl, you know, because she
> had parents but they didn't worry about her. She was more
> like a daughter to me. I was protecting her against my own
> son. My life was very confused.

Within a marriage, it seems to be more common for the husband to make unfavourable comparisons between his wife and his mother – why can't you make gravy like she does? – than for her to compare him unfavourably with his father-in-law. However, in most cases the difficulties between wife and mother-in-law are confined to the early years of marriage, and the arrival of grandchildren is often the event which finally causes the hatchets to be buried.

But why do we find being a grandparent so rewarding, and do all grandparents see their role in the same way? Surveys of grandparents suggest that their lives are enriched in a number of different ways. The first relates to the theme of generativity we discussed in the last chapter. Grandchildren provide a sense of *biological renewal*: the species goes on and one's own family line will continue. In this way grandchildren can make us feel more comfortable about the prospect of dying, and they may be one reason why people in their fifties are less frightened of death than those in their forties. It is also reassuring for older adults to discover that children are still playing many of the same games they played as children, because this too gives them a broader perspective, and a sense of their own place in the pageant of history. Less grandiosely, grandchildren are a source of emotional self-fulfilment for the simple reason that they're fun, and a source of surprise, even if sometimes rather shocking:

> My daughter who's four suddenly announced that she'd wait a little while, but one day she was going to have a baby in her tummy, and my mother-in-law practically choked on her dinner. She was horrified.

Some grandparents also live vicariously through their grandchildren, and fondly dream they will be able to achieve the things neither they nor their children have managed to accomplish, while others get pleasure from supplying them with things their parents cannot or will not provide, whether it be presents, money, or simply their time or the benefit of their experience. Finally, a shared pride in grandchildren may be one more factor which helps to bring husbands and wives closer together in the fifties. Not only does it give them a topic of conversation, but it allows them to see each other at their most loving, and so gives them hope for the years that lie ahead.

Different people get different sorts of satisfaction out of being a grandparent, and there are a variety of ways of playing the role. About a third of us prefer not to get involved with our grandchildren at all, usually because we don't get on with our children, but the great majority of people describe grandparenthood in glowing terms ('it's the best thing that's happened to us in years'), and many of the people we spoke to clearly found it more than adequate compensation for the drawbacks attached to reaching this point of their lives. Some of these drawbacks we have already discussed, but we have not yet considered the event which marks the end of the sixth age. As they approach the end of the fifties, both men and women know that they are edging towards their official retiring ages, and however fit they are, the knowledge that society considers their useful working life is almost over must have some effect on how they think about themselves.

An end to work

The official retiring age is an anachronism, fixed by social and administrative convenience rather than dictated by the physical aspects of the aging process. It was Bismarck who first set the retirement age for men at sixty-five, and if we allowed for the social changes which have taken place since his day, an equivalent retirement age might now be about a hundred! As it is, the retirement age still comes too late for some people (almost a third of British men retire before the age of sixty-five, three-quarters of them on the grounds of poor health), but it comes far too early for many (10 per cent of both men and women are still employed at the age of seventy-two, though most of them only work part-time). No doubt the intentions of those responsible for introducing a fixed retirement age were good – the old war-horse should not be kept going until he drops – but very little was said about the well-being of the elderly when a proposal was made in 1976 to reduce the retirement age for men from sixty-five to sixty. Instead, the arguments used to justify the move were that it would reduce the unemployment figures and free more jobs for younger workers. Ironically, just two years after the British Parliament had debated the possibility of lowering the official retiring age for men, the US House of

Representatives overwhelmingly passed a bill which raised the mandatory retirement age to seventy for most private sector workers and abolished it altogether for government employees!

An official retirement age seems to serve two functions: it entitles those who have reached it to a state retirement pension, and it also sets a norm for when we are expected to retire, which allows us to prepare ourselves for the event. But the admirable principle that people have a right to a pension when they reach a certain age is too easily translated into the repressive view that they have no right to go on working once it is passed. As we have already seen, a significant number of people carry on working well into their official retirement, even though the jobs they do tend to be more menial and much less well-paid than those they did earlier. When asked why, most of them mention money, but about a quarter of them claim that they just like working, and a similar proportion say they don't want to be bored!

But what do we feel about the prospect of retirement? It's actually very difficult to work out whether people dread or look forward to life without work, because their feelings on the subject seem to be inextricably bound up with worries about health and money. Given what industrial psychologists have to say about the intangible rewards we get from our jobs – especially friendship and a sense of purpose in life – you might expect that we would be shattered by the prospect of not having a job to go to. Certainly unemployment earlier in life can do considerable psychological damage, but we were very struck by the fact that the proportion of men and women in the forty-six to fifty-nine age bracket of the Colchester survey who said they were worried about the future was significantly lower than that in any of the younger groups. Of course it may be that the prospect of retirement is so dreadful that they cannot bring themselves to think about it, but this was not at all the impression we formed when talking to them. On the contrary, most of them seemed to be facing the prospect with equanimity and in some cases with obvious relish. As one put it,

> I just hope and pray that life is as exciting and as much fun as it is now. I think it will be – even more exciting, more fun. I've got a lot of long-term plans and projects.

This comment introduces two important issues. The speaker obviously enjoys what he is doing at present, and yet he doesn't seem at all worried by the prospect of having to give it up. We might have expected to find that people who enjoy their work are more resentful about having to give it up, and therefore adapt less well to retirement than those who get little satisfaction from their jobs. In fact, the reverse seems to be true, because studies show that people who enjoy their work are more likely also to enjoy their retirement – a clear case of to them that hath shall be given!

The second interesting point to emerge from the comment above is that the man is already planning for retirement, though he is still in his fifties and therefore some years from the official retiring age. The combination of the trends towards greater longevity and earlier retirement has led statisticians to make the prediction that the average man born in 1960 will have nine more non-working years than one born in 1900. This, coupled with the results of studies which suggest that the slump into senility may have more to do with our mental attitudes than the physical aspects of the aging process, has caused an increasing number of middle-aged people to make active and early preparations for retirement, and a whole new industry has grown up to cater for their demands. As we shall see in the next chapter, this change in attitude can have a great effect on life in retirement, but it must also be at least partly responsible for the optimism with which a surprising number of the people we talked viewed retirement. Many people in their fifties take up new interests that they will be able to pursue later (we saw in the last chapter that some start as early as the forties), and those who can afford to may buy a retirement home near to friends or relatives, or perhaps in some favourite holiday spot. Moving home on retirement does not always work out – research suggests that it's wiser to wait a year or two, to avoid having to make two major adjustments at the same time – but there can be no doubt that planning for retirement can make the pre-retirement period an exciting rather than a depressing time.

But we also talked to people who found it very hard to adjust to the prospect of life without work. To them it implies uselessness, a major upheaval in their lives, and irrefutable proof that they are now old. As one fifty-year-old woman said:

> You think, 'Oh Christ, another ten years and I'll be sixty and a pensioner.'

And it's not just in the fifties that people have very different views about retirement. Here are two contradictory opinions expressed by a man and a woman in their early thirties:

> My ambition if this business comes off is to retire. Not to be lazy, don't misunderstand me, but to work hard. And if I can retire at fifty or fifty-five and be relatively comfortable, then I most certainly will.

> I think retirement . . . must be an awful thing to have to face, because they are sort of saying to you, you are now too old to work.

So the prospect of retirement clearly affects people in very different ways: some dread it, others can't wait for it to happen. And when we examine what happens when the prospect becomes a reality, the same applies: some people lose all sense of purpose and fade away, while others seem to get a new lease of life from no longer having to work. But is there any way of predicting how an individual is likely to take to retirement? We have already seen that people who enjoy their work are more likely also to enjoy their retirement, and intelligent advance planning – especially on the financial side – can do a lot to improve the quality of life in retirement. Health is another important factor, and some sociologists believe that an elaborate farewell ceremony at work makes it easier to adjust to retirement, since this emphasizes that an era is over and another about to begin. A gradual winding down via part-time work also seems to make for an easier retirement than an abrupt switch from full-time work to none at all.

But some researchers believe that we can predict how well a man is likely to adjust to retirement many years before he reaches the official retirement age (unfortunately, the study on which they base their conclusion did not include women). They say it's all a question of personality, and I shall end this chapter and anticipate the next by describing five different types of personality, and showing how well each adapts to life without work.

People who flourish in retirement can be divided into three categories. The first group is described as *mature*, and it consists of relatively unneurotic individuals who have a realistic evaluation of themselves and get real enjoyment out of personal relationships and any projects they turn their hand to. Such men feel that they have made a success of their lives so far, and they take growing old in their stride. They don't spend much time regretting the past, nor do they complain about things which are missing from their present life. Unlike the other four personality types I shall describe, the mature personality can emerge quite late in life, sometimes in people who have had serious problems in adjusting to change earlier.

The second type of person who seems to take well to retirement has been called the *rocking-chair man*. People in this category can be identified early in life by their general passivity. They have always been content to let things happen around them, and they greet retirement with relief because at last they are no longer expected to jump up and organize things. Such men find that this aspect of leaving work and growing older more than compensates for the disadvantages.

The third type of man who seems to be well equipped to deal with retirement uses a very different strategy from the rocking-chair man. These people are described as *armoured men*, because they build up a powerful system of defences to protect them from their deep-rooted anxieties about growing old. Unlike rocking-chair men, they hate the idea of becoming passive and dependent, so they take active steps to see that this doesn't happen to them. They become keep-fit fanatics to ward off physical decline, and take on a host of commitments to keep their minds active. In short, they see to it that they have no time to worry about growing old.

However, there are two sorts of men who find retirement much more difficult to cope with, and both can be recognized quite early in life. The larger group have been labelled *angry men*. In retirement, they are obsessed by the feeling that they haven't managed to achieve the goals with which they set out, and they are bitterly resentful of 'the system', which they hold responsbile for their failure. Such men have never developed a sense of personal competence, and they have always believed that their lives were being governed by forces beyond their control. Unlike rocking-chair men, who usually manage to detect a silver lining in any cloud which passes over them, angry men have always taken the gloomy view, and they regard growing old as the final indignity an unjust world forces them to bear.

The second category of men who find it difficult to adjust to retirement also sees the past as a sequence of disappointing failures. But unlike the angry men, they turn their resentment inwards, and blame only themselves for their misfortunes. As a result, these *self-haters* are particularly prone to depression as they get older, because the effects of aging simply emphasize the feelings of worthlessness and inadequacy they have always had. Such people seem to suffer from *learned helplessness*, a state we have discussed at various points earlier in the book, and their personality characteristics make them identifiable early in life. In fact, it's not difficult to divide people up into rocking-chair men, armoured men, angry men and self-haters at the beginning of their adult lives. Not everyone will still be in the same category by the time they reach retirement – we have seen, for example, that it is possible to join the mature category quite late in life. But most people seem to remain fairly constant to the personality they establish by the early thirties and I suspect that future research will confirm that the seeds of a successful retirement are sown long before we start poring over the estate agents' lists of retirement bungalows.

So we leave the sixth age on a note of uncertainty. For men (and increasingly for women, too), a central plank in the platform on which they have built their lives is about to be removed. As most women seem to welcome an end to their responsibilities as a mother, so many men may feel that they have had enough of work, and that the time has come for a change. But welcome or not, change is inevitably stressful (psychologists define stress as anything which forces us to change), and not even unlimited wealth, perfect health and the most meticulous planning can prevent some trepidation creeping in as we contemplate the future from the vantage point of the end of the sixth age. The change we are about to make is as dramatic as any we have ever made – starting work and becoming a parent are the only events likely to have an impact equal to that of retirement – and we shall shortly be faced with the most difficult psychological conundrum of our lives – what was the point of it all?

CHAPTER 7

Life after Work

'I know some people thought I was doing too much and I ought to slow down a bit. I said – I've retired from work, I didn't retire from life.'

An eighty-year-old Colchester woman

Although we talked to many people in their sixties, seventies and even eighties as we tried to establish how important age is in people's lives, the large-scale attitude survey which forms the heart of the Colchester study on aging stopped at sixty. So before going on to examine the seventh and final chapter of life, I think we should pause for a moment and see what general conclusions can be drawn from the story so far. At the very beginning of the book I posed a number of key questions. Does it matter how old we are? How much do we change as we get older? If we do change, is it the result of a preordained life-cycle or simply because of the events which occur at certain points of our lives? I took as my starting-point the currently fashionable theory of adult development popularized in Gail Sheehy's book *Passages*, which holds that age is vitally important. The theory maintains that everyone's life consists of a series of distinct phases, each of which calls for a different psychological attitude. Since this means that we have to make a major psychological adjustment every few years, we must expect our lives to be punctured at regular intervals by periods of emotional turmoil as we struggle to get into the right frame of mind for the next phase of life. But the theory's most controversial claim is that the timing of these stages is universal and preordained, and determined simply by our age. Regardless of what is going on in our lives, we have to change at certain ages or else we will become psychologically maladjusted.

All this suggests that we ought to be extremely conscious of our age and that we should change significantly throughout our adult lives. The theory also seems to imply that people of different generations must find it difficult to communicate with each other, and that we ought to have a strong sense that behaviour which is appropriate at one age is inappropriate at others. Not one of these predictions is born out by our research, which leaves me convinced that although the crisis view of human development may apply to the people on whose experience it was orginally based – American adults undergoing psychoanalysis – it does not describe how most of us live our lives.

The 541 adults who took part in the Colchester survey were quite happy to talk about the concept of age, and had no difficulty in answering any of the questions we put to them. But a great many of them obviously didn't see what all the fuss was about, although they were much too polite to tell us that we were wasting our (and their) time! Certainly they were aware of their age when asked to think about it, and had views on what different stages of life were like, based either on their own experience or on their observations of other people. But very few people seemed at all preoccupied with their age, except perhaps for a few days before and after significant birthdays, like the beginning of each decade.

Nor did age seem to play a vital part in their dealings with other people. Paradoxically, the majority of people we interviewed think that there *is* a generation gap, but like other researchers we did not get the impression of widespread misunderstandings between people of different ages. Nor do our results support the idea that someone's personality changes much after the early thirties. And so far as the notion of age-appropriate behaviour is concerned, the current attitude seems to be one of benign tolerance. About a quarter of our sample agreed that there are things people should stop doing as they get older, but they almost invariably turned out to be thinking of bad habits like smoking, neglecting their health or worrying too much. We expected a substantial number of them to mention 'mutton dressing as lamb', but in fact only 3 per cent of all those we talked to made this complaint.

Far from being obsessed with our age, wishing we were younger or dreading the future, we actually seem to be remarkably content with the age we are, whatever that may be. Some ages are more popular than others, but we found very little evidence that people have serious problems coming to terms with any age. They just seem to accept it, knowing that there is nothing they can do to stop the passage of time, and on the whole enjoying the advantages each new age brings rather than complaining about its drawbacks. Of course, this is an eminently sensible strategy, because, as one thirty-year-old woman pointed out to us:

If you felt life got mouldier as you got older, you'd just jump off the nearest bridge!

Perhaps we are deluding ourselves in denying that certain ages are awkward and in refusing to accept that the advantages of reaching a certain age are ever outweighed by the drawbacks. But I don't see that this matters from a practical point of view. So long as we can convince ourselves that we enjoy being whatever age we are, it makes no sense to talk about age-related crises. Similarly, if we live our lives on the assumption that we are as old as we feel, then I think the proposition becomes true – you *are* as old as you feel! An eighty-two-year-old woman we spoke to shows how realistic we are about this:

If I'm well I feel twenty-eight, but if I'm ill that's different – I feel eighty-two then.

And the same old lady provides a splendid example of how we turn even the drawbacks of a particular age to our advantage:

> When you get to a certain age, if they don't like what you say, they think you're a bit batty anyway, so you get away with it.

We have not yet explored the final, and in some ways the most difficult stage of life, but nothing I shall have to say in this chapter contradicts the two major conclusions I think can be drawn from all the evidence, both new and old, discussed in *Seven Ages*. The first is that we ought to bury the notion of universal, age-related life crises. Many people pass through the entire life-cycle without experiencing any discernible psychological crisis, and, when crises do occur, they tend to be caused by events which just happen to fall at roughly the same point in most people's lives, rather than because a person has reached a certain age. So life-crises are neither universal nor age-related.

My second conclusion is much more general: age has remarkably little effect at any stage in life on how we think of ourselves or on how we view the world. This can be seen from the comments made by two people who were both well into the seventh age. The first is a Colchester woman:

> I haven't really thought much about being eighty. I don't put things into blocks. If you just think, 'Well, I'm only one day older than I was' ... you don't really feel very much different.

The second speaker is the French philosopher Jean Paul Sartre, in an interview which took place shortly before his death in 1980. Sartre reiterates a point made earlier in this book, that although we are aware of the objective fact that we are getting older, and of the effect this has on other people, our own feelings change very little. Here is his reply when asked whether the experience of old age has altered his way of thinking:

> No. I understand from observing others what old age means to those who look at it from the outside. But I don't feel my age – so my old age is not something that in itself can teach me anything. What does teach me something is the attitude of others towards me. Old age is an aspect of me that others feel. They look at me and they say 'that old codger', and they make themselves pleasant because I shall die soon, and they are respectful. My old age is other people.

In summary, although we are aware of how old we are, we are not obsessed with it. We accept and even exploit our age, but it is not a major source of worry. So far as our feelings and behaviour are concerned, it has some effect, but more on how other people regard us than on how we see ourselves. To the extent that we are aware of changing as we get older, we don't seem at all put out by it. It's not that we don't notice the restrictions imposed for example by new responsibilities or physical decline, rather that we are content to accept them as part of a bargain, in exchange for the advantages and new opportunities each age offers.

Where the first six ages are concerned, I hope I have managed to persuade you that the bargain is more or less a fair one. Each has its drawbacks, and each offers new rewards. But it is in the seventh age that our equanimity about age seems likely to face its sternest test. The losses are all too obvious, but where are the compensating gains?

The age of uncertainty

I described the prospect which faces the newly retired

as uncertain, on the grounds that life without work seems almost a contradiction in a society based on the Protestant work ethic. But perhaps the most uncertain feature of life after retirement is its length. The average man and woman can expect to live well into their seventies, while a significant number of us don't live to reach retirement at all. The uncertainty makes it inevitable that thoughts about death should colour the final stage of our lives, and we shall see how they affect us later in the chapter. For the moment, however, it is important to notice that whatever other effect it may have, the prospect of dying does not seem to destroy our ability to make the best of whatever age we happen to be, as you can see from the comments two old ladies made on the subject:

It's a gift after three score years and ten, isn't it? A gift from God, those extra years. So you try to make the best of them.

It's no good planning for next year, or six months from now. I live from day to day. I make the most of each day.

It is also important to realize that the seventh age of life after work is divided into two distinct phases. The first runs from retirement to the mid-seventies, and many people pass through these years without developing any of the 'symptoms' of old age. At this stage of our lives we are elderly, but we quite properly resent being lumped together with the senescent and senile. The stage begins where we left off at the end of the last chapter, with the arrival of the first pension pay-out, a moment which few people greet with unalloyed pleasure, as you can see from two of the comments made to us:

The first week I drew my pension I felt very embarrassed. I felt like a fraud. I felt – there's me with a pension book in my hand – and I don't feel anything like pension age. I came out of there like a criminal. I bumped into one of my neighbours, and I hastily put my pension book in my coat pocket so she wouldn't see it.

When I went to draw my pension I felt they were trying to push me into old age and I wasn't ready to go into old age.

The second woman not only illustrates the resentment many people feel about being made to retire before they want to, but also shows how misleading it is to place everyone over the official retiring age into a single category labelled 'the old'.

The proportion of the population which consists of retired people has risen steadily in recent years, and this has been matched by an increase both in the facilities provided for them and in the amount of research devoted to their problems. Some pensioners are grateful for the changes which have taken place. As one of them remarked to us:

Pensioners today have never been so well off. Look at the facilities we have. Our mothers never had day-centres and all the things we have, did they?

But there are also dangers in the upsurge of official concern. We have come to think of the old as a problem, and old age has acquired a gloomy image based on those it hits hardest, rather than on those whose relatively problem-free approach to the end of their lives does not bring them to the attention of health professionals or journalists in search of an exposé of the scandalous conditions in old people's homes. But which gives the more accurate picture of life in the seventh age – an immobile, malnourished, lonely old widow, incapable of stringing two thoughts together and with no perceptible interest in the world around her, or a jaunty old granny, perfectly capable of looking after herself, in full possession of her faculties, and delighted that she at last has the time to devote to her wide range of interests and amusements?

Before examining in detail the changes which take place during the seventh age, there are several general points to be made about getting old. The first is that although we talk of 'the old' as if they were a single, homogeneous group, and the experience of aging a universal process which affects everyone in roughly the same way, nothing could be more misleading. The older they get, the less likely it is that any two individuals will have the same life histories, so individual differences are actually more marked among the old than among the young. Alex Comfort has described the popular stereotype of old people as 'unintelligent, unemployable, crazy and asexual'. But it is perfectly possible to live to an advanced old age without displaying any of these characteristics, and it's certainly not the case that any of them is an inevitable consequence of the biological aging process.

My second point concerns the biological process of aging, and it is as simple as it is surprising: for all the millions of dollars which have been spent trying to crack the mystery of aging, we still don't know why we get old and eventually die. Some theorists believe that aging and death are simply the result of years of physical wear and tear, or the cumulative effect of all the diseases we have experienced. They suggest that the body eventually runs out of energy to cope with stress and disease, and at that point we die. But even if most diseases – including cancer, heart disease and pneumonia – were to be eliminated, and if all accidents could be prevented, people would still die. So there must be something more basic working on the life process, and two different sorts of suggestion have been made as to what this might be.

The first idea is that all living creatures have a basic life substance, and that how long they live depends on how economically they use this substance. For example, all living animals generate heat, and if we measure how much heat is produced over a lifetime, it seems that the total amount generated is very similar in most species. A formula based simply on heat doesn't predict the average longevity of all the different species, but a slightly more elaborate version of this idea does give us some astonishingly accurate predictions. The key to the theory is the notion of *entropy*, which describes how well a particular system is organized and how much energy it has to carry out the tasks it must perform in order to survive. This is applied to living organisms by estimating their ability to adapt to and control the environments in which they live, and the prediction is that the better a species is at gaining and using information which helps it to control its environment, the longer it will live. The fact that the longest-living species tend to have the most favourable brain-to-body-weight ratios seems to support the entropy explanation of longevity, but it applies only to *species* differences rather than to differences in how long individual members of the same species live. So entropy theory cannot explain why one person lives longer than another.

To understand this, we need to abandon such grandiose notions as life-substances and entropy, and concentrate on changes in the individual cells of our bodies and the relationships between different cells. There are three basic characteristics of biological aging. The first is that the number of specific, non-dividing cells in our bodies declines throughout our lives. For example, we lose something like ten thousand brain cells every day, and similar losses take place in many other bodily systems. Lost cells are not replaced, and waste product builds up in cells which survive. Other changes can also occur inside cells to make them less efficient. A second change which may be important is that two key proteins – *collagen* and *elastin* – become progressively stiffer as we get older. About a third of all the body's protein is collagen, and it serves a binding function in skin, muscles and the vascular system. Elastin is a similar, though more supple substance, and both proteins become much less flexible as we grow older. The third change concerns those cells which reproduce themselves. There is a limit to the number of times this can happen, and each time a cell divides, the resulting daughter cells seem to be slightly less effective than the parent cell. As a result of the errors and mutations which can creep in during cell division, it has been calculated that there is probably at least one irregularity in every cell in the body of a person who has reached the age of ninety. But although there is a link between aging and cellular mutation, the rate of mutation is too slow to be the only explanation of the changes which occur in advanced old age.

This brings us back to my assertion that we simply don't know why we – or any other species – grow old. We know that the changes I have described take place, but not why they do so, and until the process is properly understood it's impossible to provide an answer to the question, why is it that one person lives longer than another? All we can say at the moment is that it seems to depend on five things: health, money (the rich on average live longer than the poor), genetic inheritance (longevity runs in families), personality (I shall have more to say about this later), and pure luck (we have to throw this in because the combination of the other factors doesn't give us a completely reliable estimate of how long someone is going to live!). However, a number of ingenious theories have been put forward as solutions to the riddle of biological aging, and although none of them provides the whole answer, all help us to understand why we change as we do in the final chapter of our lives, and they also make some suggestions as to how we might be able to slow down the process.

Some theorists maintain that the key to aging lies in the *autoimmune system* which is responsible for destroying the foreign bodies which appear for example during viral or bacterial infections. One suggestion is that this system attacks not only foreign bodies but also harmless mutant cells and neighbouring healthy cells, so that the body in effect destroys itself as it gets older. There are two reasons why this cannot be the whole story, however. The first is that some organisms do not have autoimmune systems but nevertheless grow old, and the second is that women are more prone to several diseases (arthritis, for example, which reflect malfunction of the autoimmune system, and yet still tend to live longer than men.

Having failed to find the answer to aging in the processes which occur inside individual cells, researchers have recently turned their attention to changes in the proteins which link one cell to another. As a result of this research, some scientists now maintain that the solution to the mystery of aging lies in the very processes which are at the heart of the body's campaign to stay alive, notably cell metabolism. Cell metabolism involves oxidation, and this simple process may contain the key to both life and death. We have to oxidize to stay alive, but every act of oxidation has by-products, two of which may lead eventually to our death. The first are chemical agents known as aldehydes which cause protein molecules to become bound or *cross-linked* to their neighbours. Cross-linking gives tissue a tanned, leathery appearance, and it is involved in the changes which take place in the texture of our skin as we get older. But it also leads to a deterioration in our muscles – including those in the heart and lungs – and it reflects the fact that the tissue in our bodies contains progressively less water from the moment after birth until we die.

Cross-linkage is thought to affect not only collagen and elastin, but also DNA and RNA, and the mutations which occur in cell divisions may be the result of DNA molecules becoming cross-linked. If this is the case, there is a direct connection between the cross-link theory of aging and the autoimmunity theory we have just discussed. And if the cross-link theorists are right, dieticians are going to find themselves in even greater demand than they already are, because nutrition seems to be an important factor in determining the speed at which cross-linkage occurs. For example, over-eating can increase the number of cross-linking agents in our bodies because food is not properly metabolized. Low-fat diets and fasting may slow down the formation of cross-linked molecules, and some experts believe that Vitamin E helps the body to excrete cross-linking agents. One exponent of the theory has suggested that we may one day be able to manufacture agents capable of breaking down cross-linked cells, which would allow the body to rejuvenate aging systems with new, strong elastic protein. In short, the cross-link theory of aging offers the prospect of a modern elixir – take Vitamin E and double your life-span!

However, it's important to realize that these are only theories we are describing, none of which can account for all aspects of the aging process. There is another theory which is closely related to the cross-link theory, leads to equally optimistic conclusions, and has the added benefit of making exactly the same dietary recommendations! This is known as *free-radical* theory. Free radicals are molecules with an unusually high or low number of electrons. Electrons can be gained or lost during chemical reactions involving oxidation, so free radicals are a second by-product of this crucial process, which explains why these two theories lead to the same dietary recommendations.

Free radicals are disruptive elements which bond with other molecules to disturb normal cell function, and they seem to be implicated in many of the biological changes for the worse which occur as we get older – the cross-linkage of collagen, damage to chromosomes, the accumulation of waste in cells, the provocation of self-destructive auto-immune responses via damage done to DNA or RNA, and the deterioration of cell membranes. Exponents of the free-radical theory of aging also recommend the consumption of products which contain Vitamin E (fish, eggs, vegetables, wheat-germ, and so on), since it suppresses oxidation. However, it must be said that there is as yet no hard evidence that this or any other sort of diet reliably slows down the aging process.

But do we really want to slow down the aging process? As things stand at the moment, it's clearly unrealistic to want to live forever because the wish cannot be fulfilled. But suppose that advances in medical science made it possible at least to prolong the life-span substantially. Would it be right to do so? There is one theory of aging which insists that it would not, and a final theory which claims that we are never going to reach a position where the choice needs to be made. The sociobiologists maintain that aging and death must have some evolutionary advantage or else they simply wouldn't happen. They believe that any species must continue to evolve if it is to survive, and anything which slows down the process of evolution must therefore be to a species' disadvantage. Since they also believe that evolution of a species depends on the death of its individual members, anything which keeps individuals alive once they have produced and reared offspring can only be counter-productive.

The final theory of aging we shall consider also takes the view that it is in the nature of things that cells – and we, the creatures they comprise – must die. This theory involves the notion of a *death-clock*, which is an unspecified biological process whose function it is to count how many times the cells in our bodies have divided themselves. Normal human cells divide about fifty times, after which they stop doing so and die, and the theory claims that this happens because our genetic programme no longer instructs them to reproduce themselves. No explanation is given of why the programme should change, but if this theory turns out to be true, there will be little point in pursuing any further the details of the biological deterioration which occurs as we get older, and none whatsoever in looking for magic formulae to extend the life-span. If death really is simply the final instruction in the genetic programme with which we are born, then all the ingenious theories of aging I have described will have to be replaced by the simple statement that we die of old age! At present, however, the genetic programme theory of aging is simply one theory among many, with no more evidence to support it than any of the others.

Fit for nothing?

We may not know why we grow old, but we do know quite a lot about the effects of this mysterious process, and I think the time has come to leave the theorists to their speculations and concentrate on building up a picture of what life is like in its final chapter. The full effects of the changes which take place at the level of individual cells and the proteins which link them may not become apparent until we are well into our seventies, but the social and psychological changes which distinguish this age from those before it can be seen very much earlier. Not all of them are for the worse. As with all other ages, the reality of old age seems to be less fearsome than its anticipation because when we are younger we are very selective in the inferences we make about old age from our observations of the elderly.

Adults with aging parents are all too aware of their physical limitations and they are constantly on the lookout for any sign that the old boy's mind isn't what it was. But they tend not to notice, or perhaps just refuse to believe, that old age can bring significant advantages as well. Nor is it just lay-people who have an unnecessarily gloomy picture of old age. For example, a recent survey of 2000

American medical students revealed that a third of them believed that impotence was universal amongst men over seventy, whereas in fact many couples continue to enjoy satisfying sexual relations into their eighties and beyond. (The secret of a long sex life for men lies in being very active sexually in your thirties, according to sexologists Masters and Johnson, who also advise us to remember the old adage, if you don't want to lose it, use it!) Similarly, many of the surveys which have explored the attitudes of the old are written in a way which makes it clear that the usually young or middle-aged investigators find it hard to believe that old people are not more discontented with their lot. We can summarize the findings of these surveys by saying that although the old are not as happy as younger adults, the change in how they feel about their lives is nothing like as great as the change in their objective circumstances would lead us to expect. To take just one example, the average income of the retired man is approximately half that of the average worker, and yet surveys find that money worries do not increase significantly after retirement. In other words, we may be only half as rich, but we don't *feel* it. We seem to adapt to this aspect of growing old as efficiently as we adapt to all the earlier changes in our lives, incredible though this may seem to researchers who are themselves at a stage of life where such a drop in income would be a tragedy of epic dimensions!

There are two reasons why old people might be less miserable than the young expect them to be. It could be that old age brings positive advantages, and we shall return to this possibility later. But first I think we should look more closely at the negative side of aging, to check that we don't have an exaggerated view of the extent to which the old deteriorate, physically and mentally. This task is more difficult than it sounds, because the health, strength and ability of people over sixty varies almost as much as their life expectancy. But these three factors are not unrelated –

tne first (health) is crucially important in determining the others. In fact, perhaps the most striking finding to emerge from all the research that has been carried out on old age is that it is impossible to overestimate the significance of an old person's health. Whatever aspect of age we look at, we find that health overshadows all else. Whether we are talking about changes in personality or a deterioration in mental skills, it's almost as if there were two different old ages, one for the healthy (a very small minority) and one for the diseased (the vast majority of old people). The difference is so great that some researchers have denied that there is any such thing as a biological aging process at all. They say that all the effects we usually attribute to this process are really just consequences of the fact that the biological changes described earlier in the chapter make the old increasingly prone to chronic (i.e. irreversible and incurable) illnesses. However, this is taking it too far, because, as we shall shortly see, even people who have never had a day's illness in their lives still show some physiological deterioration in old age.

Since 85 per cent of all people over sixty-five suffer from at least one chronic illness, we know very little about what *healthy* old age is like. In practice, the consequences of getting older are almost invariably confused with the effects of illness, which may go a long way towards explaining why we are still speculating about the nature of the biological aging process. But there is one classic study which leaves no doubt that many of the changes we usually attribute to aging are really the result of disease, and I shall describe the result of this study in some detail, since it gives a fascinating picture of what life can be like in old age, and one which could hardly be less like the popular stereotype embodied in Shakespeare's description of our seventh age.

In this study, forty-seven American men between the ages of sixty-five and ninety-one, who had been diagnosed as extremely healthy by their own doctors, came into the laboratory for an extensive range of medical, physiological, and psychological tests. Closer examination showed that, where their health was concerned, they actually fell into two different categories: twenty-seven of them were in perfect health in every respect, while the remaining twenty, though without clinical symptoms, turned out to have mild diseases. This difference turned out to be very significant, since on nearly all of the subsequent tests, the men in perfect health differed from the rest.

The tests on the men in perfect health produced some astonishing results. For example, they were as vigorous and capable of exercise as a group of average twenty-one-year-old men, and there was no difference between the two groups in either the flow of blood in the brain or in the amount of oxygen consumed during exercise, despite the fact that their average ages differed by half a century! In twenty-one out of twenty-three tests of intellectual performance, the old men in perfect health outshone those with a mild form of disease. On measures of intelligence which called for fast answers, and on tests of speed of reaction, both the older groups did significantly worse than the younger men, which confirms that slowing down is an inevitable consequence of aging which not even perfect health can prevent. But on measures of verbal intelligence like the size of their vocabulary, the average scores of both groups of older men were actually superior to those of the twenty-one-year-olds.

Eleven years later, the old men returned to the laboratory for a further batch of tests. Since their average age was now eighty-one, it is not surprising that about half of the original sample had died. But in this respect too there was confirmation of the enormous significance which even mild disease has in old age: whereas only 30 per cent of the men who had shown mild symptoms earlier were now alive, 63 per cent of whose who had been in perfect health were still going strong. And they *were* going strong, too, since the researchers found remarkably little change in their performance on the battery of tests they were asked to carry out. But perhaps the most significant finding to emerge from this study is that two factors stood out above all others in distinguishing the survivors from those who had died in the years which separated the two test sessions. The secret of survival seemed to lie in not smoking and in having an organized and reward-ing living pattern. We don't need to be told that smoking is bad for our health, but the very strong link between life-style and staying alive confirms what many people have long suspected, that the timing of a person's death is not just decided by biological factors.

These healthy old men stand as an object lesson of what old age *can* be like, but sadly they are the exception rather than the rule. For most of us, old age is a very different experience. So far as the outer shell is concerned, our skin becomes wrinkled, age spots and warts appear, and the small blood vessels become increasingly frail and break, producing black and blue spots. We tend to develop a stoop, as shrink-ing muscles accentuate the effect of many years of poor posture. Our bones also become hollower and weaker, and so more likely to break. Such changes are probably inevitable, but they don't seem to be a source of great bitterness to the old people who experience them. Old people expect them, as they expect a degree of physical infirmity, and they even get a sense of relief from knowing that their age excuses them from certain things, as you can see from two of the comments made to us by old people in Colchester. The first speaker is an octogenarian lady, whom we asked how she felt about the way her appearance had changed:

A bit depressed. Well, the skin's all horrible. Then I got a magnifying glass and had a look, and I thought I'm a real old hag now. And then I thought, you silly old thing, you're eighty-two! . . . It's silly to be disappointed at my age, isn't it?

And here is a seventy-eight-year-old widower describing some of the pros and cons of old age:

> It takes me all the damn day to get up and put my clothes on. And that's why I never put them on if I can help it . . . I please myself what I do and how I do it, and that's a great advantage.

We took this man's account of the advanced state of his physical decline with a generous pinch of salt because we knew that he is actually still a keen ballroom dancer! But he and others like him convinced us that even the seventh age has its consolations.

A deterioration in both sight and hearing seems to be an inevitable consequence of old age, though our sense of taste and smell is much less affected. But perhaps the most important result of the physiological changes described earlier is that our bodies come to respond much less vigorously to both external and internal threats, which is why our health deteriorates. Since we react less violently to infection, the symptoms of disease are much less marked in the old than in the young which is why old people's illnesses are often well-advanced before they go to a doctor. Their diminished physiological capacity to respond to change also explains the fact that old people are more affected by extremes of temperature, and why overeating, dehydration and taking in too much liquid too quickly affects them more than the young.

Although we associate old age with illness, it is worth noting that acute (i.e. infectious) diseases are actually much more common in childhood. But the old are more susceptible to chronic illness, though doctors' complaints that they 'block' hospital beds are hardly borne out by the results of a study carried out in Glasgow recently, which showed that four out of five patients over the age of sixty-five leave hospital within forty days of being admitted. Another recent study suggests that it is the old who ought to be complaining about doctors rather than vice versa. A survey of elderly patients admitted to a hospital in Manchester revealed that 10 per cent of them were there as a direct result of taking drugs prescribed by their GPs, and that more than 60 per cent of them had been prescribed drugs in unnecessarily large quantities. Several of them who were confused to the point of dementia made a remarkable recovery once they were taken off the major tranquillizer chlorpromazine (trade name Largactil), which in one case had been prescribed simply because the patient had been worried about being acutely constipated! Such horror stories cannot do much for an old person's peace of mind (there is no reason to suppose that doctors elsewhere in the country are any less culpable than their Manchester colleagues), and they suggest that, for all the advances in medical science, things have not improved all that much since the eighteenth century, when Voltaire wrote his famous indictment of the medical profession: 'Doctors pour drugs of which they know little, to cure diseases of which they know less, into human beings of whom they know nothing!'

But although nearly 80 per cent of people over seventy suffer from arthritis and rheumatism, the two most common non-fatal chronic diseases, and most of the major 'killer diseases' become more frequent after middle age (cirrhosis of the liver is one of the few which do not), it is not these diseases of the body which make younger people frightened of growing old. It is diseases of the mind.

According to popular mythology, madness is an old person's affliction. If we are talking about neurosis and psychosis, this is simply untrue, because these general forms of psychopathology are actually no more common among the old than among young and middle-aged adults. But there are three types of psychological dysfunction which are much more common among the old – suicide, depression and organic brain syndromes. The suicide rate for the over-sixty-fives in America is three times that of the general population, and suicide is often preceded by severe depression. Mild depression is quite common in old age – perhaps one in five otherwise healthy old people experience it and it can be triggered by an event like retirement or the death of a friend. Severe depression is usually the result of a combination of unfortunate circumstances, and researchers have constructed a league-table of the events old people find most stressful. The death of a spouse comes at the top of this list, followed by being put into an institution, the death of a close relative, major personal injury or disease, losing a job, and divorce, in descending order of importance. But being widowed comes far ahead of all the others, and it seems to affect men more severely than women, no doubt for the same reasons that men suffer more at divorce, which we discussed in Chapter 4.

Like other forms of disease, organic brain syndromes fall into two categories: those which can be reversed and those where full recovery is not possible, though substantial improvement may be. Their causes are very varied – they include metabolic malfunctioning, vitamin deficiencies, alcoholism, the use of certain drugs, or a stroke – and the list of possible symptoms encompasses a wide range of intellectual and personality disturbances, in varying degrees of severity. But although the symptoms can include gross disorientation and the inability even to remember one's own name, it is important to know that in about a quarter of all cases, organic brain syndrome is completely reversible, and even in those where it is not, proper treatment and therapy can often lead to substantial improvement. Sometimes a stroke can lead to a chronic brain syndrome. Strokes are more common in men, and the blood clot which suddenly disrupts the supply of oxygen to a part of the brain is the result of many years' accumulation of cholesterol leading to 'hardening of the arteries'. Typically, a stroke is just the latest of a series of symptoms of the development of cerebral arteriosclerosis, and sufferers often get advance warning in the form of loss of memory, headaches, blackouts or palpitations. By no means all strokes lead to chronic syndromes, and the best way of preventing them is to avoid the combination of too much cholesterol and too little exercise in middle age.

The second type of chronic brain syndrome is senile dementia, and this is less well understood. It seems to be caused by the dissolution of brain cells independently of arterial changes, its average age of onset is about seventy-five, and it is more common in women than in men. We don't know why the brain cells degenerate in this way, nor why senility affects only some people. Its symptoms are well known – gradual decay of memory, deterioration of personality, and an increasing inability to look after oneself, which may eventually lead to institutionalization. But there is no simple connection between the extent of brain damage and the severity of symptoms. How severely old people are affected by senile dementia seems to depend on a complicated mixture of their previous personality, their genes and the circumstances they are living in. This illustrates the very important point that although we know a little about the physiology of aging and rather more about how people's personality and behaviour change as they get older, we are still very much in the dark when it comes to the question of how these two vital aspects of the seventh age are related to each other. Before leaving the subject of dementia, it is worth noticing that many people's idea of old age is based on the small minority of old people who become senile. Two statistics show how wrong this is. Only 1 to 2 per cent of the population are admitted to hospital suffering from a mental disorder at any point of their lives, and only 5 per cent of us end up in any form of institution.

All change, or more of the same?

So far as changes in personality and intellectual ability in old age are concerned, the picture is very much what you would expect to find on the basis of what has been said in this and in earlier chapters of *Seven Ages*. Those of us fortunate enough to remain in good health can reasonably expect to reach even advanced old age without becoming radically different from the people we were in middle age. At the other extreme, brain damage can change an old person out of all recognition. The majority of old people come somewhere between the two. However, the impression given by most studies of old age that there is a small but significant change in many aspects of personality and intellectual functioning is probably misleading. The truth of the matter is that some people change a lot and others hardly at all, and it is only because researchers tend to lump the two together that we get the impression that everyone changes significantly. This applies particularly to memory and to problem-solving ability, both of which can hold up remarkably well in old age, as can general knowledge and most types of know-how. So far as memory is concerned, the popular idea that old people 'live in the past' seems to be a fallacy. Research shows that when memory fades, it is the older memories which go first, whether it's a question of recognizing pictures of famous people from newspaper photos taken over the years, or recalling events from different times in one's own life. Nor is it the case that old age inevitably makes us less good at controlling our behaviour in response to verbal instructions. Experiments show that this aspect of our intellectual ability holds up well into the eighties, and only falls away seriously after the age of ninety, by which time most of us are long past caring! Generally, where there are changes, it's not that we become less effective at performing tasks, just that we do them rather differently.

Nor do we necessarily find it impossible to master new material, as you can see from the results of a remarkable experiment carried out in Australia in the early 1970s. As part of a much larger investigation into intelligence in the elderly carried out at the University of Queensland, eighty volunteers between the ages of sixty-three and ninety-one (average age seventy) were invited to join a course in learning to read German. The average IQ of the group was 102, just two points higher than that of the general population, and their earlier educational achievements were not impressive: half of them had had only primary schooling, and only one had a university degree. The jobs they had done ranged from being a waitress to being a teacher, and many of them were widows living on their state pension. In short, this was not an élite group, but simply a bunch of ordinary, reasonably intelligent elderly men and women, whose only distinguishing characteristic was their willingness to take part in a project which many of them were certain had no chance of success! Most of them were in good health, though a number of them had arthritis, and the ninety-one-year-old was actually suffering from a terminal disease.

Teaching methods were deliberately tailored to fit the students' needs. Since many of them were worried about 'going back to school at our age', care was taken to avoid a classroom atmosphere. They were not encouraged to compete with each other, but to proceed at whatever pace suited them best. Teaching methods and materials were designed to exploit the students' greatest asset – their experience of life and familiarity with their own language. A certain amount of rote learning is obviously necessary to learn any language, but this was made less painful in the early stages by presenting it in the form of cleverly constructed card games. The results of this experiment put paid once and for all to the idea that old age puts an end to intellectual activity. Fifteen of the original starters dropped out, but forty-seven of the remaining sixty-five passed the test usually taken by children after three years of studying German at secondary school, within three months of starting the course! After another three months, thirty-eight members of the group had reached the equivalent of O-level standard, while some of those who had failed the easier exam the first time now passed it.

So the old *can* learn, and they will, provided the teaching allows for and even exploits their age. The Queensland study also shows that a person's experience of old age can be transformed by successfully completing a project like the one I have just described. Most of the students were initially staggered by the progress they were making, but they soon came to revise their opinion of themselves and adjusted their thinking about old age.

But unfortunately, the Queensland German speakers, like the old men in perfect health we discussed earlier, only show us what old people *can* do, not how most old people do actually spend their lives. Most of them have swallowed the propaganda, and would share the Queenslanders' original conviction that they simply weren't up to a task like mastering a new language. Here is what one seventy-eight-year-old Colchester man had to say about his declining powers:

A job we could have done in an hour takes us all day, and then you say, 'What have I been doing?' We're much slower on the uptake, it takes longer for things to sink in. You have to say to somebody, 'What did you say?' And when they've said it again, you still wonder what they've said.

This comment reminds us of the fact that a general slowing up must be expected as we get older. The fact that the Queenslanders passed in three months an exam which secondary schoolchildren take after three years does not mean that they were faster or even as fast as children at taking in individual pieces of new knowledge. They had a wider range of background knowledge to draw on and, unlike children, they could devote all their intellectual energy to one subject.

Talk of slowing up brings us to the question of personality changes in old age, because some researchers believe that old people work slower not merely because their brains now take longer to respond, but because they like to work at their own pace, and refuse to be hustled into doing everything as quickly as possible. This is thought to be part of a more general change of personality towards *interiority*, which is perhaps the most significant psychological characteristic of the final chapter in a person's life.

As we approach the end of our lives, we become less interested in the outside world and more concerned with ourselves. In the earlier chapters of the book, I identified a series of psychological tasks we have to solve at various stages of our lives. Each one forces us to change our attitudes, which is why Erik Erikson refers to them as crises, and the most important of them are the trust-versus-mistrust crisis of infancy, the identity crisis of adolescence, the intimacy-versus-isolation crisis of the twenties, the generativity-versus-stagnation crisis of mid-life, and, finally, the psychological task which becomes increasingly important the nearer we get to the end of our lives – the integrity-versus-despair crisis.

In many ways, the last is the most difficult psychological task we are ever confronted with. Some old people find it beyond them, and the bafflement, bitterness and sometimes despair this can cause is the most heartrending aspect of old age. The task is to come to terms with yourself, to find some justification for your life, and to reconcile yourself to the fact that it is going to end. What makes it so difficult is that the objectives appear to be mutually contradictory: the easier you find it to convince yourself that you are a worthwhile person whose life has been useful and important, the more difficult it may be to come to terms with the fact that you are going to die. But as we shall shortly see, most old people do manage to come to terms with their own death, and, paradoxically, it is the person who believes that his or her life has been most worthwhile who seems to have least qualms about the prospect of it coming to an end.

Given the difficulty of the task, we can hardly be surprised if old people become less involved in what is going on around them and more interested in their own thoughts. And it may have some bearing on a very important practical question. What is the recipe for a successful old age? Some people say that unless old people keep themselves active, busy and engaged, they are bound to turn into vegetables and become a misery to themselves and a burden on others. Others take quite the opposite view. They say that an old person who continues to devote his energy to wordly matters cannot possibly have time to solve the psychological problems of old age, and so will become increasingly frightened since he will not have come to terms with his approaching death. We now know that there is no single pattern which can be recommended as the recipe for a successful old age. As so often, it seems to be a case of different strokes for different folks. Some old people obviously thrive on a diet of constant activity, though research shows that a small number of deeply rewarding interests seems to be a more successful formula than a large number of more superficial ones. There seem to be three different types of 'active' approach to old age. You can either treat it as a challenge, and pursue activities like our seventy-year-old's ballroom dancing which make no concessions to your age, or you can take up new hobbies and interests which are thought to be more appropriate for the retired. According to one recent British study, some 38 per cent of men and 35 per cent of women adopt one or other of these approaches to life after retirement. Alternatively, you can invest your energy in people rather than activities, and become the hub of a large network of friends and relatives. The same source calculates that a further 35 per cent of retired men and women fall into this category.

But rather less than a third of the retired people in this study had settled for a very different approach to life after work. They followed the pattern described earlier of withdrawing into themselves and confining their interest in the outside world to watching television and perhaps reading newspapers. In fact, any one of these approaches can lead to a happy old age, and which one a given person is likely to be happiest with is largely determined by their earlier personality, as we saw in Chapter 6. Personality changes less in old age than many people imagine, and most of the changes that do occur can be understood as a response to the psychological tasks old people are trying to solve. The shift of emphasis towards the more feminine side of a man's nature which we discussed in the last chapter continues, and the reverse may happen with women. Whether women's increasing dominance and men's greater submissiveness is the cause or an effect of the fact that the balance of power between the two sexes tilts more and more in women's favour during the seventh age is not certain. But there is a definite change, and it may not be to a man's disadvantage that he is no longer expected to be a doer, if it allows him more time to ponder the meaning of it all.

Old people do become more inward-looking and egocentric, if not actually eccentric, and they may seem increasingly dogmatic. But it's not so much that their personality changes, more that they become more like themselves. The final search for self-understanding accentuates existing characteristics, and if old people become increasingly unwilling to debate issues or to look at every side of a question, they can surely be forgiven for thinking that they have more important things to think about. The move towards interiority has a number of other important practical consequences.

The old often start to show a degree of age exclusiveness unmatched since young adulthood. Husbands and wives can become tremendously important to each other in old age and many studies show that people are more satisfied with their marriages now than at any other stage of adult life. Of course it could just be that only well-matched couples are still married, and the fact that only a minority of the marriages which have survived divorce will not have been ended by widowhood before the beginning of the post-retirement era must bring the surviving couples closer together. But whatever the reason for it, a recent American study found that more than 90 per cent of old married couples describe their relationship as very happy or happy, and the majority of them say their marriages have improved over the years. If more proof is required of the importance the old attach to their marriages, we need look no further than the results of a recent British study which found that the death rate among men and women in the year after they are widowed is ten times higher than that among people of the same age who are still married. If that isn't dying of a broken heart, I don't know what is, and it surely confirms that marriage is another respect in which the seventh age can be a real improvement over what has gone before.

Friends and *confidants* also become very important in old age. The more an old person becomes involved in making sense of his life and his impending death, the more likely it is that he will come to believe that only the old can understand the old. The importance of close friends of similar age can be gauged from two sets of research findings. The first shows that the death of a close friend is one of the most stressful events in old people's lives, and the second that old people who have *confidants* are considerably less likely to become mentally disturbed than those who do not. But this does not seem to apply to everybody, since there is evidence that people who have never had close friends at any stage of their lives are not particularly unhappy in old age. So it seems that where friends are concerned, what you've never had, you don't miss.

Old people who do value friends know that it is risky to confine their friendships exclusively to others of the same age. An eighty-year-old woman we talked to in Colchester was clearly aware of the dangers:

I think some quite eminent person said one had to constantly repair the wall of friendship because it crumbles . . . otherwise you're left alone without protection. It's not good to stay in one age group, but to make friends with people younger than yourself as well as people who are older. It means you're not so bereft.

The same woman went on to illustrate another significant advantage old age brings:

One meets more people and one learns how to find something in which you can make a point of contact. It's easier to make the approach than it is when you're younger – one doesn't worry quite so much about the impression one makes on people. When you're young you're terribly anxious that you shouldn't make a bad impression . . . But one learns one doesn't always lose people by saying what one thinks.

The last years

The question of loneliness in old age is one that concerns health professionals greatly. The average woman can expect ten years of life as a widow, and about half the over seventy-five-year olds in this country live alone. But once again, surveys don't find that living alone necessarily makes old people feel lonely. As one old lady touchingly put it to us:

No, if you live alone you don't have to be lonely. If people like you, that's the main thing . . . If people like you, and say, 'Hello Biddie, nice to see you,' that's everything to me, the greatest thing, friendship and love. To love and be loved.

This brings us to one of the most controversial topics concerning how the old should be treated. What is the best and kindest solution to the problems of old people who reach a point where they can no longer look after themselves? Contrary to popular belief, this is not a new problem, nor is there any reason why we should reproach ourselves for being less humane in our treatment of the old than our ancestors were. The idea that there was ever a golden age for the old is not supported by the study of literature. The Ancient Greeks, for example, whose average life-expectancy seems to have been about thirty years, regarded old age as a disease to be resisted, and Shakespeare was only reflecting sentiments widely held at the time in the devastating portrait of old age he puts into Jacques' mouth in *As You Like It*. But the fact that younger adults have never found that sympathy and understanding for the old comes naturally to them does not absolve us from our responsibilities towards today's old people.

When one of them becomes unable to live an independent life, there are usually only two practical alternatives – moving in with younger relatives or moving into an old persons' community or home. There is some disagreement among the experts as to which course of action is preferable, and there is probably no general answer. Different cases call for different solutions. But although old people's homes do not have a very attractive image, the differences in lifestyle between different generations, and the problems an already confused old person may have in adjusting to a régime presided over by someone she once held sway over are sufficient to convince me that the decision to 'have mother come and live with us' is, more often than not, the wrong one. A young mother in Colchester describes some of the strains this arrangement can impose on all three generations involved:

> There are lots of problems in many ways with the young and the old . . . grandchildren play her pop music and mother can't adjust herself to it at all. It makes it a bit of a strain for me, keeping the peace between the young and the old . . . It does cause me a lot of worry – a lot of strain – and I'm always on edge all the time; but we survive.

This family did survive, but the arrangement of having the old woman living with them did not. She had moved in after having a heart attack, but she eventually decided that the problems of three-generational living outweighed the risk of having a second thrombosis when there was no one to come to her assistance.

> You see, Sylvia and Johnny were at their home. It wasn't mine and I accepted it . . . I've accepted things all my life and I accepted that. But since I've got better I would like a place of my own.

So at the age of eighty-three she moved into a small flat on her own, and although both she and her daughter were aware of the risks, both seemed to be convinced that the change was for the better. Here is how the old lady viewed the situation:

> I've never been lonely. I knit and crochet and occupy my mind so I never get lonely . . . My legs will never be right, I know that it's thrombosis in my legs. I've got everything to live for now. . . . Good look-out there, isn't it [referring to the view from her flat]? It's not big but it's mine.

Her daughter, too, was relieved, if worried and slightly guilt-ridden:

> I shall make sure that mother is all right and I shall feel a lot happier because of not being nasty . . . I love my mother and I love my family and it puts me in rather an awkward position, to keep the peace . . . I think she'll be better, you know, for her peace of mind and also for mine . . . There are plenty of us to come and see her, she'll never be lonely and she's got plenty of friends.

To quote the report of a recent World Health Organization working-party on the subject, 'solutions compelling the family to take charge are not always the most efficient, economical or humane.' Perhaps the nearest thing to an ideal solution to a problem which can only become more acute as the number of old people rises, is to be found in old people's communities in Australia and America. These provide a range of accommodation, from flats in which the old people live virtually independent lives to full hospital care, with easy transit in both directions between the two. But of course there are examples of old people coming to live with their relatives to the satisfaction of all concerned, and I can only repeat that there is no single right course of action which should always be followed.

Solutions can be found to the practical problems of old age, but how successful are the old at solving the psychological problems posed by the seventh age? Perhaps the most useful characteristics we can possess at this stage of our lives are flexibility and acceptance. There *are* changes which need to be made, and the unpalatable fact of our own mortality to be accepted, and there is some evidence - still tantalizingly incomplete – that we can predict in advance how easy an individual will find it to come to terms with the final realities on the basis of how well they have made adjustments earlier in life. For example, according to the results of one study which followed the progress of a group of Americans for more than forty years of their adult lives, people who have problems in resolving the intimacy-versus-isolation crisis in their twenties, and find it difficult to maintain an intimate relationship at the age of thirty, seem to have most difficulty in coping with the final psycho-social crisis of old age.

Those who make the earlier adjustments without difficulty need not be afraid that their ability to adapt to new circumstances will suddenly desert them when they need it most, and even those who have problems with the earlier adjustments sometimes acquire an unexpected maturity and serenity when faced with the final hurdle. Younger people often complain about the way the old ramble on about the past, but research shows that the tendency some old people have to review the events of their lives can actually serve an important psychological function, especially for those who feel most bitter about the way life has treated them. We saw earlier that such people often find it most difficult to come to terms with old age, but there is evidence from a study of old people living in London that life-reviewing can be therapeutic for such people, and that it increases their chances of facing death with equanimity.

We saw in Chapter 6 that people in their fifties seem to be less frightened of death than those in their forties. Some of the strongest fears of death expressed to us in interviews came from people in their teens and twenties, and we found among the old that advancing age seems to produce a greater interest in death, but certainly no greater fear. As one old woman put it to us:

I feel that from the day you're born, your life is mapped out for you. As for death, well, whatever way that comes, I can't stop it, so it doesn't worry me.

The same woman makes the point that the reflections of the old often lead to tranquillity:

When I look back, I had a lot of worries from one thing and another. But as you get older you finally grow up, and I think you have more peace of mind.

An eighty-two-year-old woman was equally philosophical, and she shows the solace that many old people derive from religious faith:

Am I afraid of death? No. It's an inevitable experience of life, and if you have faith and believe in the after-life, well, you start again, I hope.

There are people whose fear of death grows as they get older – we saw in Chapter 5 that narcissists are particularly vulnerable in this respect – but most of the people we talked to seemed more worried about the inconvenience their death might cause other people than about the fact that the world would soon have to manage without them. Here is how the eighty-year-old lady with whose robust comment on retirement I began the chapter described her feelings about death: -

Dying doesn't worry me. The only thing I do worry about is if I go unexpectedly and leave a muddle for everyone to clear up. I don't think I'm afraid of dying. I think I lost my fear of death a long time ago.

It is more than four hundred years since the French essayist Montaigne dismissed death as but an end to dying, but I do not think we have become any less philosophical about it in the intervening centuries. We remain resolutely pragmatic about our age until the end, accepting the drawbacks and making what we can of the new opportunities that even the final age offers. So I see no reason to revise the conclusions drawn at the beginning of this chapter. For most of us, age never ranks high on our list of worries. We are aware of how old we are, but very few of us have any problem about adjusting to the passage of time, and even fewer lose sleep wondering how they will come to terms with being older. On the contrary, we seem to be incorrigible optimists on the subject of 'the next age', for how else can we explain the fact that so many people reach the end of the seventh age fervently hoping that there will be an eighth!

Technical Appendix
The Colchester Survey on Aging

by

Jane Ritchie, Social and Community Planning Research

The research study of mid-life years, carried out by Social and Community Planning Research (SCPR), was funded by London Weekend Television. The general purpose of the study was to determine how people view the process of aging at different stages of adult life. More specifically, the study aimed to examine how attitudes, behaviour and circumstances change with age and to identify any critical stages that occur during adult development.

The research was conducted in two stages. At the first stage, a qualitative study was undertaken involving individual in-depth interviews and group discussions with people aged between 19 and 60. This was followed by structured individual interviews with a probability sample of adults ages 29 to 58.

The Qualitative Study

At the qualitative stage, 8 group discussions and 20 individual depth interviews were conducted. The groups were designed to involve people of similar ages and to represent different stages of life events, and there were 6–8 people in each group. They were structured as follows:

Ages 19-25: half men, half women; half single, half married without children (2 groups).

Ages 30-37: half men, half women; all married; half with youngest child 5 or under, half youngest child over 5 (2 groups).

Ages 38-45: half men, half women; all married; half with youngest child 11 or under, half with youngest child over 11 (2 groups).

Ages 50-60: half men, half women; all married; half with children still at home, half with all children left home (2 groups).

The 20 in-depth interviews were conducted with both men and women from four age groups (30-36; 37-43; 44-50; 51-60), again representing different marital and family circumstances. An analysis of the qualitative stage is described in a report prepared by SCPR.

The Interview Survey

The interview survey was carried out during the winter of 1979/80 in the Borough of Colchester. The decision to confine the study to one area had the advantage of eliminating regional variations from the results, a factor that would have been difficult to allow for within such a limited sample size.

It was intended that the survey should provide 500 interviews with adults aged between 29 and 58 inclusive. Within this age range, it was required that approximately equal numbers of men and women should be interviewed and that the sample should contain roughly similar proportions of middle-class and working-class respondents.

Sample Design and Selection

The sample was selected in three stages. At the first stage, 20 polling district areas were selected from within 18 wards in Colchester. In order to accommodate roughly equal proportions of middle- and working-class groups, the areas were selected from available data so that half would contain a high proportion of middle-class households and the other half a high proportion of working-class households. The main index for determining the selection was the type and tenure of housing in the areas as identified by the local authority and small area statistics.

Once the 20 areas had been selected, a random sample of *addresses* was selected from within each. Before making this selection, an estimate had to be made about the number of households that would contain eligible (i.e. aged 29-58) individuals. From information in the General Household Survey on the age structure of households, it was estimated that 60-65 per cent of households would contain a person in the required age range. There was, however, uncertainty about the precise proportion in Colchester. Moreover, an allowance had to be made for non-response and other non-productive addresses. In total, 1500 addresses were issued sequentially as the levels of eligible and productive interviews became known.

The third stage of selection took place at the address itself, since only one interview per address was required. The interviewer therefore had to ascertain whether anyone at the addresses was within the specified age range and, if so, to list all eligible people. To ensure a random selection of individuals from the addresses, a modified form of the 'Kish grid' was used.

Table 1. Statement of response at fieldwork stage

	Number
Sampled addresses	1500
Not covered	87
Total covered	1413
Addresses out of scope (i.e. vacant, business/industrial premises, demolished, not traced)	46
Total addresses in scope	1367
No eligible individuals (29–58) found at address	573
Assumed to contain no eligible individuals	52*
Total ineligible addresses	625 (46% of addresses in scope)
Total addresses where eligible person found	742 = 100%
Interviews achieved	461 = 62%
Interviews not achieved	281 = 38%

Reasons for non-response

Refused interview	164 = 22%
Refused to give information for selection	31* = 4%
Broken appointment – could not be recontacted	18 = 2%
No contact with selected person	24 = 3%
No contact with anyone at address (no selection possible)	21* = 3%
Selected person away/in hospital/ill/ incapacitated during survey period	19 = 3%
Other reasons for no interview	4 = 1%

Note: Where no information about the age structure of the household was obtained, estimates (marked*) have been made about the number which would have proved eligible, based on the proportions found (by ward) in the remaining population.

Fieldwork

The 31 interviewers who worked on the project received a one-day personal briefing before embarking on the fieldwork. In total, 1413 of the 1500 addresses were covered by the interviewing team. The outcome at these addresses is summarized in Table 1.

Two features of the response rates are worthy of note. First, 46 per cent of households did not contain any individuals aged 29-58, a 6 per cent larger proportion than the maximum anticipated to be out of scope. The second, and more striking feature of the response, is the high rate of refusal to participate in the study. This poor response may have been partly a result of the door-step selection process; but there was also more resistance to participate in an interview than is usual.

There are several possible explanations for this. Asking for ages at a very early stage of the contact may have alienated potential respondents. Similarly, the purpose and content of the interview may have seemed rather vague and uncompelling. The fact that the study was being undertaken partly to provide information for a television series may also have made people uneasy about participating.

Another explanation for poor response, supported to some extent by the data, is that people who felt vulnerable about the process of aging would not wish to answer a lengthy questionnaire on the subject. The levels of response were lower among the 30-year group. This would suggest there may be some bias in the responses obtained related to the subject matter of the survey.

The extent to which any of these factors were the cause of the low response rate is uncertain. It is felt that all of them may have played some part, resulting in a cumulatively high level of refusals. Although the effect of the poor response cannot be quantified and no correction for it is possible, it does need to be borne in mind in the interpretation of the data.

The Interviews

Information was collected from respondents by means of a personal interview and a self-completion booklet. The broad areas of coverage within the interview, some of which arose from the qualitative stage, were as follows:

Socio-demographic characteristics
Pattern of live events to date (e.g. marriage, children, etc.)
Views on stages in adult development
Attitude/behaviour changes
Changes in life priorities/values
Physical aging
Perceived changes with aging
Employment/careers
Friends/counsellors/mentors
Leisure activities
Health and physical fitness
Anxieties/dreams/treats
Generation gap
Age related/appropriate behaviour
Anticipation of aging
Chosen ages

The average duration of the interviews was 45-50 minutes, while the self-completion booklets took an average of 10-15 minutes to complete.

Coding, Editing and Analysis

The interview questionnaires contained a number of open-ended questions where verbatim answers were recorded. Codes were later assigned to these answers, which reflected the range and diversity of the material collected. All the questionnaires were subjected to a clerical edit to check the consistency and continuity of the data. The information was then transferred to punchcards and a full computer edit of the data was carried out before any analysis began.

Before any tabulations could be run, the data had to be weighted to correct for the sample selection of individuals. This was necessary because a single interview per address meant that an individual's chance of selection was inversely proportionate to the number of eligible people at the address. In all tabulations, weighted and unweighted bases have been shown.

For the purposes of the social class analysis, middle class was defined as social class groups I, II and III (non manual), and working class as all remaining social class categories.[1] The data were not reweighted a second time to correct for the over-representation of middle-class respondents.

The age and sex distribution of the people interviewed is shown in Table 2, together with the proportions we might have expected from small area census data. As noted earlier, the proportion in their late 40s and 50s is lower than would be expected. Although some of this difference may be accounted for by sampling error, it is likely that it reflects a higher refusal rate among the higher age ranges.

[1] The Registrar General's classification of occupations was used to define the respondents' social class using the occupation of the head of household.

Table 2. *Comparison of age and sex distribution of sample interviewed and area population*

Age	Men	Sample Women	Total	Population Men	Women	Total
	%	%	%	%	%	%
29 – 34	32	31	31	23*	22*	23*
35 – 44	33	36	36	33	32	33
45 – 54	26	22	24	31	33	32
55 – 58	9	10	10	13*	13*	13*
Base: total						
aged 29-58	100%	100%	100%	100%	100%	100%
Weighted	350	458	808	12276	12780	25056
Unweighted	199	262	461			

*Estimates have been made in these categories where age ranges did not exactly correspond with the survey groups.

Further Reading

For the benefit of readers interested in pursuing the subject further, the following pages contain a list of the more important books and articles I used as source material for *Seven Ages*.

Abrams, Mark, *Beyond Three Score and Ten*. London: Age Concern Publications, 1978.

Allman, L. R., and Jaffe, D. T., *Readings in Adult Psychology: Contemporary Perspectives*. New York: Harper and Row, 1977.

Amster, L. E., and Krauss, H. H., 'The relationship between life crises and mental deterioration in old age'. *International Journal of Aging and Human Development* 5, pp. 51-6, 1974.

Aries, Philippe, *Centuries of Childhood*. London: Jonathan Cape, 1962; Harmondsworth: Penguin, 1973.

Belsky, J., and Steinberg, L. D., 'The effects of day care: a critical review'. *Child Development* 49, pp. 929-49, 1978.

Berndt, T. J., 'Developmental change in conformity to peers and parents'. *Developmental Psychology* 15, pp. 608-16, 1979.

Birren, J. E., and Schaie, K. W., *Handbook of the Psychology of Aging*. New York: Van Nostrand Reinhold, 1977.

Blackstone, T., and Weinreich-Haste, H., 'Why are there so few women scientists and engineers?' *New Society*, 21 February 1980.

Blythe, Ronald, *A View in Winter*. London: Allen Lane, 1979.

Bower, T. G. R., *A Primer of Infant Development*. San Francisco: Freeman, 1977.

Brown, G. W., and Harris, T., *Social Origins of Depression*. London: Tavistock, 1978.

Bryant, P. E., *Perception and Understanding in Young Children*. London: Methuen, 1974.

Butler, R. N., 'The life review: an interpretation of reminiscence in the aged'. In B. N. Neugarten (ed.), *Middle Age and Aging*, Chicago; Chicago University Press, 1968.

Clarke, A. M., and Clarke, A. D. B., *Early Experience: Myth and Evidence*. London: Open Books. 1976.

Clausen, J. A., 'Glimpses into the social world of middle age.' *International Journal of Aging and Human Development* 7, pp. 99-106, 1976.

Coleman, J. C., *Relationships in Adolescence*. London: Routledge and Kegan Paul, 1974.

Coleman, P. G., 'Measuring reminiscence characteristics from conversation as adaptive features of old age.' *International Journal of Aging and Human Development* 5, pp. 281-94, 1974.

Conger, J., *Adolescence: Generation under Pressure*. London: Harper and Row, 1979.

Crawford, M. P., 'Retirement rituals: the farewell to work'. *New Society*, 20 December 1973.

Crawford, M. P., and Hooper, D., 'Menopause, aging and family'. *Social Science and Medicine* 7, pp. 469-82, 1973.

Dalto, C. A., Ajzen, I., and Kaplan, K. J., 'Self-disclosure and attraction: effects of intimacy and desirability on beliefs and attitudes'. *Journal of Research in Personality* 13, pp. 127-38, 1979.

Damon, W., *The Social World of The Child*. San Francisco: Jossey-Bass, 1977.

Dennis, W., 'Creative productivity between the ages of 20 and 80'. *Journal of Gerontology* 21, pp. 1-8, 1966.

Donaldson, M., *Children's Minds*. London: Fontana, 1978.

Erikson, E. (ed.) *Adulthood*. New York. W. W. Norton, 1978.

Farrell, C., *My Mother Said*. London: Routledge and Kegan Paul, 1978.

Fogarty, M. P., *Forty to Sixty: How We Waste the Middle Aged*. London : Centre for Studies in Social Policy, 1975.

Franklin, H. C., and Holding, D. H., 'Personal memories at different ages'. *Quarterly Journal of Experimental Psychology* 29, pp. 527-32, 1977.

Gillis, J. R., *Youth and History: Tradition and Change in European Age Relations, 1770-Present.* New York: Academic Press, 1974.

Gould, R. L., *Transformation: Growth and Change in Adult Life.* New York: Simon and Schuster, 1978.

Haan, N., 'Personality organization of well-functioning younger people and older adults'. *International Journal of Aging and Human Development* 7, pp. 117-27, 1976.

Haan, N., and Day, D., 'A longitudinal study of change and sameness in personality development: adolescence to later adulthood'. *International Journal of Aging and Human Development* 5, pp. 11-40, 1974.

Helms, D. B., and Turner, J. S., *Exploring Child Behaviour.* Philadelphia: Sanders, 1978.

Ivester, C., and King, K., 'Attitudes of adolescent towards the aged'. *Gerontologists* 17, pp. 85-9, 1977.

Katz, M. M., 'The effects of aging on the verbal control of motor behaviour'. *International Journal of Aging and Human Development* 5, pp. 141-56, 1974.

Kimmel, D. C., *Adulthood and Aging.* New York: Wiley, 1974.

Kuypers, J. A., 'Ego functioning in old age: early adult life antecedents'. *International Journal of Aging and Human Development* 5, pp. 157-79, 1974.

Levinson, D. J., *The Seasons of a Man's Life.* New York: Knopf, 1978.

Livson, F. B., 'Patterns of personality development in middle-aged women: a longitudinal study'. *International Journal of Aging and Human Development* 7, pp. 107-15, 1976.

Lombardo, J. P., and Wood, R. D., 'Satisfaction with inter-personal relations as a function of level of self-disclosure. *The Journal of Psychology* 102, pp. 21-6, 1979.

Lowenthal, M. F., Thurnher, M., and Chiriboga, D., *Four Stages of Life.* San Francisco: Jossey-Bass, 1976.

Maccoby, E. E., Doering, C. H., Jacklin, D. N., and Kraemer, H., 'Concentration of sex hormones in umbilical-cord blood: their relations to sex and birth order of infants'. *Child Development* 50, pp. 632-42, 1979.

McKinlay, S. M., and Jefferys, M., 'The menopausal syndrome'. *British Journal of Preventive Social Medicine* 28, pp. 108-15, 1974.

Moore, T., and Clautour, S. E., 'Attitudes of life in children and young adolescents'. *Scandinavian Journal of Psychology* 18, pp. 10-20, 1977.

Neugarten, B. N., (ed.), *Middle Age and Aging*. Chicago: University of Chicago Press, 1968.

New Society, *The Seven Ages of Man*. London: Heinemann, 1964.

Newman, B. M., and Newman, P. R. *Development through Life: a Psychosocial Approach*. Homewood, Illinois: Dorsey. 1979.

Newson, Elizabeth and John, *Four Years Old in an Urban Community*. London: Allen and Unwin, 1968.

Newson, Elizabeth and John, *Seven Years Old in the Home Environment*. Allen and Unwin, 1978.

Nicholson, J. N., *Habints: Why You Do What You Do*. London: Pan, 1978.

Nicholson, J. N., *A Question of Sex*. London: Fontana, 1979.

Nuttall, E. V., and Nuttall, R. L., 'Child spacing effects on intelligence, personality, and social competence'. *The Journal of Psychology* 102, pp. 3-12, 1979.

Oakley, A., *Becoming A Mother*. Oxford: Martin Robertson, 1979.

Office of Population Censuses and Surveys, *Older Workers and Retirement*. London: HMSO, 1980.

Pahl, R. E., 'Living without a job: how school leavers see the future'. *New Society*, 2 November 1978.

Q-Search, *Quest Entering Motherhood*. London: Schlackman Research Organization, 1979.

Rapoport, R., Rapoport, R. N., and Strelitz, Z., *Fathers,*

Mothers and Others. London: Routledge and Kegan Paul, 1977.

Richards, M., *Infancy.* London: Harper and Row, 1980.

Rosenberg, S. D., and Farrell, M.P., 'Identity and crisis in middle-aged men'. *International Journal of Aging and Human Development* 7, pp. 153-70, 1976.

Rutter, M., 'Maternal deprivation, 1972-1978: new findings, new concepts, new approaches'. *Child Development* 50, pp. 283-305, 1979.

Rutter, M., *Changing Youth in a Changing Society.* London: Nuffield Provincial Hospitals Trust, 1979.

Schofield, Michael, *The Sexual Behaviour of Young People.* Harmondsworth: Penguin, 1968.

Sheehy, G., *Passages: the Predictable Crises of Adult Life.* New York: Dutton, 1976.

Stevens-Long, J., *Adult Life: Developmental Processes.* Palo Alto: Mayfield, 1979.

Tanner, J. M., *Foetus into Man.* London: Open Books, 1978.

Thornes, B., and Collard, J., *Who Divorces?* London: Routledge and Kegan Paul, 1979.

Thurner, M., 'Midlife marriage: sex differences in evaluation and perspectives'. *International Journal of Aging and Human Development* 7, pp. 129-35, 1976.

Tolor, A., 'The generation gap: fact or fiction?'. *Genetic Psychology Monographs* 94, pp. 35-130, 1976.

Welford, A. T., 'Motivation, capacity, learning and age'. *International Journal of Aging and Human Development* 7, pp. 189-99, 1976.

Won-Doornink, M. J., 'On getting to know you: the association between the stage of a relationship and reciprocity of self-disclosure'. *Journal of Experimental Social Psychology* 15, pp. 229-41, 1979.

Zajonc, R. B., and Markus, G. B., 'Birth order and intellectual development'. *Psychological Review* 82, pp. 74-88, 1975.

Index

Index

Edward Shorter

THE MAKING OF THE MODERN FAMILY

How has marriage changed over the past three centuries? Is the nuclear family disintegrating, and why? Has women's new freedom affected the traditional sexual balance? And what is the role of children in the family, past and present?

In this remarkable history of the family in Western society, Edward Shorter draws on a wide range of research into such areas as courtship, illegitimacy, child care, sexual practices, family planning, and the sharing of household responsibilities. He describes not only changes in structure, but changes in how people, rich and poor, thought and felt about themselves. He shows how the Victorian 'sexualization' of marriage contributed to the development of the enclosed nuclear family, and suggests that in the future the couple, rather than the family, may be the key unit.

'a compulsively readable book'   J. H. Plumb

'the material . . . is irresistible'   Jonathan Raban

'vivid, admirably digested, immensely lively and full of ideas'
New Statesman

'A most important contribution to historical understanding'
The Times Literary Supplement

Katharina Dalton

ONCE A MONTH

Once a month, with demoralising regularity, over fifty per cent of women feel tired, confused, irritable and incapacitated due to the effects of premenstrual tension. Many others are indirectly affected – husbands, children, colleagues, workmates and friends.

Premenstrual syndrome is responsible for the timing of half of all criminal offences in women, for half of all suicides, accidents in the home and on the roads, hospital admissions, incidents of baby battering and alcoholic bouts. These are the calculable effects – how much greater are the less obvious changes in a woman's daily life, in her behaviour, appearance and health?

The problems might seem insurmountable – but are they? This book is a popular and easily understood account of menstrual difficulties by a doctor with many years of professional and research experience in their causes and treatment. Katharina Dalton shows that in most cases women can treat themselves, and that in severer cases progesterone treatment can be highly effective. It is a book which many readers – male as well as female – will find informative, sympathetic, helpful and above all practical in relieving the suffering caused by premenstrual syndrome.

Sheila Kitzinger

WOMEN AS MOTHERS

How does a woman's behaviour change when she becomes a mother? Are there clear definitions of the 'right' and 'wrong' ways for mothers to behave? What kind of status do mothers now have in Britain and America?

In this wide-ranging study of motherhood, Sheila Kitzinger shows that maternal behaviour, far from being inborn and unchanging, is a direct response to the society the mother lives in. In closely-knit tribal societies, mothers will tend to keep their children with them all the time. In Western society, which places great value on independence and autonomy, every 'mother's aid' (pram, playpen, baby bouncer) is designed further to separate mother and child. Conception, pregnancy and childbirth itself are surrounded by quite different kinds of ritual and expectation, and Sheila Kitzinger examines the rituals of, for example, an American maternity ward and a birth in the African bush.

At a time when mothers in the West feel their role as an increasingly challenged and difficult one, and when women are re-examining their lives and status, Sheila Kitzinger's examination of one of the most important areas of a woman's life is illuminating and invaluable.

Fontana Paperbacks

Fontana is a leading paperback publisher of fiction and
non-fiction, with authors ranging from Alistair MacLean,
Agatha Christie and Desmond Bagley to Solzhenitsyn and
Pasternak, from Gerald Durrell and Joy Adamson to the
famous Modern Masters series.

In addition to a wide-ranging collection of internationally
popular writers of fiction, Fontana also has an outstanding
reputation for history, natural history, military history,
psychology, psychiatry, politics, economics, religion and
the social sciences.

All Fontana books are available at your bookshop or
newsagent; or can be ordered direct. Just fill in the form
and list the titles you want.

FONTANA BOOKS, Cash Sales Department, G.P.O. Box
29, Douglas, Isle of Man, British Isles. Please send purchase
price, plus 8p per book. Customers outside the U.K. send
purchase price, plus 10p per book. Cheque, postal or money
order. No currency.

NAME (Block letters)

ADDRESS